Tripping the Prom Queen

A Passion for More:
Wives Reveal the Affairs That Make or Break Their Marriages

Sisters:
Devoted or Divided

The Men Out There:
A Woman's Little Black Book
(with Michele Kasson, Ph.D.)

Second Wives:
The Pitfalls and Rewards of Marrying Widowers and Divorced Men

Mothers-in-Law and Daughters-in-Law:
Love, Hate, Rivalry and Reconciliation

Reclaiming Ourselves:
How Women Dispel a Legacy of Bad Choices

Women of Divorce:
Mothers, Daughters, Stepmothers—the New Triangle

The New Wife:
The Evolving Role of the American Wife

Tripping the Prom Queen

The Truth About Women and Rivalry

Susan Shapiro Barash

St. Martin's Griffin
New York

A Note to the Reader: Reference in this book to Web sites and other resources as potential sources of additional information does not mean that either the author or the publisher has control over, or is responsible for, the content or policies of this material.

www.stmartins.com

Book design by Irene Vallye

Library of Congress Cataloging-in-Publication Data

Barash, Susan Shapiro, 1954–
    Tripping the prom queen : the truth about women and rivalry / by Susan Shapiro Barash.
        p. cm.
    ISBN-13: 978-0-312-33432-1
    ISBN-10: 0-312-33432-X
    1. Women—Life skills and guides. 2. Women—Psychology. I. Title.

HQ1221.B245 2006
302.5'4'082—dc22

                                                      2005044416

For my mother,
the fairest of them all

Author's Note

This book is based on extensive personal interviews with women and experts in the fields of psychology and counseling. Names have been changed and recognizable characteristics disguised for all people in the book, except the contributing experts, in order to protect their privacy. Some characters are composites.

Contents

In the misfortunes of our best friends we always find something not altogether displeasing to us.

—La Rochefoucauld

She must learn to compete . . . not as a woman, but as a human being.

—Betty Friedan

Tripping the Prom Queen

Facing the Dark Mirror

All my life, I've relied upon the kindness of women.

I had a terrific relationship with my mother, who supported my earliest efforts to explore the world and discover a sense of myself. I had wonderful girlfriends, pals who were good for everything from a carefree shopping trip downtown to long, serious discussions about the meaning of life. When I got to college, I was fortunate to find female professors and mentors who nurtured and challenged me while offering a wide variety of role models for how to make my own way in the academic world. When I began teaching gender studies at Marymount Manhattan College, I found smart, interesting, and supportive colleagues with whom I could discuss the latest developments in our respective fields while sharing my feelings about the complicated business of balancing marriage, motherhood, and a career. And as I watched my own daughters become lovely young women with a world of promise before them, I cherished the thought that they were so much more self-confident than I had ever been, and would have so many more opportunities than I'd ever had.

I knew that partial credit for my good fortune went to the women's movement, which had proclaimed in the early 1970s the value of sisterhood. Women, oppressed by men for generations, had finally realized that we needed to look out for each other. Luckily, solidarity came without effort to our kind and generous natures, once we had seen through the dangerous illusions of patriarchy.

Okay, what's wrong with this picture?

In fact, it's all true. I *have* been blessed with wonderful friends, colleagues, and family. And the women's movement *has* contributed enormously to our understanding of the kinds of bonds that women can build with one another.

But, like virtually every other woman I have ever met, I've also known the dark side of female bonding. I've had conflicts with my mother, my daughters, my girlfriends, my colleagues, with women whom I thought were my friends, with women whom I learned not to trust. I've been the subject of gossip, betrayals, backstabbing, catfighting. I've found myself enmeshed in relationships marked by unexpected competition, envy, and jealousy. And in both my own life and the lives of other women, I have seen how female friendship can be both empowering and disabling, a source of rock-solid strength as well as a mire of treachery, deceit, and misunderstanding.

I'm reminded of my friends Cynthia and Elinor, whose bitter falling-out sent shock waves through our entire circle of friends. These two women had been close since college, having settled in the same midwestern city, and their blend of intimacy and rivalry seemed to work for them. When Cynthia went into business for herself as a marketing consultant, it was largely Elinor's mixture of support and prodding that had gotten her to take the leap. A few years later, Elinor began thinking of setting up her own consultancy—and Cynthia was there to challenge and encourage her. For nearly two decades it seemed that their friendly competition was actually good for them both, spurring each woman on to new achievements even as she continually measured her accomplishments against those of her friend.

Then Cynthia got engaged. Both women had had brief, unhappy first marriages and a long stretch of relatively satisfactory dating, but when Cynthia found her new love, Elinor was going through a dry spell, feeling lonely and unappreciated. The lack of male attention was particularly hard on Elinor, a stylish, exuberant woman who was known for taking center stage at any party.

Although Elinor herself didn't particularly want to get married, she had a hard time watching Cynthia snag what society still considers a woman's ultimate prize. And when she learned that her wedding invitation was for one only, she was outraged.

"How can she expect me to show up at her wedding without a date?" she fumed to any of us who would listen. "All of her other friends are married. There won't even be anyone there for me to dance with! It's her big day, sure—but does she have to rub it in that I'm alone?"

Cynthia, for her part, was deeply wounded that Elinor seemed more interested in her lack of dance partners than in Cynthia's wedding. "I've waited so long to find someone, and now that I have, she can't even be happy for me," she'd say tearfully to me and our other friends. "Can't she ever think of anyone besides herself?"

Eventually, Elinor confronted Cynthia in an angry conversation that left both of them hurt and upset. By mutual agreement, Elinor stayed away from the wedding, and the twenty-year friendship ended. When I thought of how much the two women had meant to each other and how intensely each of them had approached this final encounter, I was shaken by the idea that female rivalry could run so deep. What had seemed a friendly and useful competition had turned into a painful contest.

It wasn't only my friends who suffered from female rivalry. I remember when I was just sixteen years old, during spring vacation, being whisked off to an early lunch by my best friend's brother, only to discover, to my astonishment and hurt, that she was expecting some college boys to drop by and didn't want me there to compete with her. When I started college at Sarah Lawrence, I soon noticed that while some of my classmates were indeed true friends, others seemed to resent that I had a boyfriend. It didn't help that Sarah Lawrence, a former girls' school, included very few straight men among its student body— an early lesson in how competing for items in short supply often brings out the worst in women.

In graduate school, the stakes got higher, and the competition got stiffer, a trend that continued when I went on to vie for a limited number of academic jobs. I always had friends and colleagues with whom I could have trusted my life—but I also found women who seemed to view not only me but all other female academics as their rivals.

This sense of rivalry became more painful when I divorced my first husband. Many of the friends I depended on for comfort and support suddenly began to view me as a threat. Some took me out to lunch to get the dirt, then dropped me soon after. I think they found it disturbing that I had left my unhappy marriage while they were still committed to theirs. For other women, the threat seemed more immediate—twice I was told in no uncertain terms that I had better stay away from someone's husband, despite my protests that I would no more go after a friend's husband than I would stay friends with a woman who went after mine.

Thankfully, I also had some true friends who remained loyal and supportive during one of the most difficult times of my life. To this day, I trust them implicitly, with the kind of faith you reserve for the people who have proved themselves under fire. But I've also never forgotten the shock and disappointment of discovering how quickly those other friendships turned to rivalry.

Nor was the problem limited to other women. Reluctantly I began to admit that I, too, had felt competitive, envious, even jealous of my fellow females. I, too, had walked into a dinner party and done a quick tally of how I stacked up. Was I as talented as the other women? As pretty? As prestigiously employed? During my divorce, before I met my second husband, I, too, had looked longingly at the few women I knew who seemed truly in love, thinking, "Oh, to have what they have." I, too, had caught myself viewing my daughters with something close to envy for their youth and self-confidence, for the advantages their generation would have that were so far beyond my own. I had even wandered through my local bookstore while I was working on my first book, checking out the other women writers, envious of their apparently secure place on the bookshelves when I wasn't even sure whether I could find a publisher.

Meanwhile, of course, I was continuing to write about the topic that has preoccupied me for the last fourteen years: women. I wrote books about sisters, second wives, and women having affairs. I met women who were struggling with their roles as daughters, mothers, workers, and lovers, seeking to create new identities for themselves, trying to make traditional arrangements work. I talked to women from all ethnic backgrounds and social classes, from struggling Jamaican immigrants to the trust-funded descendants of *Mayflower* passengers. Everywhere, no matter what other topics I was asking about, I found hints of a dark secret, a problem that everyone seemed to sense but no one was willing to talk about: women's rivalry.

When I went to the movies or watched television, I saw similar signs of trouble in paradise. Although male friendships in the media abound—from buddy movies to the warm, collegial relationships among the guys on cop shows—I saw precious few portraits of female relationships. The handful of examples that I did find rarely offered any sense of how women could form friendships based on love, trust, and a sense of separate identities. In the romantic comedy *Jerry Maguire*, for example, female friendship is portrayed as a powerful obstacle to romance. The heroine's sister and her feminist friends sit around carping about how badly the men in their lives have treated them, trying to entice the younger, more hopeful heroine to join them. But the heroine insists that she "just likes men" and eagerly forgives the wayward Jerry ("You had me at hello."). Her youth, beauty, and romantic success make her the envy of the other women, who clearly would rather bond over their common misery than help each other to find individual versions of happiness.

Although I had heard many real-life stories that echoed this negative image, I didn't want to focus on such a dismal view. I didn't like feeling that I might be playing into the sexist stereotypes that had portrayed women as conniving little man-hunters; nor did I enjoy reliving my own painful experiences with female rivalry. But finally, I had to face the truth: this was too central an aspect of women's lives for me to ignore. My next book would focus directly on jealousy, envy, and competition. Perhaps by looking closely at this problem, I could help women find new ways to overcome their dark side and form healthier, more satisfying bonds.

So I designed a study whereby I could interview five hundred women—again, from a wide range of ages, classes, ethnicities, and religions—asking them directly about their experiences with these feelings. I wanted to know the role that women's rivalry had played in their lives, their experiences as both targets and perpetrators of female envy. I was eager to understand how these dynamics had shaped my subjects' life choices, their relationships with people of both sexes, and, most important, their sense of self. I wanted to know why some relationships seemed to transcend these problems, while other bonds were marked by bitterness and betrayal.

What I found astonished me. I heard from women whose colleagues, best friends, and sisters had stolen their boyfriends and husbands. I talked with women whose fear of female rivalry was so strong that they chose to live in small towns, "so there would be less competition"; women who avoided certain parties "because I don't want my husband to meet too many single, beautiful women." I heard about girlfriends dropping a woman when she snagged a promotion at work, or finally found a great guy, or even when she became pregnant. Women described the wear and tear of constant competition, of continually comparing themselves to friends, coworkers, sisters, even to their daughters. Many women confessed that they had spent their lives trying to steer between two painful courses: reaching for the advantages that other women seemed to have and struggling to defend themselves from other women's envy. Although I had known that female rivalry was a theme in many women's lives, I emerged from my research feeling as though it must be a theme in *every* woman's life. *We're just not allowed to talk about it.*

In fact, when I recovered from my first wave of shock at the extraordinary stories I was hearing, I was able to boil down my findings to three conclusions:

1. Despite all the efforts of the women's movement to change this troubling pattern, we're still willing to cut each other's throats over what we value most—jobs, men, and social approval. Although we've moved into the workplace and the public arena as never before, we tend to ignore men when it comes to competing, focusing our rivalry almost entirely upon each other.

2. We'll do anything rather than face up to female envy and jealousy—especially our own. Between traditional social pressures to be the "good girl," and feminist expectations of female solidarity, we sweep all evidence of a bleaker picture under the rug. Indeed, in these postfeminist times, women are often rewarded for romanticizing female friendship and punished for telling the truth about female rivalry.

3. Even though my focus is on female rivalry, I have also found some wonderful examples of female bonding—within families, between friends, among colleagues. In these positive instances, I found that the key was for women to have realistic expectations, of themselves and each other. When we stop demanding total, unconditional support; when we accept our loved ones' differ-

ences as well as similarities; when we own up to our own rival-rous natures; and when we confront problems rather than ignore them, we can create extraordinary bonds that nourish us throughout our lives.

A New Look at Female Competition

I walk into a party with my husband and immediately feel everyone's eyes upon us—perhaps more upon him. I notice that when he goes to the bar to get drinks, one woman in particular follows him. Although she has to know we are together, she proceeds to move close to him, beginning a seemingly intimate conversation. I am talking to a group of friends I have not seen for quite a while. By the time I get back to where my husband is standing, the woman is telling him that she loves to play golf and can go to the range with him any Saturday. I look at my husband, who seems to be enjoying the attention, and realize that he has been sought after, regardless of ownership. This woman moves away reluctantly when I introduce myself as his wife, but manages to find my husband repeatedly throughout the night. I ask my friend, the hostess, about her and she tells me that this woman is absolutely a flirt and will steal anyone's man if she can.

Later, when we get home, I tell my husband that if he ever speaks to that woman again, I will be gone. While I am indeed protecting my turf, I am also well aware that this woman is a sexy blonde. I am not in despair, but my antennae are up.

As you can see from this anecdote about my husband and me, I'm no stranger to female rivalry. Perhaps because the subject is so personal, this has been the most challenging of all the books I've written. It hasn't been easy coming to terms with these painful issues, either in myself or in the hundreds of women I interviewed.

But once I acknowledged that female rivalry *was* a problem, I started to see it everywhere—in the media, in my personal life, and in the lives of my daughters, as well as in the experiences of the five hundred women who shared their stories with me. Consider, for example, the story of this real-life high school queen:

> It was a freezing cold day when my best friend, Allison, and the other two candidates for homecoming queen stood on the football field, shivering in their gowns, waiting to see who would be crowned. The bleachers were packed . . . and people actually held banners with a name of each contestant written in big letters.
>
> Allison didn't win, and she was devastated. I remember how she tried to hold it together. She changed into jeans and sat with me for the rest of the game, as hard as that was. At first she asked me if I thought that the winner was prettier than she was. Then she asked me if the winner was more popular. That was an odd question, since the obvious answer was yes.
>
> Finally, as we were driving home from the game, Allison began to cry. She said she wished the winner ill and that she didn't deserve to win. Allison said she hated her for winning. All I could think of was how the winner stood on that field, alone with her crown, while the others moved to the side. Nobody was even happy for her.

Certainly, I had recognized female rivalry in my previous books. On each project, I heard tales of envy, jealousy, and competition. When I wrote about sisters, I ran into sibling rivalry. When I wrote about single women and dating, I heard how much they envied married women. When I wrote about married women having affairs, I heard about how much they envied their lovers' wives, or their own happily married friends, or the single women whom they knew. Stepmothers and mothers envied each other, as did first and second wives. Divorced women envied the still-married or remarried; married women envied the divorcées who had gone off to greener pastures.

Finally I realized that it was time to do a study focusing on how women treat each other, a study that would show both the external pressures and the internal dynamics that lead to envy, jealousy, and competition. I was particularly concerned to show where this female rivalry begins: in women's insufficient options. In a world where there simply isn't enough to go around, women compete. In a world that limits women to narrowly defined roles, women compete with each other.

I also wanted to explore the ways in which female rivalry has intensified as women have moved from 1950s-era housewifery and child raising to the expanded options of the twenty-first century. Ironically, as women's options have grown, so has our rivalry, from the old-fashioned sphere of hearth and home to the brave new world of career and professional success. Although each new breakthrough for women has opened up wonderful new opportunities, it has also created more occasions for competition. "It is definitely a problem how many avenues are open for women to compete with each other these days," comments Dr. Claire Owen, professor of psychology at Marymount Manhattan College, whom I interviewed in connection with this study. "If there is a pretense of getting along, it only exists at a superficial level. Underneath, there is the urge to outdo one another."

We can't understand female rivalry without understanding the pressure to conceal it. Although the women I interviewed spoke readily of competing with mothers, sisters, coworkers, and friends, many of them also seemed to buy into the myth of female solidarity, lamenting their own isolation from what they saw as a world of camaraderie and support. Women also described feeling betrayed when they realized that an apparently close friend was also a rival, a theme that was taken up by Mary Duenwald in a September 10, 2002, *New York Times* article entitled "Some Friends, Indeed, Do More Harm Than Good." Duenwald cites research showing that "the ill effects of friendship are more devastating than experts thought." Although previous studies had suggested that friendship—male and female—could be a powerful antidote to stress, more recent research indicates that broken promises, dashed expectations, and other side effects of friendship gone wrong can actually raise the level of stress in our lives, often to disastrous effect. In light of this new perspective, understanding why female friendships go wrong—and how to put them right—seemed more urgent than ever.

So I went on to design my research study, which covered five hundred heterosexual women of all ages, races, and backgrounds. My first step was placing the following ad in flyers for YWCAs and health clubs:

Writer in search of tales of female envy, jealousy, and friendship. Anonymity guaranteed. Call collect.

When women responded, I asked them if they could recommend friends, relatives, or coworkers who might also have interesting stories to tell. Because such a wide range of women answered my ad, I had access to a diverse group of subjects. I also conducted interviews and research with psychotherapists, scholars, divorce lawyers, and even with plastic surgeons, who were surprisingly insightful about the ways that women's rivalry over appearance affects us all.

I found the whole process fascinating, and surprisingly frustrating. To a much greater extent than in my other books, my interviewees often began by glossing over their deeper feelings, trying to portray themselves as "good girls" rather than admitting to the envy, jealousy, and anger that they actually felt. Frequently, the women were guarded and measured, so that I had to dig deeper than usual to get at their true feelings. As a result, I spent considerably longer conducting most of these interviews than I had for the ones in my previous books.

Although I've empathized with many of my interview subjects over the years, I felt a sense of kinship with these women that was more intense than usual. In some cases, I identified so profoundly with a woman's story that I found myself wanting to speak to her as a friend, wishing I could share my own history with her and hear her perspective on my own friends and rivals. At other times, I was appalled at the degree of bitterness, anger, and resentment my subjects expressed, and saddened by how difficult some women found it to overcome their early rivalries. Many women made such statements as, "Since high school, beautiful women have made me feel insecure," or "My friend and I have been competing for the past thirty years," or "Even though I'm happily married today, I find myself consumed with bitterness whenever I remember how my best friend stole my boyfriend in junior high."

It wasn't only the stories of past rivalries that haunted me. Women told me that they had blatantly set out to steal another woman's husband, lover, friend, or job. They described the times that friends had stolen jobs or relationships from them. They detailed the bitter envy that they still felt for or from their mothers, sisters, and in-laws. And I shuddered at the apparent freedom so many women felt simply to take what they wanted without regard for other women's feelings. It was as though we were all crazed customers at some kind of year-end shoe sale, shoving our fellow females out of the way as we clutched desperately at the few remaining pieces of merchandise. I had the discouraging sense that our culture had created female monsters, dooming us to play out these intense and bitter rivalries almost against our will.

But whether I felt close to my subjects as kindred spirits or horrified at the world of female jealousy they portrayed, I was always fascinated, particularly when I started compiling my data and realized how widespread the problem really is:

- More than 90 percent of women of different social strata claim that envy and jealousy toward other women colors their lives
- 80 percent of women say they have encountered jealousy in other females since they were in grade school
- 90 percent of women in diverse jobs report that competition in the workplace is primarily between women, rather than between women and men
- More than 65 percent of interviewees said that they were jealous of their best friend or sister
- More than 70 percent of interviewees were familiar with the

concept of women stealing a friend's husband, lover, boyfriend, or job

- 40 percent of interviewees reported themselves the victims
  of another woman's theft of a husband, lover, boyfriend, or
  job
- 25 percent of interviewees reported that they themselves
  had stolen a friend's husband, lover, boyfriend, or job

Although hearing the stories of female competition was often disturbing, I concluded my study with a feeling of optimism. Yes, at first
glance, this portrait of hidden rivalry and cancerous envy seems bleak
indeed. But facing up to this gloomy picture is the first step toward a
better future of more authentic, loving bonds among women. If we are
willing to look closely at this issue, we may be astonished at the rewards
we stand to gain.

Shades of Rivalry: Competition, Envy, and Jealousy

As I sorted through the stories I was hearing, I began to realize that female contests took three forms: competition, envy, and jealousy.

Competition is probably the most benign form of female rivalry.
When we compete with one another, we're saying, *I'm willing to fight
you for what I want.* This isn't necessarily a bad thing, particularly when
we're competing for limited resources. A woman who withdraws from
consideration for a job, for example, simply because she knows other
women are also up for the position would be almost pathologically unwilling to engage in the normal, healthy competition that is simply a
part of life. Likewise, a woman who refused to consider dating a man
merely because she knows other women find him attractive would not
be coping with competition in a healthy way. Indeed, one of the great
benefits of the women's movement has been its permission for us to
claim our ambitious natures, freeing us to go after what we want without always worrying about whether someone else wants it, too. In some
cases, competition can even be a powerful force for good, motivating us

to perform better, to be more honest about what we want, and to marshal our resources on our own behalf.

The problem, according to my research, appears in two places. First, despite the efforts of the women's movement to open every type of job to women, we still tend to compete only with each other. The reality series *The Apprentice* makes this all too clear. Rather than presenting a group of competent professionals, male and female, all vying equally with each other, the series conveyed the idea that women's primary rivals are other women. The miniskirted apprentices were not competing on the basis of competence and knowledge alone; they were also battling each other on the basis of looks and sexual allure. A more sober presentation of workplace rivalry might not have had such high ratings, but the very popularity of the show's catfights reveals the pressure women feel to size each other up while leaving the men alone.

Second, sometimes healthy competition for what we want turns into a problematic desire to have something merely because a rival already has it. We didn't want that guy, until we saw him with our best friend. We weren't so interested in getting into an Ivy League school, until we found out that a classmate was going to Harvard. We were content to put off getting pregnant for another few years, until our best friend told us that she was due in June. Suddenly we've created a contest based less on our own authentic wishes than on rivalry with a competitor.

At this point competition shades into **envy,** which might be expressed as *I want what you have.* Now, even this feeling has its positive aspects. If envy of a pregnant girlfriend causes us to realize that our own childbearing years won't last forever, we've used that feeling to get in touch with something that truly matters to us. Although the envy may be uncomfortable, it's helped us understand ourselves better, and to take positive action on our own behalf.

Or perhaps it never occurred to us that we could become a successful stockbroker or journalist, or that we could dare to try for such a glittering prize. Then a friend achieves that type of success and we realize,

Hey! If she can do it, why can't I? A little envy can be the catalyst that spurs us to aim a bit higher, try a bit harder, make our own dreams a little bit bigger.

In the same way, the momentary wish that we, and not our girlfriend, were dating that hot new guy can be a useful way to get in touch with our own feelings about romance. Maybe there are problems with our current relationship or with our solitude, and we haven't been willing to act on them. Perhaps we've been pretending to ourselves that things are fine, and only a sharp jab of envy wakes us up to the realization of how dissatisfied we really are. If we are willing to explore those uncomfortable feelings, we might make some important discoveries that can ultimately enrich our lives.

Or we could go in the other direction and focus all of our discomfort upon our rival. This is the stage of female rivalry that I call **jealousy,** which might be expressed as *You've got something I want—and I want you dead.*

All right, maybe "dead" is putting it too strongly. None of the women I interviewed actually confessed to murder, though some real-life stories come fairly close. One bizarre case of a mother accused of plotting to kill another mother suggests that women can indeed become toxic if their jealousy gets out of hand. In this instance, the daughters were cheerleading rivals and the scheming mother wanted to upset her daughter's competition as a way to take her out of the race. But even when we don't take our jealousy to murderous extremes, it's important to understand how we sometimes project our own desires and frustrations onto other women. Instead of figuring out what we want and how to get it, we focus on what they have and why we hate them for it. My research showed me that the more powerless we feel, especially when competing for "scarce goods," the more prone we are to turn healthy competition into a corrosive jealousy that can destroy our relationships, our peace of mind, and even our sense of self.

Consider the story of Brenda, a forty-eight-year-old registered nurse who had been married for about nine years:

Once I married Roy I expected to be satisfied, but a weird thing happened. I became jealous of other women's lifestyles. . . . Those with families seemed to be the most enviable of all. . . .

Suddenly, I had to have a baby. I hadn't even considered it a possibility, and now I was consumed. I ended up in a support group for infertile women and when two of the members became pregnant, I went nuts. . . .

Once Roy and I adopted a baby, I settled down, and today I feel blessed. But I find myself competitive now over my daughter and other mothers and their children. I think this jealousy is just a big part of who I am.

Fear or Fascination? Our Preoccupation with Female Rivalry

Once I started exploring this topic, it seemed as though stories about female rivalry were everywhere. Not only were numerous movies and TV shows structured around this ever-fascinating theme but the media seemed to report endlessly on feuds, competitions, and catfights between famous women in entertainment, business, and politics. Jennifer Aniston versus Angelina Jolie; Hillary Clinton versus Monica Lewinsky; Camilla Parker-Bowles versus the late Princess Diana—it seemed that few stories were as popular as two women competing over the same man.

Almost as intriguing was the spectacle of women competing for the same job, as evidenced by reality shows like *The Apprentice, America's Next Top Model,* and *The Starlet.* Or, if we preferred, we could watch women competing over each other's families, in programs like *Trading Spouses: Meet Your New Mommy* or *Nanny 911.* In each of these programs, women were ostensibly competing in only one category—as professionals, or as mothers. But every show demonstrated that, in fact, women's competition is total, including professional competence, looks, fashion sense, and sex appeal, all indiscriminately considered as elements within a single competition without boundaries.

Advertisements drew even more explicitly on the theme of female envy, as in the publicity for the weight-loss program represented by former model Anna Nicole Smith. After years of being overweight and ignored, the ads explained, the slimmed-down Smith was finally getting the acclaim she deserved—acclaim that the (presumably female) consumer could acquire simply by buying this product. But attention and admiration were not the only goals to be sought. The ads pointed as well to female rivalry with their succinct slogan: "Be envied."

Although Smith was supposed to be the target of our envy for her miraculous weight loss, the ads drew on the implicit contempt that women (and men) felt for Smith after she'd gotten fat. Indeed, malicious stories about the woes of prominent women—Martha Stewart's legal problems or Kirstie Alley's weight gain—seemed to be a never-ending staple of popular culture, particularly in media targeted to women.

Why, I wondered, were we so fascinated by the miseries of famous females? In an era when women were making unprecedented gains in politics, business, and the arts, we seemed to have an endless appetite not for inspiring stories but for tales that fed our own competitive natures. What was the appeal of watching powerful women fail? Why not just cheer them on, viewing them as inspirational role models who offered us hope rather than icons whom we needed, obsessively, repeatedly, to tear down?

As I reviewed my research and thought about my own experiences with envy, it seemed to me that our fascination with female rivalry had three sources. First, there was our own sense of despair at the ways in which modern society, apparently so open to female success, still makes it so difficult for women to get ahead. Whether we're talking about the shortage of good men, the scarcity of women at the top of the financial tree, or the impossible pressures on women to remain perpetually youthful and beautiful, it seems clear that female success is still elusive for most of us. Although we may be able to achieve more than was possible for our mothers and grandmothers, the glass ceiling and the unrealistic standards for female beauty still hold us back. In such a context, looking at women who seem to have succeeded where we have failed can become almost unbearable. We need to believe that our heroines have feet of clay, that they'll gain weight and grow old just like the rest of us, that they, too, worry about losing their men to younger, prettier rivals. If we worry that a lust for success makes us somehow less feminine or desirable, how can we help savoring the hardships of high-achieving women such as Hillary Clinton and Martha Stewart? Their success seems to mock our failure even as it tempts us to take steps that we fear may make us less feminine and alluring. It may seem preferable to put the conflict to rest by tearing these women down and watching them fail.

Second, even healthy competition for women is still largely taboo. It's very difficult for most of us to admit that we want to win, to snag the promotion at the expense of our coworkers, to rise to the top of our profession. Although the recent prominence of female athletes has given us at least some models for women who openly admit their desire for victory, most of the successful women we see in our culture have been forced to hide their ambition. Women like Hillary Clinton and Martha Stewart have obviously put a great deal of effort into achieving their prominent positions. No one wins a senate election or builds a multimillion-dollar company without making an enormous amount of effort—effort that by definition includes the wish to defeat one's competitors. Yet both Clinton and Stewart were excoriated for their ambition, even as they tried their best to act as though they weren't, in fact, competing. Clinton's infamous attempt to portray herself as "just a housewife" by offering her recipe for chocolate-chip cookies backfired—no one could believe her in the housewife role, and both homemakers and career women resented her pretense. Stewart's ambition likewise shone through her role as contented homemaker, leading to numerous attacks on her supposedly cold and heartless nature.

The message couldn't have been clearer: women may rise to the top, but they must *seem* as though they don't care whether they win or lose. Nice girls care only about being nice. They win only by accident or by someone else's efforts. For those of us in real life, however, this is an impossible injunction—we *know* that success takes hard work and a will to win. So how can we avoid hating the women who seem to succeed so easily when we ourselves are trying so hard?

Significantly, both Clinton and Stewart became much more popular when they were shown to fail. Clinton, thrust into the role of the wronged wife, became a figure with whom many women could identify. Rather than hate her for her success, they could empathize with her failure. Despite her political qualifications, I wonder whether Clinton would have been elected to the Senate in the absence of the Lewinsky scandal. Likewise, Stewart's jail time seemed to humanize her. Instead of envying her seemingly facile rise to the top, women could pity her harrowing fall.

A third reason for our fascination with other women's failure is, I believe, rooted in the nature of female identity itself. For virtually every woman in this society, our definition of ourselves is bound up in our perception of other women. We see ourselves through comparisons with our mother, our sisters, our friends, and our colleagues. For a whole host of reasons—some psychodynamic, some social—we have a hard time seeing ourselves as separate individuals with destinies of our own. Instead, we view our identities as a kind of zero-sum game: we succeed *where our mothers fail;* we gain *what other women lose.* We can't envision succeeding or failing on our own terms; we can only measure ourselves against other females. So first we envy the powerful women we see in the media, and then we symbolically triumph over them as they crash and burn. After all, we can never compete against them. Who can be as beautiful as a movie star or as powerful as a princess, a president's wife, or the head of a business empire? If we can't beat them ourselves, at least we can enjoy the sight of them competing with one another, and we enjoy even more seeing them fail.

However, we pay a terrible price for this vicarious victory. Every time we cheer the downfall of a powerful woman, we're giving ourselves the message that power is bad and we shouldn't desire it. Every time we revel in a beautiful woman's aging or weight gain, we reinforce the idea that we, too, are less valuable if we are old or overweight. Every time we gloat over a woman's loss of a husband to a younger, prettier rival, we are reminding ourselves that our own relationship is unstable, that someday our man, too, will move on to greener pastures.

Moreover, in savoring women's defeats and seeing other females as our rivals, we lose out on the chance to make women our allies. Who better than other women to understand what we are going through— on the job, with men, in friendships, with our family? Who else should we look to for support, empathy, and assistance? With whom should we join together to improve conditions for us all? But we cannot expect other women to join us in true solidarity if we are continually reminding ourselves that these very women are our enemies.

Beyond Our Dirty Little Secret

All right, so what's the good news? What do we have to gain from delving into the grim world of female rivalry, from taking a closer look at the backstabbing, undermining, and self-hatred that color so many of our female relationships?

As the early days of feminist consciousness-raising made clear, when we look more closely at a problem, we can feel relieved just by acknowledging it. Although everyone I spoke to had encountered jealousy, envy, and competition in some form, most women hadn't been able to talk about these issues. They felt pressured by traditional views of women, and by feminist platitudes. Many women expressed a sense of obligation to focus on the positive, to stress how important their mothers, sisters, and friends were to them, to tell only good stories about the other women they knew. To many of my subjects, women's rivalry seemed like a dirty little secret, and they were afraid of how they might look if they were honest about it. One of my hopes for this book is that it will help women start talking freely about the full range of their experiences, including the negative aspects of female bonding.

More important, I believe that if we confront this problem honestly, we can create some new alternatives for ourselves. But the first step in solving a problem is understanding it. So Parts 1 and 2 of this book are a mirror of what female rivalry looks like. Then, once we have faced the dark side, we can look forward to better days. Thus, in Part 3, "Revolutionizing Rivalry," I explore how awareness of this problem and the willingness to confront it can help us create richer and more nourishing bonds. If we can learn to make competition, envy, and even jealousy work for us rather than against us, and if we can resist the "urge to merge" by accepting our differences as well as our similarities, we can look forward to a new world of healthy and productive female bonding, free at last of the rivalry and destructiveness that have characterized our relationships for too long.

Part 1

From Diapers
to Dior

The Myth of Female Solidarity

When I began my research, Clara was one of the first women with whom I spoke. She was an urban working woman of fifty-two, twice divorced, who told me frankly that she had always considered herself superior to other women. So I admit to feeling a bit disappointed when she said emphatically, in her silvery, aristocratic voice, "I know female rivalry exists, but I haven't had to deal with it. I am lucky because I have never felt that way about anyone. I doubt I'm much help to you."

I thought perhaps I was on the wrong track, after all. Perhaps what I would find as I worked my way through my study was that female rivalry was a relatively limited problem, one that may have affected the women whom I'd studied in my previous books, but not really of general interest.

A few days later, I had occasion to speak with Marie, the woman who had recommended Clara to me in the first place. "How did it go?" she asked. "Did Clara give you some good material?"

"Actually," I admitted, "she said she's never really encountered female rivalry. For her, it doesn't seem to be an issue."

Marie burst out laughing. "That's ridiculous," she said when she finally caught her breath. "Clara is the most jealous woman I know. That's why I thought her interview would be interesting."

Apparently I had learned more from Clara than I had bargained for. I found out what a charged topic this is, and how few women want to acknowledge the presence of envy, jealousy, and competition in their lives. Yet over and over again, even as women insisted to me how much they valued their girlfriends or how rarely they had ever felt jealous of another woman, they went on to share scenarios like these:

The Women's Charity Luncheon

You walk into the huge hotel conference room filled with large round tables covered with white cloths and adorned with centerpieces of demure pastel flowers. The noise is deafening as women, mostly aged thirty-five to sixty, talk hurriedly in small clusters, eager to get in as many minutes of networking as possible before the program begins. Only the most secure stay in one place for long; the others move abruptly from group to group, frantically trying to check out the other guests while allowing themselves to be seen. The competition begins here: who approaches you, and whom do you approach? Important messages about each guest's status can be read in the urgent traffic patterns.

Everyone is dressed to the nines, further evidence that women dress for women and not, as the official story has it, to attract or impress men. The competitive juices are flowing as women covertly scan their rivals. Who looks younger than last time, and why? Was it botox, collagen, a minituck? Who are those younger women in the corner—how did they get invited, and whom do they know? Who here might help you get your child into the right private school or college, or perhaps offer your offspring a prestigious summer job? Are there any business contacts here who might be useful to you or your husband?

Afterward, you're exhausted. It's partly the fatigue that comes from knowing that the slightest details of your face, your body, and your per-

sonal life have been under scrutiny from several dozen people who see you as their rival, if not their enemy. (You may see them that way, too.) But even more disturbing than the relentless competition is the mask of friendship beneath which it hides. You wouldn't mind the contest, you find yourself thinking, if only it were out in the open. But having to pretend that you're all friends is a tricky business.

Singles Night

You're a woman somewhere between the ages of twenty-five and sixty, and you're at this event looking for a date. You haven't wanted to come alone, so you've brought a couple of friends—both women, of course. That's why you're here, because you're having trouble meeting men.

The event planners seat you all in a big circle and ask you to take turns giving a one-minute introduction. Although you're supposed to be keeping track of potential partners, you find yourself so preoccupied with the other women that you barely notice the men. Who here is younger than you? Prettier? Sexier? Thinner? Whose introduction is funnier? More inviting?

Then it's time for people to circulate, meeting the partners of their choice. You manage to approach a few guys, but you can't help noticing the other women in the room, many of whom seem to be standing in the midst of a small circle of admirers.

As the event is winding down, you find your friends. One says scornfully, "I didn't meet anyone—what a bunch of losers!" The other says, "Oh, I found two guys I really like, and they both asked for my number." You and your fellow rejectee roll your eyes, trying not to let your more successful friend see your response. Afterward, the two of you will engage in a long, consoling phone call in which you agree that your other friend is far too easily satisfied.

Beneath your remarks lurks a sense of betrayal. You went to the event together to help each other. But your third girlfriend "put herself first," succeeding on her own rather than failing with you.

The Office

It's your first day at work. You're nervous as you walk into your new of-
fice, but you relax a bit when you notice how many other women work
here. At your last job, your colleagues were mainly men, and while you
got along fine with most of them, you couldn't help feeling a bit left out.
You expect that things will be different here.

Your colleagues seem quite nice. Throughout the day they take turns
coming over to your desk and asking you lots of questions. Are you mar-
ried? Divorced? Do you have a boyfriend? How did you get this job?
Where did you get that great skirt?

They're all so friendly, you find yourself telling them about your ter-
rific boyfriend, the night-school classes that will be your ticket out of
here, and the new diet you're on. You're thrilled to be in such a warm,
supportive environment, and you look forward to being friends with all
of them.

The next day, some question comes up about an office procedure.
"Why don't we ask Lana how to settle this?" a woman suggests, pointing
to you. "When she gets her wonderful new degree, she'll be off to a bet-
ter job, so we should take advantage of her while she's here!" Your boss,
who didn't know about your plans, gives you a funny look. You wonder
if the coworker let the information slip on purpose.

Later that week, another colleague stops by your desk. "I know you're
dieting," she says sweetly, "but I just had to bring you one of my home-
made muffins. Don't you just love chocolate?" When you try to refuse
the temptation she places in your path, you can see how hurt she is—or
is she angry? You begin to wonder if maybe you've been too friendly.

As I spoke with the women who responded to my query, I heard
story after story like these. Women seemed to compete with each other
in every conceivable realm, from third-grade quarrels over who was
most popular to elderly women comparing their grandchildren. I heard
about women competing over clothes, hair, and makeup; boyfriends, female friends, and popularity in general; colleagues, employees, and

bosses; children, siblings, and parents. Women compared themselves to other women at home, at work, on vacation, even in terms of death. For example, one woman told me a harrowing story about becoming a widow in her midfifties, explaining that her husband's funeral had more guests than the funeral held for her friend's husband. Both women were relatively young widows, but instead of banding together, they competed—first over the number of funeral guests, then over their relative degrees of pain: the first widow insisted that her widowhood was more harrowing than her friend's because she'd been so much closer to her husband and her marriage had been so much stronger.

Then there were the two sisters who competed over planning their mother's funeral. As Edie, a thirty-nine-year-old postal worker, explains it, her older sister, Leeanne, took all the credit for the arrangements:

My mother would have wanted us to share this ordeal equally. I was closer to my mom . . . but Leeanne was the daughter who had done better, who had married a wealthy guy and lived a certain lifestyle. So Leeanne kept saying to me that our mother would have wanted everyone to come to *her* house to pay their respects, that it would have made Mom proud. She kept saying that my home wasn't acceptable, that it would actually shame our mother to receive the funeral guests there. I felt like I couldn't win—and I didn't understand why this had to be a competition. . . .

She acted like it was *her* mother, not our mother, by the end. . . . It's hard to believe it came down to this. In my mind it should have been the two of us getting through the week together, each using our own strengths.

Clearly, female competition—that great, unstudied subject—is a powerful theme in women's lives. The topic is all the more powerful, I realize, because for most of us, it has been taboo. Like Clara, we have insisted that we ourselves had never been jealous, envious, or even competitive with a female rival. Instead, we clung for all we were worth to the myth of female solidarity.

Catfight or Dogfight? How Male and Female Competition Differ

Some women, of course, did come clean. When I first described the idea for this book to a close friend, for example, she readily agreed that women are often rivalrous, and even shared a couple of anecdotes with me about her own bouts of envy.

"But, Susan," she went on, "aren't men even more competitive?" After all, she pointed out, men are the ones who devote themselves to sports, who seek to get ahead in their careers, who have it drummed into their heads almost from infancy that "real men" are winners, programmed to avoid at all costs the shame of losing. Why write about *female* rivalry, wondered my friend, when it's men who've raised competition to a fine art?

At first I was taken aback. Certainly I, like many others with feminist leanings, wanted women to have the opportunities that men had always had. If competition had been a part of male success, perhaps female competition was a *good* thing, a sign of our success. And isn't competition in general simply a part of life, particularly in our individualistic, achievement-oriented society?

Then I looked at my data and realized that there are two problems with the way most women express their rivalry:

1. By and large, women compete primarily with each other. In the heady days of second-wave feminism, many women imagined entering the workplace and the political orbit, competing against the men who had previously refused them entry. In this optimistic scenario, we were each other's natural allies, helping one another to get ahead, while men were, if not our enemy, at the very least, our rivals. Many of us imagined a powerful network of sisters cheering each other on as we finally got the positions, money, and power that men had always had.

Unfortunately, my research suggests, women mainly compete not with men but with each other. In a law firm for example, some women partners may indeed be at the top of the hierarchy. But most firms usually operate to the tacit understanding that only a few partner slots are "reserved" for women, so that every woman must compete against her "sisters" for those few places. It seems unthinkable that 40 or 50 percent of the partners might be female, let alone 60 or 70 percent! Thus virtually every successful woman I spoke with told a story like Theresa's:

> I've been at this law firm for ten years, and I have seen some of the men make partner while I am waiting. Yet the men don't bother me, because in a sense, there is nothing I can do about their success—it's a given. There are three women in my position, all waiting to find out if we will be chosen. . . .
>
> We've been envying each other all along. If a senior partner even looks in someone's direction, the other women lawyers envy that person. . . . Every move that is made in this firm puts us on edge and makes us think that another female . . . has something over us. So I admit, I can be envious of a younger female attorney who walks in and gets everyone's attention. And I can be envious of the women lawyers on a day-to-day basis. . . .

Theresa says that the relentless competition on her job extends to the off-hours as well:

> I'll go out at night with my friends who have high-powered jobs, and then everyone is envious of the person who makes the most money and has the best title. The only time any of us really rallies for another is if someone hits hard luck. If I am passed over for partner and this other woman gets it, then I know my friends will be there for me. If I get the job and get a raise, they'll be envious.

Early feminists believed that once our generation became successful, we older women would mentor the younger ones, using our power to make it easier for the next generation. What they didn't count on was the queen bee syndrome—the tendency for a powerful woman to get used to being the only female in the group and to decide she wants to keep it that way. Many women told me stories about female bosses, teachers, or senior colleagues who were actually less helpful to them than their male counterparts. Theresa herself admits to envy of her younger colleagues, particularly since they do enjoy more advantages and acceptance than she had at their age.

Besides competing at work, women also compete over boyfriends, husbands, and children—but once again, their rivals are only women. High school girls rarely go out for the football team; they're trying to make cheerleader. And even when the new generation of female athletes manages to bond over soccer or basketball, they're still competing off the field over weight, hair, clothes, and (if they're heterosexual) boys.

Competition doesn't stop in the teen years. When heterosexual girls grow into women, they compete with other females for that hardest-to-find of all commodities, "the good man." When they have children, they ask not "Who's the best parent?" but "Who's the best mother?" In virtually every sphere of competition, men are irrelevant, only women are each other's rivals.

2. Female competition tends to be total, extending to every detail of a woman's life. Guys compete, sure, but their contests tend to be specific, goal oriented, and limited. They may fight to the death over who scores the most points in a pickup basketball game, who snags a much-desired promotion, or drives the bigger car, but these contests are generally limited to one specific area of competition, and when it's over, it's truly over. The networking at business lunches may be as relentless as at the charity affair I described. But while men are cutting each other out of deals and potential clients, they're usually not also looking at who's gained weight, whose kids are failing geometry, or who's having a bad hair day. Women's competition, by contrast, extends simultaneously into all realms, so that the women in the office scenario, envious of "Lana's" bright future, fight back with high-calorie muffins as well as sly insinuations to the boss.

Why is female competition so totalizing? I think it's partly because, despite our many gains, we're still socialized to view ourselves in relational terms. In too many cases, our currency remains *who we are* rather than *what we do*. Because men's competition tends to be about external achievements, they can go out for a beer with their rivals after the contest is over. Even if men never feel quite safe with their buddies, hiding their vulnerability at all costs, they still tend to create "no-contest" zones where certain aspects of their lives are protected. Women's competition, by contrast, is about our identities—*and*, unlike men, we tend to expect total union and sympathy with our same-sex friends. We have a much harder time setting boundaries to our competition, which makes it all the more destructive.

I also believe that most women are still struggling with the good-girl role that forbids us to be angry or competitive. Men tend to accept their competition as a natural, even a healthy, part of their lives, and as a rule, they're less afraid of their own anger and ambition. Because we're less comfortable with our ambition, our repressed desire for power, money, or success finds expression in all sorts of inappropriate places, including contests over looks, men, and children.

Consider the movie *Working Girl*, a textbook example of mixed messages about female ambition. A glamorous executive played by Sigourney Weaver seems to offer mentorship and support to an upwardly mobile office worker (Melanie Griffith). Griffith welcomes Weaver as big sister and role model, until she discovers that Weaver is only using her as a pawn in office politics. Ultimately, Griffith wins both Weaver's love interest and her job, gaining the heart of male lead Harrison Ford and the support of fatherly boss Philip Bosco, who fires Weaver with a nasty remark about her "bony ass."

Although Griffith's character emerges the clear winner, the movie is relentless in its insistence that only Weaver was competing. Griffith wins almost against her will, insisting for most of the movie that she admires Weaver and doesn't want to hurt her. In real life, Griffith would be the false friend, the one you'd learn to mistrust because she was stabbing you in the back even as she gave you an innocent smile. "Win every battle, but look as though you didn't even know there was a contest," the movie seems to say, encouraging women in the audience to drive their competitive urges underground. Moreover, it's not enough for the movie—clearly intended to satisfy the fantasies of a female audience—that Griffith wins the promotion. She also has to get the guy and hear the alpha male criticize Weaver's ass. She wins the trifecta—looks, men, and career success—but only because she never seemed to be competing.

Such mixed messages make it difficult for women to experience healthy competition or even to put boundaries on unhealthy rivalry. But ignoring these emotions only makes them more powerful. And it encourages us to channel our natural wishes for power and success into all sorts of spheres where they don't belong, from how many valentines we get in sixth grade to how a prestigious middle school has just accepted our son.

Female Friendship: The Double-edged Sword

As I reviewed the interviews in my study, I was struck by one prevailing contradiction: on the one hand, women relied intensely on their female friends, expecting them to provide emotional support whenever any other relationship fell short. A girlfriend was supposed to be there whenever things got rough in family, work, or love, offering advice, comfort, and double-chocolate ice cream. The women of *Sex and the City* are the model for this kind of "girlfriend love," to the point that their four-person relationship is often the most enduring feature of the TV series, outlasting boyfriends, marriages, and career choices. The older women on *The Golden Girls* also shared comfort, coffee, and cheesecake, calling each other "family" and vowing to be there for each other always.

Yet most of the women I spoke with seemed to live in perpetual anxiety. They worried about not succeeding in a male-dominated workplace, about not being able to snag the right boyfriend or land the right husband, about having children too early and ruining their careers, or putting off childbirth and losing their fertility. Women of all ages told me that everything they wanted—love, marriage, work, family—was in short supply, and that only the best-looking, sexiest, and most ambitious women could "have it all." So whenever things got tough, guess what women felt they *could* sacrifice? That's right, the beloved girlfriend. Wasn't she supposed to be always there, perpetually understanding and tolerant? Why *not* sacrifice her to the less forgiving demands of men, work, and motherhood?

Being sacrificed by a friend is painful enough. But being locked into a rivalry with her is even worse. And in this contest for survival of the fittest, women's natural rivals are each other. If every woman is competing against every other, then your best friend is also your most serious rival.

Thus, says Dr. Donald Cohen, a marriage and family therapist, "Women are expected to do too many things. They cannot excel at any one thing when their responsibilities are so spread out. The result is that they take what is not rightfully theirs."

"On an everyday basis, women are very insecure," agrees Dr. Ronnie Burak, a clinical psychologist with a primarily female practice. "If they have not accomplished enough in their lives, they will be envious of those who have done more. This applies to women at every age and stage."

Once again, *Sex and the City* illustrates the point, revealing the double bind of women who are supposed to support each other even as they measure themselves against their friend's achievements. In one episode, Charlotte, married and obsessed with her infertility, discovers that Miranda, single and uninterested in having a child, is unexpectedly pregnant. Charlotte feels not only cheated but betrayed. Of course, Charlotte understands on a rational level that Miranda has not "stolen" Charlotte's child or her fertility. Still, she can't help feeling that, by contrast to Miranda, she has failed. It's only a short step to competition, envy, and on to jealousy. In a world where a childless woman is largely judged as a failure, Charlotte struggles not only with her sorrow over not having a baby but also with her envy of Miranda for being more successful at a woman's "primary task."

This painful bind—depending on women and yet needing to compete with them—marks women's lives from childhood through adulthood and on into old age. Indeed, Victoria, a thirty-nine-year-old divorced mother of two, told me that female rivalry seemed to have shaped her entire life:

> I admit that I was jealous of friends by the time I was in junior high. . . .
> But when I got married at the age of twenty-eight, I thought I could finally stop feeling so jealous. . . . I had gotten a great guy . . . handsome and smart. I was hoping that someone noticed that I was the winner here. . . .
>
> Then I had trouble getting pregnant the first time and several of my friends already had babies, and that feeling began all over again. . . .
>
> I was never in it with my girlfriends on these things, sharing events and highlights, being each other's ear, like we were supposed to be. Instead, I was always trying to stay afloat, hoping no one was so far ahead of me that I'd feel left behind again. . . .

When I reviewed Victoria's interview, I found the most poignant sentence to be the one near the end: *I was never in it with my girlfriends on these things, sharing . . . like we were supposed to be.* The myth of female solidarity made Victoria feel even more inadequate. Whenever Victoria compared herself to her girlfriends, she came up short. Then, when she compared her friendships to what she thought was the ideal, she came up short there, too. The only solution was to step up the competition, hoping that someday, somehow, someone would notice "that I was the winner here. . . ."

Sometimes women find creative ways of balancing their need to compete and their need to be close. The ritual of selective obligation, for example, involves trading confidences and gossip according to a complicated and unspoken hierarchy, figuring out which information must remain confidential and which secrets you're entitled to betray. For example, a group of office coworkers shares a loose affiliation. Alice and Betty are particularly close, however, and so Alice never gossips about Betty with the other women. Alice and Cathy, on the other hand, have no particular obligation, so when Cathy tells Alice a secret, Alice feels no compunction about sharing it with Betty. Nor does she mind telling Betty that Cathy looks tired, has gained weight, is slacking off a lot lately, or is getting on her nerves with all those stories about her fabulous dates. But she would never say similar things about Betty to Cathy—although she might gossip about Betty to Dina, a longtime best friend who works somewhere else.

Thus, Alice has no obligation to Cathy, a slight obligation to Betty, and a more serious obligation to Dina—a web of selective obligation in which the rules change depending upon the relationship. Alice probably expects Cathy to talk behind her back, but she'd be hurt if Betty did so, and devastated if Dina betrayed her in that way.

When selective obligation works, it can be an effective way of managing female rivalry and establishing female bonds. Even though you never openly acknowledge your rivalry, you find ways to allow for a little bit of competition and backbiting, and you make sure to always have one or two girlfriends whom you trust completely. But when the system breaks down, the sense of betrayal is all the stronger. "How could you have told her *that?*" the betrayed woman cries, unaware that she herself has just completed a complicated minuet in which she now betrays, now honors, a confidence. "You were supposed to be my friend!"

Three Myths and the Price We Pay for Them

As I looked more closely at the myth of female solidarity, I discovered that it was, in fact, three myths. Each one of these seductive patterns of belief seems to be common among women of all ages, classes, and ethnic backgrounds. And, like the smooth-talking boyfriend who inevitably lets us down, each seduction contains the seeds of its own betrayal.

1. *The Mommy Mystique*. Many of us tend to seek unconditional love and support from one another, the kind of total, boundless mothering that we wish our mothers had shown us. Instead of looking for adult relationships based on honesty and mutual challenge, we project all our unfulfilled childhood wishes onto our female friends. With expectations like these, our friends, colleagues, and mentors will certainly disappoint us, leaving us ill-equipped to cope with legitimate expressions of rivalry, competition, and difference.

With rare insight, Alexandra, a forty-year-old massage therapist who lives in a suburban town, attributes her breach with a lifelong friend to her own confusion between friendship and mothering:

> My best friend, Gayle, is ten years older than I am and was a role model when we were younger women. I met Gayle when I was in college and I moved into her apartment building. At that time we were both young married women and she owned a small gift shop in town. We seemed like equals, but I always thought that Gayle was the one leading me, setting an example, since she was older. When I confided in her that I wanted to be divorced, even though I had young children, she said she understood, and she agreed that my husband and I were not a good match. So I thought I had her full support. She helped me find a job through one of her friends and we met almost every day. I doubt I could have gotten divorced without her—we were that close.
>
> The strange thing is that as soon as the divorce came through and I started to have a single life, Gayle pulled away. She stopped offering to watch the kids while I went on a date and she became cool to me. I guess her attitude was that she was tired of being there for me. She didn't like that she'd had to listen to my story and help me clean up my mess all along. So she just stopped spending time with me and stopped being my confidante. First Gayle gave me the courage to leave a bad marriage and then she stopped being my friend.

Alexandra is unusual among the women I spoke with in that she went beyond her sense of betrayal to question her own role in the conflict. Instead of clinging to her wish for a "mommylike" best friend, she discovered that she needed to redefine her definition of friendship, envisioning a more open, less dependent relationship.

Likewise, when Marylee became a young widow, she was forced to move beyond the mommy mystique to a more egalitarian and adult view of friendship:

During my husband's illness, my friends took care of me. But once he died, I felt that I was being judged by some friends and dropped by others. It was sort of like the crisis was past, except it wasn't that way for me. I . . . still needed to feel protected.

I had one friend in particular, Jama, who was single at the same time I was widowed, and she sort of took charge and planned things. We gathered our kids together on weekends when we didn't have dates, and we shopped for work clothes at discount stores together.

It felt really close, and then our time together was interrupted. We had a big falling-out when Jama ended up being relocated. I felt like she left town to be away from me. . . . The relationship went from Jama planning our time together to her not even living nearby. . . .

I admit, I wasn't so fair with her. But we eventually got back together, after several years. This was a mature decision on both our parts, and for me it was a turning point. I realized how much I missed her and how I could cope with my own life without her guidance and just enjoy the friendship.

2. *The Twinning Syndrome*. Women often expect their friends to mirror them exactly, to join them in a merged state in which both parties proceed on identical journeys with matching attributes. Then, when one woman changes her life path, overcomes a long-standing obstacle, or achieves a new goal, her friend, sister, mother, or colleague feels abandoned.

Certainly, when we're perfectly happy with our own lives, we're less likely to feel deceived at a friend's "departure" into her own script. But who among us has never felt twinges of doubt, fear, and sorrow as we think about "the road not taken" and bristle at the limitations in our own choices? Thus, the thirty-something woman with three children envies her single girlfriend, imagining the freedom of not having to deal endlessly with diapers, preschools, and all those play dates, while the childless woman sits at her friend's family dinner table and wonders if she is doomed to a lifetime of loneliness.

Again, a little competition is only human, and we've all felt twinges of envy, jealousy, and self-doubt. Psychologist Jo League, whose practice focuses on women's issues, remarks that "It is human nature for women to compete. We want to have good things for ourselves and are resentful when we are not the chosen one." But when women identify so closely with their girlfriends—and particularly when they depend upon them, as good friends are entitled to do—it can be threatening when a friend makes a radically different choice. Instead of remembering that we each have our own path in life, we worry about how our friend's decision reflects on us.

Sybil, a thirty-five-year-old freelance editor, found that her married friends suddenly disappeared once she divorced her husband:

I think that my friends were worried that it was contagious, getting divorced. I guess they also wanted only to be with women who were living the same lifestyle that they were. This was hard for me since I lived in a small town, and I felt as though everyone had ostracized me. My two closest friends were the worst—they acted like I didn't fit in their world, like I had cooties or something. I was no longer invited to the Monday morning breakfast after the kids were dropped off at school. I wasn't on any committees at school with them anymore, as though the committees I was on were suddenly unpopular. I was no longer a part of the clan, because I was doing something different and that made me different.

In the end, Sybil found the banishment so painful that she moved to another town—for financial reasons, but also for social ones: "It was so lonely, getting divorced and losing my girlfriends at the same time."

3. Foul-Weather Friends. Sybil felt that she lost her friends when her social status fell. But women also told me about friends deserting them when their lives improved. Sadly, the old cliché is frequently true: "Men punish the weakest member of the group; women punish the strongest." All too often, we are there for our friends when they're feeling fat, lonely, underpaid, and unappreciated. But when they lose weight, get a guy, or land a much-deserved promotion, we disappear. Struggling with our own problems, we may feel sold down the river by friends who succeed in areas where we feel inadequate, and that sense of treachery can become the occasion for rivalry, backstabbing, and the loss of friendship.

Thus, Amanda, a thirty-eight-year-old business woman, can chart the ups and downs in her friendship with Julie based on how well she herself is, or isn't, doing. During college, Julie was there for Amanda when Amanda's brother became very ill. "Julie was totally supportive, nurturing," Amanda recalls. "She knew how painful it was for me and was willing to listen to all of my stuff. She even came with me to visit him in the hospital. I don't think I could have gotten through without Julie during that time."

Julie's friendship extended through a second difficult time, when Amanda's serious boyfriend, whom she'd planned to marry, broke up with her. "It was Julie who was there, who got me through again," Amanda told me. "She even tried to find me a few dates. Whatever has happened to me that's been tough, Julie has been the one who I could count on."

As a foul-weather friend, Julie was terrific. But when the weather improved, Julie's friendship cooled. "When I got a great job, and then a promotion, and finally got engaged, Julie was icy and not even interested," Amanda said. "In the past few years, I've been pretty solid, and

Julie hardly calls. I think she only likes to be with me when I'm in a crisis. When I'm in a good place, she's distant or even gone."

Sadly, many other women told me stories that echoed Amanda's. Women often form temporary, intense bonds with women whom they either pity or view as equally miserable. If one of the friends in this group of damaged goods lands a husband, finds a terrific job, or loses weight, it causes a schism. The end of mutual misery often means the loss of the friendship.

We Need More Pie!

The U.S. Census informs us that 64 million women are in the workplace today. Clearly, we've finally moved into what was once considered a man's domain. Yet we're still earning only seventy-six cents to every man's dollar. On some level, we know we haven't yet arrived at full equality, and because we're competing primarily with other women, our sisters seem to be responsible for our straitened circumstances. When you compete for a limited slice of the pie, you naturally tend to focus all your anger on your rivals. But who's really responsible for restricting the pie supply?

My own sense is that we'll never overcome the tendency to compete with one another until we focus not on the contest for limited goods but on the larger goal: making more good things available to everyone. Economically, we need better-paying jobs, improved childcare options, and more opportunities for women to advance. Socially, we need more men raised by mothers who believe that women are their equals, more men who are looking for strong women and lasting relationships. Personally, we need to find ways of broadening our standards of attractiveness, so we don't feel the need to enter ourselves in the perpetual beauty contests that seem to be a key feature of many women's lives. Winning these measures will lessen the pressure to continually rate our age, our looks, and our fashion savvy against those of every other woman in the room.

The need for a larger view is all the more urgent now that women are, in fact, operating in a wider domain. "What women cannot readily have is what makes them jealous," comments Dr. Claire Owen. The expanded choices for women in today's society, she says, have also opened up more territories for female competition: "The more options for women in today's society, the more we see these feelings of jealousy and envy in play." In the past, women's competition might be focused on clothes, husbands, children, and lifestyle. Now we're also competing at work, politics, and sports, with increasing pressure to have it all and to succeed in every field.

Still, men tend to keep their power while women battle it out. "Women despise one another on Wall Street," a forty-five-year-old veteran stockbroker explains. "We have no friends at work, simply other women wanting to get ahead and make money. If we need anything, we go to the men. They are still the bosses, for the most part."

Even when women see females in charge at a lower level, they know the top of the pyramid is populated mainly by men. The manager of a New York City nail salon told me that her fifteen female employees compete voraciously for clients. "Who gets better tips, who has the most clients, is what matters," the manager explains. "Then who has a date on Saturday night, who gets engaged. Finally, who will open her own boutique." Although the fifteen women work for a female manager, they're still competing for male-controlled rewards in the form of boyfriends and husbands. And they know that if they do open their own salon, they'll almost certainly be asking male bank officers for loans and seeking to rent real estate from male landlords. Even when women have achieved some small measure of power—owning more than 50 percent of all small U.S. businesses, according to the U.S. Census Bureau, including 6.2 million privately held companies that employ 9.2 million people and produce $1.15 trillion in revenue—men still vastly outrank us.

"If the pie is very small," explains sociologist and professor Dr. Nechama Tec, "then women are not likely to share a piece of it and so they are territorial and not giving, but jealous instead." After all, 64 million women are working, yet only 14 percent of those working women fill managerial positions.

Cutting Off Our Nose to Spite Our Face

One thing became crystal clear to me as I worked on this book: there is something irresistible in tripping the prom queen. No matter how good our own lives are, no matter how much we know better, no matter how we try to remember the importance of female solidarity, every single one of us has at least one moment of looking at a powerful female rival and savoring the fantasy of bringing her down.

So why not give in and do it? What is wrong, after all, with our rivalrous impulses, and why should we not act upon them whenever we get the chance? Even if we don't act out our envy and jealousy, why not at least enjoy the pleasure of watching a rival falter and fail?

I believe that when it comes to female rivalry, none of us can cast the first stone. As I confessed in the introduction to this book, I, too, have had to battle the temptation of seeing other women as my rivals. But the more I have learned about this topic, the more clearly I've seen that this is a temptation we must resist.

First, if we compete with other women over men, looks, and children, we are dooming ourselves to a lifetime of perpetual insecurity. Today we are the one who trips—tomorrow, who knows? We may find ourselves the one whom others seek to trip. Stealing another woman's man, or even taking vicarious pleasure when a woman loses her husband or boyfriend, consigns us to continual worry that our own relationships may be in jeopardy. Reveling in another woman's loss of beauty reminds us that one day, we, too, will face a younger, prettier rival. Seeing our lives as a grand contest among women means entering a competition that we can never finally win.

Second, competing with women at the workplace creates practical problems as well as psychological difficulties. Not only do we deprive ourselves of the companionship of female colleagues, we keep ourselves from relying upon those who should be our natural allies. If women see other women as their primary rivals on the job, we won't gain power but will only lose ground. Instead of focusing on doing the best job possible and on competing, if necessary, with every other employee in our field, we will narrow our energies to petty contests with other women, and our rivalry can easily backfire.

Eloise, a thirty-three-year-old hospital administrator, discovered that competing with a woman on the job only sabotaged her own efforts to succeed:

> I've been promoted twice in the past year. When my boss, a man, brought in a young woman to take over my last job, I decided that she could never do as well as I had done. To that end, whenever she did something smart, I would keep it from our boss.
>
> But when I was on vacation, an emergency came up, and he saw how capable she is. In the end, my seeing her as a competitor took away from my own quality of work. And she got promoted beyond me! If I had only befriended her and thought of it as teamwork, with our male boss and our male coworkers, too, everything would have worked out differently. Next time I'll know not to want someone else to suffer or look like less.

Eloise's soul-searching didn't stop there. Now she wonders, "If I had been able to undermine her, would I be remorseful? Or is it only because I got caught, in a way, that I am rethinking this?" My own hope is that we don't have to keep "getting caught" to see that competing with other women is a dead end. Instead of tearing other women down, we need to broaden our horizons on a wider vision of teamwork, as Eloise suggests, even as we put our efforts into improving our own chances for success.

2

Mommy Dearest and the Evil Sister

[T]he queen . . . turned yellow and green with envy. From that hour, whenever she looked at Snow White, her heart heaved in her breast, she hated the girl so much. And envy and pride grew higher and higher in her heart like a weed, so that she had no peace day or night.

She called a huntsman, and said, "Take the child away into the forest. I will no longer have her in my sight. Kill her, and bring me back her lung and liver as a token."

—"Snow White," the Brothers Grimm,
translated by Margaret Hunt

Rapunzel grew into the most beautiful child beneath the sun. When she was twelve years old, the enchantress shut her into a tower, which lay in a forest, and had neither stairs nor door. . . . "Ah! thou wicked child," cried the enchantress [when she discovered that Rapunzel had become engaged to a handsome prince]. ". . . I thought I had separated thee from all the world, and yet thou hast deceived me." In her

anger she clutched Rapunzel's beautiful tresses . . . and snip, snap,
they were cut off, and the lovely braids lay on the ground. And she
was so pitiless that she took poor Rapunzel into a desert where she
had to live in great grief and misery.

—"Rapunzel," the Brothers Grimm,
translated by Margaret Hunt

Where would fairy tales be without the wicked, envious queen or the jealous, grasping witch? These archetypal stories speak to our sense of a mother's power, and our fear, as daughters, of either competing with them or leaving them. As soon as Snow White is old enough to be considered alluring, the wicked queen orders her execution. The minute Rapunzel reaches the age of puberty, the old witch locks her in a tower, and when she discovers that the lovely girl has still managed to attract a handsome suitor, she strips her surrogate daughter of her most beautiful feature and exiles her to a lonely desert.

But jealous mothers aren't confined to old-fashioned stories. *The Graduate's* Mrs. Robinson, eager to win for herself the younger man who eventually loves her daughter, stands as a modern-day wicked queen whose name is still invoked to denote an older woman who preys on young men. And Rapunzel would almost certainly recognize the enchanting, disturbed mother in Mona Simpson's novel, *Anywhere but Here*, portrayed on-screen by Susan Sarandon in the movie adaptation of the same name, a woman whose possessive love alternately attracts and repels her teenage daughter. ("Strangers always love my mother," the narrator comments at the novel's beginning. "And even if you hate her, can't stand her, even if she's ruining your life, there's something about her, some romance, some power.")

It's no wonder that mothers loom so large in our psyches and play such a significant role in our later relationships with other women. As psychologist Jo League puts it, our mothers are our first mirrors, and their interpretation of us can last a lifetime. "Whatever message the mother gives to her daughter, it is very powerful," League points out. "And when sisters are involved, the relationship becomes even more influential. . . . This is where the patterns get laid down, and they are often carried over to other female relationships."

Indeed, when it comes to determining our future relationships with women, our feelings about our sisters, if we have them, are almost as important as our relationship to our mothers. "It all begins with the family and how the females work together," League remarks. "The daughter processes the modeling and then takes it out into the world with her."

Certainly twenty-nine-year-old Celia, recently engaged, sees her adult sense of rivalry as rooted in her early experiences of her older sister and her mother:

I believe that I have always been envious of others. My sister, who is two years older, is also an envious person, and when we were kids, we would be envious together. We knew who the smartest girls were and who the wealthiest girls were. We knew who had the prettiest mother. But our mother, although she looked good, always worried about who was better, and so we became like her. She taught us to marry well and to ensnare a man. And we did, because we are good pupils.

My mother and her sister were always envious of one another, and at the same time, they did everything together. . . . My mother wanted to travel and my father refused. My uncle and aunt traveled extensively, and this bothered my mother. My mother was the one with the more successful husband and she made it clear to my sister and me that we should have extremely successful husbands and that neither of us should settle, like my aunt.

Now I am about to marry someone who is just as she wanted him to be, and my mother approves. Suddenly I am in the limelight and my mother is paying attention to me, not to my married sister. When I went to find an engagement ring, my fiancé suggested I take my sister. She steered me toward the less beautiful rings because she didn't want me to have something she would envy.

Some days she and I are close, and sometimes I can't escape. Even in
planning my wedding, my sister didn't want it to be too fancy or she
would regret hers, which was only last year. I blame my mother for making us envious of each other from the time that we were kids.

For most of us, our very first lessons in female bonding come from
our mothers and sisters. They teach us to envy and compete, to support
and nurture, or a bit of both. And whether we embrace or reject their
lessons, we often spend a lifetime coming to terms with them.

Good Mother/Bad Mother

For many of us, the image of mother is marked by a profound split. On
the one hand, we adore the all-loving good mother we believe or wish
we had; on the other hand, we fear the all-powerful bad mother, the basis for fairy-tale witches and wicked queens. Cinderella, for example,
has her fairy godmother and her cruel stepmother, while Dorothy, in
The Wizard of Oz, is helped by Glinda the good witch even as she is
threatened by the Wicked Witch of the West. The popular TV show
Gilmore Girls translates this split into modern terms: Lorelai, the hip,
young, thirty-something mother, has a warm, close, almost sisterly relationship with her daughter, Rory, whereas Lorelai's mother, Emily, is
cold, judgmental, and manipulative.

Almost a century ago, pioneering psychoanalyst Melanie Klein, a
specialist in infancy and early childhood, identified this split as basic to
our understanding of our mother's role. Significantly, Klein also wrote
extensively about envy, believing that this painful emotion often characterized the mother-child bond.

In the beginning, Klein suggests, is the breast, source of all nurturance and the baby's first primary experience of satisfaction, the basis
for our fantasies about an all-nurturing mother who will always be
there when we need her. But what about those painful times when
baby is hungry and the breast isn't there? Maybe the mother is in the
other room, on the phone, caring for another child, or simply hasn't

heard the baby's cries. Even if a mother comes running as soon as she hears the infant cry, those hungry, lonely minutes can seem like a lifetime to a newborn, and the young child is filled with resentment. In response, the infant develops the idea that the mother is cruel, manipulative, and withholding.

It's hard for us to reconcile these two experiences—the blissful satisfaction of our mother's response and the painful humiliation of our mother's apparent abandonment or withholding. On this primal level, nothing that a mother does can keep her baby from envying and resenting her power, even if the infant also feels loved, secure, and well nourished.

So here we have our first experience of envying and resenting powerful women, an experience made all the more painful because our mother is usually a woman whom, as infants, we also idolize and adore. And if our mothers are also envious, either of other women or of us, the mother-child relationship is complicated even further. Already upset about our lack of power, we feel even more anxious when we realize that our beloved (and envied) mother envies *us*. Twenty-year-old Sarah describes the conflict vividly:

My mother would comb my hair for hours when I was a little girl. She would tell me that I had hair like spun silk. She would dress me like her: we both had black skirts and yellow sweaters; we both wore jeans, sneakers, and pink sweatshirts. But if I displeased her in some way, she wouldn't let me dress like her. She wouldn't let me be close to her. That was the punishment. And if strangers went on and on about me in the convenience store, my mother would get mad, and she would tell me later, in the car, that she had been an even prettier little girl than I was.

I . . . started to hope that no one would talk about my blond hair when we were out, or my big eyes. I dreaded any compliment, since I never knew if it would please my mother or piss her off. *She* would compliment me as much as she wanted, that was always okay. I just couldn't get too much attention from other people, even my aunts and uncles and cousins, or it would make her angry that she wasn't the best.

Sarah's story demonstrates clearly how, at a very early age, we develop the notion of an idealized "good mother" alongside fears of a demonized "bad mother." In some cases, as in Sarah's, these double identities are based in our mother's actual "dual natures." In other cases, we are simply unable to accept our mother's faults, so we split our hope of a "perfect mother" from our negative fantasies about the "awful mother." This split comes back to haunt us, though: first in unrealistic expectations of other women, then in the inevitable anger and disappointment when once again, our expectations of unconditional love and boundless nurturing are not met.

Sarah's story also reveals how much the envious mother needs her daughter to mirror her exactly. Sarah's mother insisted on wearing the same clothes as her daughter and on seeing her daughter as a little reflection of herself. Yet this need to be identical contains the seeds of envy: if Sarah and her mother are so similar, any deviation threatens to reveal Sarah's superiority, making her the victor in a contest she didn't even know she was in. Like Snow White, Sarah quickly learned that once strangers found her attractive, her mother would be upset. Like Rapunzel, she realized that only her mother was allowed to admire her.

This good mother/bad mother split is such a basic part of our culture that we see it everywhere—in fairy tales, TV shows, even in serious literature. Sleeping Beauty, for example, has both the wicked fairy godmother, who curses her with death at age sixteen (like Snow White's wicked queen, the evil fairy seems to be particularly jealous once the princess is of marriageable age), as well as the protective good fairies who commute her death sentence into a hundred-year sleep. The long-running sitcom *Everybody Loves Raymond* also plays out the split: Ray's wife, Debra, is the good, sensible mother upon whom both husband and children can always rely. Ray's mother, Marie, is the demon mother—overbearing, self-involved, smothering, and particularly jealous of the women whom her sons choose in preference to her.

The bestselling novel *White Oleander* continues but reverses the fairy-tale dichotomy, portraying a daughter torn between a nearly perfect foster mother (played by Renée Zellweger in the film version) and an evil biological mother (Michelle Pfeiffer). The evil mother actually destroys her daughter's foster mother, more concerned with her rivalry than with her daughter's well-being.

If the good mother/bad mother split was confined to our family life, that would be difficult enough. But, as we saw in Chapter 1, we experience a similar conflict with our female friends. Just as we needed our mothers when we were small, we need our female friends and colleagues when we grow up. Part of why *Sex and the City* is so popular, I believe, is because it holds up this image of "girlfriends for life" and reassures us that we're right to count on our women friends. But then, having depended on our girlfriends so much, we find it all the more painful when they fail to provide the unconditional love we so desire. Sometimes our female friends actually betray us; other times, they may simply fail to live up to our (realistic or unrealistic) expectations. Either way, the experience tends to echo our early disappointment with our mothers: we feel that we can no longer count on the one relationship we thought would always sustain us.

As we saw in Sarah's case, the problem is compounded when our primary female role models themselves feel insecure. Adrienne, a forty-one-year-old interior designer, attributes her own sense of insecurity to her mother's modeling of envy:

> When I was in grade school I felt jealous of my friends, one in particular. She was prettier and she came from a better family. We were very close, my friend, Denee and I. We even got our first birth control together and we stayed in touch through college. But I was always jealous of her and how her life was turning out. . . .
>
> In the end, I married a very successful man and I joined his business,

heading up the design team. I saw that I was ahead of Denee at that point—but how could I ever really be ahead? My mother had always pointed out that Denee had a better figure. She was dating like crazy when we were single and she had a good job right out of college. She would always look better and be thinner than I was, I knew that.

I sort of felt we were even when I married first. . . . When Denee married finally, she married a guy with no money and I figured it was some kind of justice. My mother thought so, too.

When I reviewed Adrienne's interview, I was struck by how she repeatedly invoked her mother's authority when describing her own envy. It seemed that Adrienne and her mother had bonded over their shared envy of other women, reinforcing both women's sense of inferiority even as they found a kind of mutual comfort in their common misery. Significantly, Adrienne even envied Denee her more loving mother:

I'm an opportunist on some level because for years I didn't have what I wanted and Denee seemed to be fine. It also had to do with her mother and sisters, since they were always so chummy and my mother was not like that at all.

Sadly, Adrienne felt that her early pattern of envy and insecurity was now a fixed part of her identity, even though she had objectively become more successful:

I'm not proud of these feelings, but I've always been like this. I have great clothes and a beautiful apartment, but I look at everyone else and try to size it all up. I've been like this for so long, it won't be changing now.

I'm more optimistic than Adrienne. I believe we *can* overcome our patterns of envy and jealousy once we understand them. But, as always, recognizing a problem is the first step to solving it.

Three Problematic Patterns

Although many mother-daughter relationships are often tense, the tensions may take different forms. Over the course of my research, I've come to identify three primary ways in which mother-daughter bonds can set us up for lifelong rivalry with other women:

1. The Competitor

Annie, forty-four, is an art teacher and a single mother who has raised two daughters in the suburb of a southern city. Her own mother, she says, competed with every other woman she knew, including her own daughters:

> My mother taught me to never trust another woman. She was not close with her own sisters and she had no women friends. My mother was a great beauty—according to her. . . . I never thought I was pretty until much later on because she wouldn't allow me to be pretty. . . . She wouldn't let me think that way. It never got better, not when I was in high school or college—I could never get it right with her.

Annie's mother is a classic competitor. She trusts neither other women nor her own daughter. As a result Annie and other competitors' daughters must grow up with no images of positive female bonding. The only way they know how to relate to other women is by competing with them. This is Snow White's wicked queen come to life, continually asking the mirror who's the fairest of them all, and consumed with anxiety over the answer.

2. The Merging Mother

Mirthe, thirty-eight, lives in a northeastern city, where she works for a small dress company. Like Annie, she felt that her mother competed with her, especially over looks and male attention. But Mirthe also felt that her mother wanted not a daughter but a clone:

I . . . fight the impulses to not be nice to women because that was what
my mother showed me. She was always jealous of me since I was my father's favorite and I had a desire to work and to get a business degree.
She wanted me to be like her, and at the same time she let me know I
could never be as good as she is. . . .

Merging mothers often give their daughters mixed messages like these.
On the one hand, they invite their daughters to be like them—a clear af-
firmation of their own worth. On the other hand, they convey to their
daughters that if they compete with their mother, they'll always lose. "Be
just like me, but not as good" is the motto of these merging mothers.

The heroine in *Anywhere but Here* sums up the problem: "The thing
about my mother and me is that when we get along we're just the same."
When the daughter feels identical to her mother, she's also competing with
her. Instead of discovering her own unique abilities and desires, the daughter sees herself reflected in her mother's face and feels she must compete.
Saying "We're just the same" invites the inevitable afterthought: "My
mother is smarter, stronger, and more experienced, so she must be a better
version of me than I am." Even if one day the daughter feels that *she's* the
better version—younger, sexier, more ambitious—she's still locked into a
competition that one woman must win and the other must lose. The merging mother thus relates to her daughter through envy, rivalry, and jealousy,
though these emotions may lurk under a mask of affection.

3. Queen Lear

Remember how Shakespeare's King Lear set up a contest among his
daughters? He planned to divide his kingdom, giving the daughter who
loved him most the largest share:

*We have this hour a constant will to publish / Our daughters' several
dowers, / Which of you shall we say doth love us most, / That we our
largest bounty may extend? . . .*

Mothers, too, often set up competitions among their daughters, suggesting that they will give their "largest bounty" to the prettiest, smartest, most successful, or most loving. Sometimes, as we saw with Celia, daughters resent their mother for setting the sisters at odds. In other cases, as with thirty-four-year-old Nicola, the mother's role goes unnoticed and the sisters reserve all their hostility for each other. Nicola insists that she and her sister are "amazingly similar," devoted siblings who will do "anything" for each other. "We share clothes and thoughts, and both of us are tall and blonde," she explains. "There is no competition between us. . . ." But when Queen Lear comes onto the scene, the dynamic changes.

> The problem is when our mother is around. . . . It causes my sister and me to get very competitive. I will be wearing a new sweater and my sister will say, "Did Mommy get you that?" . . .
>
> I'm like that, too. I will see my sister carrying a new bag right after our mother has left town and I'll be upset. . . . I don't know who sets this up since our mother is very fair, but we even compete over what she buys our kids. . . . Besides that, my sister and I get along really well.

Unlike King Lear, who comes right out and asks his daughters to compete, Queen Lear usually disguises her role. Thus Nicola's mother allows her daughters to play out their envy while she remains above the fray. As a result, Nicola alternates between competing with her sister and insisting how alike they are, as if any sign of difference would instantly become the grounds for a new contest.

Ruth's envious mother set up a competition with a sister who wasn't even physically present:

> I had a sister who died before I was even born. This was in the '50s, when growing up an only child was somewhat unusual. So if I was envious of one thing, it was that I'd lost my chance to have a sister. Plenty of my friends had sisters, which made it worse. I would hear that they were go-

ing shopping with their sisters or going on a family vacation, and I felt alone and without something very important. I couldn't tell my mother about this because she was already so sad about my sister all the time.

I always felt my mother missing my sister and envying me my existence. I thought that she was thankful to have me after her loss, but also conflicted. Whenever she looked at me, she saw what she had lost, that I was an only daughter and that she was supposed to have had double that. It was my loss, too, but I doubt she ever saw it that way. My mother was an excellent teacher and she felt she had to protect me from the world. She taught me early on that everyone would love me, and so I operated on this premise. I think she poured everything into me because of my sister who died. But I could feel that envy of hers, that I had what my sister could not have—a life—and that somehow it was my fault.

These three roles are not always so cut and dried. Many mothers alternate between two or more patterns; many mothers, too, offer nurturance and support alongside the envy, as we saw in Sarah's case. My goal here is not to blame mothers—I am one, myself, and I know what a struggle it is to free ourselves completely from these powerful patterns. But I do want us to see how rivalrous the mother/daughter bond can be, even—or especially—when mothers and daughters are also close and loving.

The Never-ending Contest

It's not only our mother's envy of us that is the problem. Many of the women I spoke to described their mothers as envying other women, and then encouraging their daughters to follow suit.

Lourdes, a thirty-three-year-old southwestern social worker, says bluntly, "My mother taught me to never trust a woman. She identifies with males and not with women and she definitely taught me to do the same." Although Lourdes has no sisters, she grew up feeling competitive with her brothers. Nonetheless, Lourdes attributes her current conflicts with female friends to the lessons she learned from her mother.

Despite that, she tried hard to separate from her mother and hew to a different course, and she's frustrated by the way her mother has affected her relationship with other women:

> My mother prefers my three brothers to me and always has. She is male identified, which she claims is on a moral basis. She has no trust in women. She has been divorced twice and widowed once, so she has had this life based on men, as they come and go. If men are wealthy, that matters to her. . . .
>
> I have not looked to be like my mother. I want my girlfriends to matter to me and I want to matter to them. But maybe because of my mother, I keep choosing the wrong women friends. I keep wanting deep relationships with women because my mother wasn't there and she had no close girlfriends. But I keep misjudging my friends because I've had no one to show me how to act and what to expect. It is disappointing because I can't find any friends who are actually giving enough. I misjudge women as friends. It has to do with my mother.

Liza's experience, on the other hand, was almost the mirror image of Lourdes's. Liza, a thirty-nine-year-old accountant, attributes her current triumphant approach to life to her mother's favoritism.

> I have always been special. I am the youngest of four sisters and I was probably a surprise to my parents. . . . I do very well at work, and am still quite pretty. . . .
>
> For me, it's great. I like to be the one everyone wants. Why wouldn't I? . . . Because of how I was raised, I have never doubted myself. It's been fabulous.

Sadly, Liza's victory seems to have come at her sisters' expense, so that even while she glories in winning the family popularity contest, she notes the price paid by the "losers":

> My older sisters felt ordinary in comparison to me and it has always been
> a problem for them. They love me but are also bothered by the way it is.
> I have the handsome husband who makes the most money, and I live in a
> city while my sisters live in the boonies. I doubt they can stand all of this,
> and so they wrestle with their emotions.

Liza never spoke directly to me about how her early experience shaped her current relationships with other women. But it's clear to me that even though she sees herself as a winner, she lives in a perpetual contest. She can't describe her handsome, successful husband without comparing him to her sisters' more ordinary spouses; she sees her own residence as a commentary on their less desirable location. I would suspect either that she has few female friends or that she joins with her friends in a "superiority bond" at the expense of other women. Either way, both Liza (a "winner") and Lourdes (a "loser") live in their mothers' world of continual competition.

An interesting real-life example of a mother's envy shaping her daughters' lives can be seen in the story of Rose, June, and Gypsy Rose Lee. Memorialized in the musical *Gypsy*, Rose is the archetypal stage mother who never got her own chance to shine. At first she tries to make her oldest daughter, June, into the star she could never be, neglecting her younger daughter, Louise. When June runs off to have her own career, Rose molds Louise into a world-famous stripper whose very stage name echoes her mother's—Gypsy *Rose* Lee. Not only does Rose play one daughter off against each other, she also uses both daughters as surrogates for her own frustrated ambitions, and clearly envies each daughter both her success and her eventual independence.

Avoiding the Mother's Mistakes

Some mothers seem to instruct by negative example. Elsie, a twenty-three-year-old student, loves and respects her mother, but definitely does not want to be like her:

I want a career that fulfills me. I am considering public service but everyone tells me there is no money to be made there. Not that I really care. My mother, who is the only one who supports me, feels that this might be a good thing for me to pursue because it interests me. Her example is all about wanting something too much and getting nowhere. She is a woman who worked two jobs most of my childhood. She was always worried. I want to care less and have options. I'm not saying that I don't care about my career, but that it isn't the only part of my life I need to get right. I am flexible and open, because my mother couldn't afford to be.

Reviewing Elsie's interview, I could almost hear her mother saying, "Don't do what I did, Elsie, do the opposite." Neither Elsie nor her mother seems to see Elsie's choices as a negative commentary on Elsie's mother—but to the contrary. Because Elsie's mother is able to admit her own limitations, she offers her daughter a chance to learn from them. Elsie's success doesn't have to come at her mother's expense.

Amelia also wants to avoid her mother's fate:

My mother taught me what not to be. I watched her, an early baby boomer, as she raised us. She acted like a martyr and a victim. She gave up her job and a life outside the home to be our mother. I don't know what she missed more, work or her friends. She just could not get a handle on how to incorporate friends and some kind of part-time work into her life. I saw her as very lost by her obligation to mother us, and she was not happy.

I learned from my mother that women friends are something one really has to have. My mother lost touch with her friends, and both blamed them and missed them. She was so sure that they were all doing better than she was. She hated the fact that some of her friends had money and happy marriages while she had neither. It all seemed like some kind of contest that she had dropped out of but kept thinking she was still in.

If Amelia learned about the importance of female friends from watching her mother's loneliness, Diane learned about the need to limit female friendship from observing her mother's overinvolvement with her girlfriends. As a result, reports thirty-one-year-old Diane, she herself has only a few girlfriends, and she is careful to keep them at a distance.

I never wanted to take my friends as seriously as my mother took hers. My mother would ignore us when her friends were around, and she would be short and unkind toward us while she carried on like the life of the party with her friends. They had been in a sorority together in college, and they still act like they belong to some secret club. It seemed not only hypocritical to me but like it was the wrong priority. I always felt that her friends weren't worth it and I think that they were secretly jealous of her because she was the prettiest and had the cutest husband. They also found my mother irresistible and wanted to be with her.

I'm not sure why I saw all this and my mother saw none of it. To her, her girlfriends were her life. She would sneak out of bed at night after we were all asleep, including my father, to talk on the phone to her friends. She would unplug the phone in the bedroom and have a phone date set for Annie, her best friend, to call at a special time. She would pick up the phone before the first ring was even finished so as not to wake us.

I knew I didn't want a life of that. What else did she have besides us and her friends? My father wasn't very exciting, and my brothers were trouble. I was the one who wanted more from her, but I couldn't get there, couldn't get her attention. My mother used to ask me why I didn't care more about my girlfriends. The answer was because she cared too much.

The Mother's Curse

The threat of a mother-daughter rivalry sends the daughter out into the world without self-confidence. Instead of relying on a strong sense of self-esteem, the daughter has learned that competition will always be part of a relationship between women, so that mother, mother figures, and mentors are always to be feared, as are friends, colleagues, and peers. In such a case, the daughter will find it extremely difficult to tap into the positive aspects of relationships with women.

Mothers, too, are hurt by the perpetual sense of rivalry with their daughters. Like the wicked queen and the witch with whom we began this chapter, they must live in constant fear, either of being surpassed by a younger rival or of being abandoned by a daughter who chafes at their restrictive rule. Such conflicted relationships make it doubly difficult for older women to offer mentorship and advice to younger women, either in the workplace or as friends, while setting up younger women to fear and resent women whose wisdom and life experience might be of real use.

Likewise, when we engage in rivalry with our sisters, whether biological or symbolic, we are reminding ourselves that no woman is ever to be trusted. While in the short term we may enjoy a moment of glee at a sister's defeat, in the long term, we are isolating ourselves from potential allies. Worse, we are offering ourselves as targets for both our sisters and our friends, who may someday resent or diminish our success much as we have diminished the successes of others.

Jacyntha, who at thirty-five has been married to her husband for eleven years, now senses the error of her treatment of her husband's sister.

When Luke and I were first married, his older sister, Nell, was bossy and tried to be with Luke without me. She would call him up on Saturday mornings and ask him to run in the park with her, deliberately inviting him away from me. She did this all the time, even when I was pregnant and especially when I had to take the boys to birthday parties on Saturdays and Sundays. She also wanted him to take her bike shopping, since when they were both single, he had bought her a bike that finally died. For years Luke went with his sister and left me for hours on a Saturday or

Sunday. Then Nell got married and had too busy a schedule to think about Luke. She didn't call on a weekend for a long time. Luke got used to being with us, as he should be, and I felt like I'd won somehow.

About a year ago, Nell's husband had an affair and she left him. Luke wanted me to start inviting her over on weekends so she wouldn't be alone. That was when I decided I'd had enough of Nell's pushing and pulling. I told him no, she wasn't included, I didn't care about her unhappiness, that our children came first and I had no interest in Nell joining us. I was getting back for her meanness, I suppose. Now Nell makes plans with Luke at work and every Thursday night they go out and do something really fun, like play tennis or go to a sport event. For ages I've been asking Luke for a "date night" when I would get a sitter and we could have a night to ourselves. He's never bought into it but he's giving a night a week to his sister. So my banishing her on weekends backfired.

It's tempting to speculate what might have happened had Jacyntha tried to bond with her sister-in-law rather than compete with her. Perhaps what began as a tug of war between two women vying for the same man could have become a deeper and more satisfying friendship, even a new familial bond. But by reaching first for competition rather than connection, Jacyntha isolated both her sister-in-law and herself. This may be the lesson we learn from our mothers and sisters at an early age, but it is a lesson we must find a way to unlearn.

Mean Girls and Heathers

Who among us has fond memories of those teenage years? Virtually every woman I interviewed remembers her middle school and high school years as an unceasing battle in which no one escaped unscathed. Although some of the women I spoke with described best friends with genuine warmth, most of them remembered their adolescence as a training ground for the never-ending female competition that was to mark their adult lives as well.

For example, Diana, age thirty, works for a pharmaceutical company in a large city. Today, she's engaged to be married and is happily part of a circle of female friends. But when I asked her about her teenage years, the vivid memories came pouring out:

> Girls were always mean, even in grade school. By fifth grade, we were stealing each other's boyfriends. . . . By ninth grade I would have dinner with my three best friends on a Saturday night, and two hours later, one of us was making out with one of our best friend's boyfriend somewhere else. . . .

In college . . . girls were backbiting and stole each other's boyfriends. . . . By then we were really invested in each other's achievements, and the idea that someone was better than anyone else, if she made Dean's List or got an internship, drove us crazy. So we kept getting jealous of our good friends, and we were never satisfied until we'd done some damage to someone else.

Although Diana has tried to pull away from her competitive group to create a circle of more genuine friends, she feels discouraged by the jealousy she still encounters:

This past year, I was able to buy myself an apartment. When I showed it to one of my friends, I saw the jealousy in her eyes. . . . I thought she would be happy for me; I thought I'd gone beyond friends who wanted what I had, but I was wrong. . . . Now, sixteen years later, it keeps on going.

Likewise, Melinda, a thirty-three-year-old single woman who is ambitious about her career in advertising, sees high school as a kind of training ground for the female competitiveness she would encounter throughout her life. Indeed, not only was Melinda's later life shaped by the feminine opposition she encountered, her very body has been sculpted to meet the demands of the competition.

When I was in high school, I envied the popular girls and the blondes. And I've envied any beautiful woman ever since. I have spent a fortune on procedures to make me feel better about myself, including breast enhancement, and I became a blonde in high school as soon as I could buy a bottle of bleach. I'm not competitive with my friends, but I also choose friends who are not beautiful. This has always been a problem for me, and I know it, but I can't seem to fix it.

Sandy, a forty-six-year-old full-time working mother of three young children, now has a vision of how women could support one another, a vision that makes the female competition she remembers from adolescence all the more frustrating:

> We would have these beach parties during school vacations. The highlight of our night would be writing cruel things about the other girls in the slam book. We would pepper it with compliments, but basically the fun was in trashing one another. Then we would see who was the most popular and had the fewest critics, and she would win out. . . .
>
> Only when I became a single mother did I realize how much women align, and that each of us deserves to do well. There are plenty of opportunities—with men, with work—if we could only see it that way.

Regardless of teenage girls often expressing their rivalry in covert ways, it is no less destructive—and probably more so—than the overt competition that prevails among teenage boys. In one famous *Seinfeld* episode, George and Jerry bemoan the sadistic gym teacher who used to give the boys "wedgies" and encourage them to beat each other up. "Girls don't do anything like that, do they?" Jerry asks Elaine.

"Oh, no," Elaine replies dryly. "We just tease each other until one of us develops an eating disorder."

In fact, the world of teenage girls may be the one place in our society where female competition, envy, and jealousy are readily acknowledged, both by the culture as a whole and by teenage girls themselves. Movies such as *Heathers*, *13 Going on 30*, and *Mean Girls* portray the world of female adolescence as a snake pit of backbiting, competitiveness, and unbridled rivalry, and teenage girls can't get enough of them. Actually, it was my seventeen-year-old daughter who encouraged me to see *Mean Girls*, a movie that she herself has seen at least a half dozen times.

Nevertheless, despite the growing awareness of teenage girls' aggression and hostility, all too many parents, teachers, and school officials trivialize the very real cruelty that goes on among young women. "Oh, they're all concerned with being popular," a school principal might say. Or, "Girls bond and form cliques—that's just what they do at that age," a teacher might say with a shrug. A well-meaning parent might even insist, "I know that other girls can say and do mean things. But *my* daughter would never be that way, and I know that everybody likes her, too."

The girls, however, would almost certainly tell a different story. According to a study conducted in 2002 by the National Clearinghouse on Family Violence ("Aggressive Girls—Overview Paper" by Artz and Nicolson in Ottawa, Canada), aggression in teenage girls is on the rise, with girls demonstrating more incidents than do boys of the same age. Bullying is another way that teenage girls mistreat one another—again, more common among girls than boys because it is a nonphysical form of harming a peer. My own research, conducted among women between the ages of twenty-five and seventy, confirms this pervasiveness of bullying and meanness. Whether a girl is a perpetrator, target, innocent bystander, or some combination thereof, you can be sure she is deeply affected by the climate of rivalry and competition that seems to characterize virtually every situation in which adolescent females get together. And, as my research has also shown me, both the painful memories and the aggressive behavior linger on well past the high school and college years.

Kathy, for example, was nearly fifty years old when I interviewed her, with a loving husband and four children. Still, she told me, thin, pretty women make her feel insecure about her looks, an insecurity she dates back to her student days:

> I remember in college, there was one woman who all the boys adored. We were in a program for teaching special ed, and I thought she was going to be a serious person. But her looks got in the way of that, and she was really just there to get a husband and to get out of having to teach. I could feel myself, even then, being critical of her for that. I know it wasn't fair, and

if she hadn't been the one the guys liked, I wouldn't have paid her so much attention. This girl was tall and thin and blond, but a bottle job. The fact is, she was not that pretty, and her hair was so fake it was a joke.

When I reviewed this interview, I was struck by how Kathy continued to feel envious of this woman even today. Although she admits that "it wasn't fair" to be so critical, Kathy also makes sure I understand that her rival didn't deserve the attention she got. The fact that Kathy needed to repeat these damning details is a sad testament to the way female competition continues to shape her adult life, as she herself acknowledges:

I think back on this now, and I know that this woman made me feel plain and dumpy. I had this feeling of inadequacy, which lasted for ages, whenever there was a group of chummy women around, or one really pretty woman. It took me years to figure out that I should work on myself and stop worrying about the next woman, the sexier woman. . . .

It has taken most of my life for me to stop being so uneasy with these women. For some reason I don't feel envy if someone has more money or a nicer house—and plenty do—but I will always become uneasy when someone is thin and pretty.

Ironically, the pretty girls, the ones Kathy envies, also suffer from female rivalry. Abbie, who at forty is still considered a great beauty, sees her childhood good looks as the barrier that has kept her from forming close friendships:

I have tried, since third grade, to be nice to the girls. They resented me then, and they resent me now. Even if they got married, had kids, had a nice life, even if they had plastic surgery, they still resented me. I know better than to trust a new friend, and I wonder why women are so cold to me when they meet me. Or some women are obnoxious when we are introduced, and I am so naïve, I wonder what I am doing wrong. Then I remember that it is because of how I look. Women have been envious of me my whole life, and it has taken me a long while to figure it out. . . .

Deadly Friends

This dreary view of female adolescence has been explored in a number of books by psychologists, educators, and journalists, all of whom portray the teenage years as a particularly challenging time for young women. For example, pioneering psychologist Carol Gilligan, writing with Lyn Mikel Brown, published *Meeting at the Crossroads: Women's Psychology and Girls' Development* in 1992. In this groundbreaking book, Gilligan was the first to lay out the notion that somewhere between ages nine and twelve, girls face a serious loss of self-esteem. As they enter adolescence, Gilligan argued, girls begin to mute their voices, seeking to fit in rather than to achieve. As they strive to become women, girls bow to "The Tyranny of Nice and Kind" (the subhead for one of Gilligan's chapters) and become more interested in pleasing their friends, parents, and teachers than in discovering their own thoughts, feelings, and abilities. In a memorable phrase, Gilligan suggested that young girls become anthropologists, seeking to understand and then adapt to the rules of the culture within which they find themselves, a culture that calls on them to value relationships more than either accomplishments or authenticity.

Although Gilligan doesn't focus on female rivalry per se, she does describe the "relational struggle" that teenage girls undergo, so that their friendships become a crucial part of their transition from childhood into adolescence. My own research has shown me that the competitiveness among girls may very well be the basis for the dramatic loss in self-esteem that Gilligan describes. As girls become teenagers, the world seems to remind them at every turn that the most glittering prizes are reserved for the prettiest, the nicest, and the most popular. Thus Victoria, whom we met in

Chapter 1, feels that female rivalry has shaped her life, and that her teenage years were when she first learned to despise herself for being a "loser":

> I admit that I was jealous of friends by the time I was in junior high. I saw how the boys gravitated to a handful of girls, and I wanted to be one of them. I saw how teachers preferred certain students, and I wanted to be in that circle. I knew that some of my friends had parents with money and lived in bigger houses and had more things, and I also felt denied on that front. It seems that until I was twelve or thirteen, nothing mattered but having fun with my girlfriends. . . .
>
> Then one day it all changed. Some girls looked better than me; other girls were more popular. I began to hate their successes and loathe my failures.

Psychologist Mary Pipher also details teen girls' loss of self-esteem in her book *Reviving Ophelia*. Pipher begins her poignant exploration of female adolescent anguish by recounting the cautionary story of her cousin Polly. An adventurous, athletic, and opinionated tomboy with a wide circle of friends including both girls and boys, Polly became a different person as she entered her teen years—moody, withdrawn, and apathetic. Her personality change, as Pipher saw it, was inspired by the abrupt ostracism she experienced, as her tomboyish ways were suddenly no longer acceptable to either sex.

Often, when an adolescent like Polly emerges from her depression, the carefree, daring adventurer becomes a coy teenager preoccupied with fashion and popularity, apparently content to look on admiringly while boys take the lead. This is a terrible loss for these young women, due to a cultural climate that distorts a young woman's self-image. Many teenage girls feel like outcasts amid their female peers. Rather than working together, these young women are separated in the midst of this troubling period. Thus, Shawna, who at thirty-seven has two small daughters and a comfortable life, recalls how she and her childhood friend, Jill, developed a competition that utterly preoccupied both of them.

> Jill and I competed for grades, guys, and friends in school. Whoever was
> most popular in our clique had to be closest to one of us. We would diet,
> and whoever lost more weight won that one.

As with Kathy, Abbie, and Victoria, Shawna sees her teen contests
as the training ground for a lifetime of rivalry:

> We competed for who would marry first, and I won that one. But Jill got
> engaged immediately after I did, and she had to have her wedding as
> soon as we got back from our honeymoon. We cut our honeymoon short
> for her. We competed for who had the best wedding shower, better
> wedding gifts. When my husband and I bought our house, I saw how
> jealous Jill was. . . . Everything we did had to be the same, or one of us
> felt cheated and like a loser.

Shawna and Jill's symbiotic rivalry recalls a chilling scene from the
movie *Heathers*, a black comedy in which disaffected but popular Veronica begins systematically murdering the clique of popular teenagers that
rules the school. In a sardonic commentary on how girls enforce con-
formity, all the other popular girls are called Heather. Veronica (played
by Winona Ryder) has just given a drink laced with Drano to one of the
nastiest Heathers. When she dies, Veronica gasps, "I just killed my best
friend!"

"And your worst enemy," her boyfriend (Christian Slater) reminds
her.

"Same difference," replies Veronica.

Like Veronica and Heather, Jill and Shawna seem joined at the hip
in a half-friendly, half-deadly competition. So long as they compete,
they are prevented from asking whether the game is worth the candle.
Egging each other on to continue the competition, they lose both the
chance to support each other and the opportunity to question the
terms of the fight. Who has time to ask whether marriage is what she
really wants, whether it matters whose house is bigger, why it's so im-

portant to stay thin and pretty? As long as our minds are on the contest, we can forget about anything except winning.

Mary Pipher blames the problem on what she calls a girl-poisoning culture, and I'm inclined to agree. The pressures on teenage girls go far beyond whatever messages they receive at home, extending into the larger world of media, school, politics, and the economy. But if our culture deserves to be called girl poisoning, it is often girls themselves who pass on the tainted cup, whether literally, as in *Heathers*, or only metaphorically, as among the female summer interns described by Ruth La Ferla in her August 4, 2002, article in *The New York Times* Sunday Styles section. "I dress better than you, I'm better connected than you, I'm richer than you, and I'm younger than you," was the blown-up quote used to illustrate La Ferla's article, "Attack of the Summer Intern," suggesting that these young women would have been happy to destroy their rivals with words if not in deed.

Sometimes the rivalry does turn deadly, as in the Queens, New York, stabbing incident reported by Michelle O'Donnell in the October 12, 2004, *New York Times*. Two teenaged girls aged sixteen and fifteen living in a city housing project were quarreling over a boy who had once dated the fifteen-year-old but had moved on to the older girl. Suddenly, according to the police, the fifteen-year-old girl reached out and slashed the older girl's face. A third girl handed the sixteen-year-old a six-inch dagger, which the injured girl promptly plunged into the younger girl's chest.

When I came across this article, I was horrified but not surprised. It seemed to me that the lethal culture of female rivalry could quite easily lead to actual murders, with a supportive girlfriend literally handing you the blade with which to kill your rival. The reaction of William Lake, a dazed adult who happened to be visiting his mother in a nearby apartment, was quite different. "Kids fight, but not like this," he commented. "Maybe it wouldn't shock me if it were boys. But girls . . ."

Odd Girls and Queen Bees

Gilligan and Pipher only hint at the female rivalry that can erode a girl's self-esteem and cripple her confidence. Two more recent books have made female aggression their central topic. Journalist Rachel Simmons published *Odd Girl Out* in 2002, the result of her visits to some thirty schools and her interviews with three hundred girls, from all classes, ethnic groups, and geographic regions. Everywhere she went, she found depressingly similar results: tales of female rivalry, jealousy, envy, and bullying. When she asked a group of ninth-grade girls to explain the ways in which girls' and boys' meanness differed, the group was quick to tell her:

> [Girls] destroy you from inside.
> There's an aspect to evil in girls that there isn't in boys.
> Girls target you where they know you're weakest.
> I feel a lot safer with guys.

Simmons found something that my own research bears out: precisely because girls form such intimate friendships, they have special access to the emotional areas where their friends are the most vulnerable. "In fact," Simmons writes, "it is the deep knowledge girls have of relationship, and the passion they lavish on their closest friends, which characterizes much of their aggression." And because girls are so afraid of losing their friends, the fear of loss becomes a weapon that a bully can use.

I'm reminded of Leah, a friend of mine who experienced a similar dynamic as an adult.

> Myra was one of my dearest friends—I thought. But I've come to realize that she used our friendship as blackmail. Whenever we disagreed, whenever I didn't want to go along with what she wanted—and, yeah, whenever I screwed up—she'd convey that she was so hurt and upset, our friendship was in jeopardy. I was so terrified of losing her, I'd panic

and agree to whatever she wanted. And if I ever stood up to her, she knew exactly what to say to shut me up. It was like she had a whole catalogue of my worst faults and greatest fears, and she wouldn't hesitate to mention them. It's taken me a while to realize that our relationship just wasn't worth it. I still miss her, but I don't like being bullied.

My friend was a woman in her early sixties who was saddened but not devastated by the loss of a lifelong friend. But when you're a teenager, it's not so easy to let go of an important relationship, particularly if you think you're sacrificing not just one friend but your entire social standing. Nor is it always easy to distinguish between aggression and affection. Jeanette, who works as an office manager, described a longtime friendship embodying such an interwoven pattern of companionship and rivalry that I honestly couldn't tell whether she liked her friend, resented her, or felt some complex mixture of both:

> I grew up always feeling like less, and this was because I was never pretty enough. I saw that my sister and my friends, who were prettier, were treated better. . . . I remember that my pretty best friend in grade school and high school always had something over on me. She was the one everyone gravitated to, and I was her sidekick.

Although Jeanette is now thirty-nine—very far from the awkward teenager who played the sidekick—she can't seem to stop competing with someone who is supposed to be her friend.

> It is ironic that she has not aged as well as I have. Although . . . her looks gave her an edge early on . . . today, I would say that I am ahead of the game, finally. And that is how I continue to think: Who is ahead, who is the winner, who is prettier.

Female rivalry, mixing intimacy with hostility, has continued to shape not only Jeanette's friendships but her entire self-image. Perhaps she would never say anything to her friend about not aging well; perhaps her friend never said anything to her about being a less pretty teenager. But it's clear that, in Jeanette's mind, at least, the two women's intimate knowledge of each other serves as a weapon that each woman always knows the other *might* use. Their very closeness makes their relationship that much more competitive, and that much more dangerous.

If intimacy is the grounds for betrayal, it doesn't really matter who wins—you're always vulnerable to attack from the people you *should* be able to trust. Thus thirty-three-year-old Betsey says frankly that she's always been one of the most beautiful women in her circle. But ever since she was a teenager, her beauty has made her both popular and a target:

Being beautiful is an advantage, no question. But other women hate it, and the prettiest women are always on guard. From being the homecoming queen to getting the star football player, the perks have always been there. Even in grade school everyone seemed happy to be with me because I was so pretty. . . .

My best friend from high school, who was equally cute and popular, has really aged and seems to be a hausfrau now. It's like she's just handed over all of the stuff that made her special just to be a wife and a mother. I don't want to be like that. I want to be who I always was, the prettiest and the most popular. We live in a small town, and I work hard to make sure I am in demand. I befriend all the mothers in my son's grade and I make sure that I am head of the PTA and all of that. That way, I am remembered. Then I have to work hard to make sure I am pretty for my age and as much a winner as I was in high school.

It is a lot of work and no one is really my friend, except for my best friend, the one who is losing it. She is starting to hate me for keeping my looks. And the others hate me because they never had any looks to begin with. I doubt I can win, whatever I do. So I just work on what seems best for me, even though it's sort of lonely because few women like me, because I'm still pretty. Maybe they never liked me.

Betsey's uncertainty—her questions about who is *really* her friend—have extended into adulthood, but the training for such maneuvers begins in childhood. Rosalind Wiseman, author of *Queen Bees and Wannabes: Helping Your Daughter Survive Cliques, Gossip, Boyfriends, and Other Realities of Adolescence*, likens teenage girlfriends to a platoon of soldiers who have banded together to survive adolescence. In fact, she says, teenage girls develop an entire chain of command, with the queen bee ruling the little group, catered to by various wannabes.

Jeanette invokes this worldview by referring to herself as her prettier friend's sidekick. Apparently, Jeanette's friend was the queen bee, and Jeanette managed to stay in the group only by currying favor with her. Although today Jeannette has gained some confidence in her appearance, she still feels on edge because in her mind the competition still exists.

Writer and actress Tina Fey makes the dynamics crystal clear in her screenplay for *Mean Girls*, the fictional movie based on Wiseman's book. *Mean Girls* revolves around Cady Heron (Lindsay Lohan), a pretty but naïve teenager who has been home-schooled by her anthropologist parents during their extended residence in Africa. Now Cady must face a different sort of jungle—high school—which she observes with scientific detachment, commenting with bewilderment on the cruelty, bullying, and jockeying for power that she observes.

The popular clique, known as the Plastics, take Cady into their ranks, where she gets a firsthand look at the elaborate rituals of gossip, humiliation, and proofs of friendship in which the girls engage. For example, using three-way calling, one girl telephones Cady and attempts to trick her into saying something nasty about a third girl, who, unbeknownst to Cady, is listening on the other line. The girls also explain their fashion rules to Cady—on certain days they must wear pink; on other days, they can't wear pink—with appropriate punishment for the girl who, knowingly or unknowingly, violates the code.

Like the nonfiction book on which it is based, *Mean Girls* makes it clear that female rivalry is a high-stakes game. The relentless tyranny and mockery are genuinely destructive, and girls can easily emerge from their high school experience with damage that takes a lifetime to undo.

Envy Without Boundaries

Most often, teenage girls compete over fashion, weight, looks, boys, and general popularity—all the superficial values of what Pipher calls our girl-poisoning culture. But when girls compete over brains and achievement, the results can be equally problematic.

Justine, for example, a forty-eight-year-old entrepreneur, has spent a lifetime trying to reconcile her brains and ambition with her wish for female friends. As a teenager, she explains, she got the message that smart girls would never be popular:

> My friends in high school hated me because I was so smart. My girlfriends resented it when I was awarded a scholarship to college. . . .

After Justine graduated college, she came to terms with her own ambition and went off to found a business of her own, going into partnership with a close friend. At first, she believed she had resolved the problem that had plagued her since her teenage years. Surely, she thought, she and her friend could support each other, since they were now literally working toward the same goal. But as soon as they became successful, the competition resumed:

> At first we struggled, then we became successful, and then the competition and bad feelings between us set in. And this wasn't about men against women, it was about my partner and me. I think she secretly hated my intelligence, whereas I saw it as the two of us having separate strengths. She was better at bringing in the business, and I was better at strategizing. In the end, we went our separate ways.

Today, Justine explains, she has simply come to accept that she can't trust either women in general or her friends in particular:

Today I work for a small company, and there are less headaches than in running one's own business. I am wary of women at work, and I am wary of my friends. In order to have less competition, I say very little to women coworkers about my work, and I try not to act too smart.

Although Justine concludes with an apparently strong attitude—"I have stopped worrying about who is really on my side, male or female"—it was clear to me that she had simply given up. Exhausted from a lifetime of dealing with female rivalry, she had merely decided to keep all women at arm's length. Perhaps she would be attacked, but she would never again be betrayed.

Marolina is almost twenty years younger than Justine, and she comes from an entirely different culture—her family emigrated from Ecuador when Marolina was twelve. Despite the generational and cultural differences, she speaks of girlfriends with the same wariness as Justine, expressing the same sense that women's envy is without boundaries:

Girlfriends all envy you. Whatever you do, wherever you go, whatever lifestyle you have, your friends are jealous of something. I have two friends who I can trust; with the rest, I am very guarded.

Marolina believes that she has good reason for her suspicions. Her supposed friends, she says, will stop at nothing to get what they want, regardless of whether another woman is hurt:

In my culture, there is lots of cheating in young marriages. I believe that my friends take each other's men because there is no respect between the women.

Marolina is unusual among her friends; while they struggle with the rigid restrictions of their immigrant parents, her own family allows her a bit more freedom. This, too, Marolina says, is grounds for envy:

I watch my girlfriends rush to get married just to get away from the house. It still is like that in our religion and with our families. So even if my mother does pressure me to get married, my girlfriends are jealous of the freedom that I have. I travel where I want and do what I want, and this is the reason they envy me.

Yet Marolina says her freedom is only the current pretext for her girlfriends' envy:

Before that, it was something else, that I was pretty, that my father does well. It is always something.

I asked Marolina whether she'd felt the same degree of envy growing up in her home country. Significantly, she said no:

Over there, my girlfriends and I were raised to be close, and our mothers did things together. . . . When we got here, things changed. Some of us were married off right away, and some of us wanted to go to college. It began to change the way we were together. By then we were also teenagers and we were starting to compare ourselves, our boyfriends, our clothes, our nights out. It began to get out of control. That is how it is with your girlfriends, they aren't ever friends, especially as our lives change.

From Archie Comics to *Joan of Arcadia*: Grounds for Hope?

When I remember my own teen years, I think of Archie comics, the endless battle between straightforward, down-to-earth blond Betty—hopelessly infatuated with Archie but rarely more than a pal to him—and glamorous, treacherous, dark-haired Veronica, the perpetual object of Archie's desire.

Despite the fact that I'm not blond, I identified with honest Betty, and I cherished the times when she won out over Veronica, even as I puzzled over the comic plots in which she and Veronica actually seemed to be friends. How could you be friends with someone who was your rival, I wondered. Why would Betty ever trust Veronica, knowing how often Veronica had schemed behind her back to win Archie, or how often Archie had simply ignored Betty in his pursuit of the dark-haired girl? I was also confused at the role of class and money. There was a clear implication that Veronica was more desirable, even more beautiful, because she was rich; yet the comic also seemed to criticize her as spoiled and unpleasant (the perfect match for rich-guy Reggie), while Betty's middle-class income made her both plainer and nicer (just like Archie). Finally, I couldn't understand why Veronica was supposed to be so much more beautiful than Betty, though everyone seemed to agree she was. They both looked equally pretty to me—why was it so important to know which one was better?

Looking back, I realize that important messages about female rivalry (among other things) were inscribed in those innocent-seeming Archie comics. Underneath the placid small-town exterior, the lessons came through loud and clear: Beauty is the most important factor in winning a man's heart—except sometimes it's better to be nice. Women must depend on each other for friendship—except when they're competing, as they always do. Having more money doesn't necessarily make you better than someone else (in fact, it might even make you worse)—but it does make you more desirable. In other words, the comics summed up the mixed messages that every woman of my generation received, messages that shaped the contradictory legacy of female friendship and feminine rivalry that made girlfriends both so important and so dangerous.

Archie comics continue to be sold at a remarkable rate, and my daughters still pick up the Betty and Veronica issues today, as do my female students. Clearly, even young women in their twenties are fascinated by the never-ending battle between the two female friends. And there's no shortage of more recent media imagery to teach girls that they both need girlfriends and must learn to fear them. Yet I am also struck by one of the small but significant studies of teen culture that actually shows teen girls working through their differences to create bonds that are at least somewhat more healthy.

On *That '70s Show*, for example, the Fox sitcom that chronicles the lives of five teenagers in the tiny town of Point Place, Wisconsin, the two female characters are shown to be as different as two girls could be. Jackie is the Veronica—rich, spoiled, fashion obsessed, sure of her good looks, sharp-tongued about the shortcomings of other girls, and perpetually bossing around her unfortunate but devoted boyfriends. Donna is the Betty (a redhead in the first few seasons, she has now actually dyed her hair blond)—down to earth, a casual dresser, a budding career woman, dreaming of success. She acts like "one of the guys" and is literally the girl next door, neighbor to Eric, the show's hero and her sometime boyfriend. For the first couple of seasons, the two girls were not rivals, exactly, but hardly friends: Jackie relentlessly mocked Donna's height and lack of fashion sense, while Donna joined the guys in baiting and teasing Jackie.

Gradually, though, the two girls develop a tentative friendship. When Donna is puzzled about why her first sexual experience is so unsatisfying, it's Jackie she turns to for comfort and advice. When Jackie's mother abandons her and her father ends up in jail for white-collar crime, Donna is the one who offers to take her in. "You've got to help her, Donna, she's your best friend," one of the guys tells Donna.

"God, she is!" Donna exclaims in disbelief. "How the hell did that happen?"

Although the show gets plenty of comic mileage out of the gap between Donna and Jackie, the two females are also shown to be supportive and reliable, in their way. They're so different, they can't really compete, nor can they betray each other. Although in real life, one can't imagine these girls spending five minutes in the same room, there's something sweet about a TV show creating an alternate reality in which the feminine Jackie and the feminist Donna manage to coexist without trying to change each other, let alone to destroy each other. (Typically, when other women are involved, Jackie is relentlessly competitive, while Donna is usually confident enough to avoid rivalry.)

Another show to explore teens working through their differences was *Buffy, the Vampire Slayer*, which ran for several seasons on the WB network and is currently in syndication. Buffy is "the chosen one," literally the only girl of her kind; according to legend, one vampire slayer is chosen every generation, and Buffy, the ex-cheerleader, is that one. Her best friend, Willow, is Buffy's opposite in almost every way: brunette where Buffy is blond, shy where Buffy is bold, geeky where Buffy is cool. Yet the two girls really need each other. Periodically, an episode would focus on Willow's jealousy of Buffy, or on her frustration with Buffy's sense of specialness and isolation, or on her loneliness when Buffy finally meets another slayer. Again and again, the two girls must relearn the basic lesson: each is a separate person with her own strengths, and competition only weakens them both.

For a few seasons, Buffy and Willow were aligned against Cordelia, the real "Veronica" of the show. Rich and spoiled, the raven-haired Cordelia was universally hated by Buffy and her friends. But gradually, that opposition also broke down as Cordelia reluctantly came to join the slayer group, which, equally reluctantly, came to accept her. It was never an easy alliance: it took work, and often there were fights and bitter misunderstandings. But precisely for that reason, the show offered a very positive message, which is that friendship is neither a blissful merging nor a treacherous battle. Rather, it's a dynamic relationship between two unique humans who must always work at communicating and connecting.

More recently, the CBS show *Joan of Arcadia* has made teen female friendship a central theme. For several episodes in fall 2004, Joan's best friend was Judith, an adventurous but troubled girl who admires Joan enormously. In one episode, Joan believes that her boyfriend, Adam, is cheating on her with Judith. Both Adam and Judith are tremendously hurt by the false accusation. Joan and Judith end up fighting in the hallway, for which Joan (but not Judith) is punished by being made to clean up graffiti from the school walls. When Joan finally realizes her mistake, she is overcome with guilt. Then, in a moving scene, Judith appears at Joan's side to help with the cleanup in a silent gesture of forgiveness and solidarity. Significantly, the girls don't need to talk to reestablish their relationship, whereas Joan and Adam must engage in a lengthy conversation before things are right again.

The Price We Pay for Teenage Rivalry

In this chapter, I've focused on how girls participate in teenage rivalry. But we must never forget the extent to which our culture encourages this battle between girls over boys, looks, popularity, and status, a competition that seems to begin earlier every year, setting the stage for lifelong scenarios of envy, jealousy, and competition.

The price we pay for entering this deadly arena is high. Teenage girls, knowing how difficult it is to live up to the narrow definition of the "popular" girl—thin, pretty, and perpetually nice—discharge their frustrations in bullying and covert nastiness. Meanwhile, girls are typecast with labels that may stick with them for the rest of their lives: tomgirl, slut, nerd; fat, pretty, popular. On a recent episode of *Desperate Housewives*, the slutty character played by Nicollette Sheridan, Edie, makes a telling remark to good-girl Susan (Teri Hatcher). Wasn't Susan a cheerleader and honor student, Edie asks, and Susan, of course, admits that she was. Edie, for her part, was promiscuous and ostracized, a role she continues to play today. Even now that she is in her forties, all poor Edie wants is acceptance, to be invited to the Tuesday lunch poker games that are the primary solace of women on Wisteria Lane. Edie remains trapped in the dream of high school popularity, while the other women, envious of Edie's sexual appeal, are likewise constrained by their teenage envy. The message couldn't be clearer: teenage competitiveness means that we end up viewing ourselves and other women as winners or losers based on what happens early in our lives.

But if we perpetuate these high-school-era models into our adulthood, where will the next generation of teen girls look for inspiration? If only someone—parent, teacher, career woman—would break the vicious cycle, we wouldn't have to cheer for Betty against Veronica. Instead, we could each enjoy a clear sense of our own unique capabilities and options, a sense of self that we could pass on to our daughters. We would finally be able to suit ourselves, to follow not the destiny prescribed by our looks or personality but the destiny we chose for ourselves.

Like the desperate housewives on Wisteria Lane, forty-year-old Claudia is still lamenting the scars she accrued in her teenage years. Now a director of daytime activities at a women's organization and a happily married woman, Claudia can still feel the pain of those earlier days:

> If only my mother hadn't made me feel an outcast. If only she hadn't made me feel fat and that my curly hair was hideous. She actually preferred my blond, skinny best friend. It took me years to stop reacting to that. I figured, if my mother thought that about me, then the rest of the world saw it the same way.
>
> I was also a really good student, and in my hometown, that wasn't as valued as being popular. So I would sort of disappear when I got the A and others were getting C's. The boys were nice to me when it came time to get homework in, and I was so needy, I'd let them see my finished work. But they gravitated toward the other girls—the in-crowd—even in junior high. Had I grown up this way in the '90s or today, I'd shoot myself. Then it wasn't as big a deal, although I surely suffered. But if Britney Spears and Lindsay Lohan had been on magazine covers, I don't think I would have survived.

Claudia found a way out of her teenage prison. But she insists that, despite her later success, she continues to pay the price for adolescent rivalry:

> What happened that worked for me is that I read enough and learned enough to understand a world beyond looks and popularity. So I made

my own way. I got into a good school on a scholarship because I figured out that was important. I admit, I also lost weight and straightened my hair and finally got a boyfriend by eleventh grade, after years of suffering. . . . I only wish someone who mattered, like my mom or her sisters, had been able to reinforce this and help me out with it.

Part 2

Best Rivals and Worst Friends

4

The Perpetual Beauty Contest: Envy over Appearance

"How Much Younger Can You Look in a Week?"
"Which Woman Will Keep Her Looks the Longest?"
"Get Beautiful! Look Like You, Only Better."

The headlines, from *Harper's Bazaar*, *Marie Claire*, and *InStyle*, say it all. Women are engaged in a perpetual beauty contest that extends to every aspect of their lives, competing with other women, younger women, even with themselves. The message is clear: women are judged relentlessly, not only by how we look but by how we measure up to an impossibly rigid set of standards.

Women competing over their looks is such an old story that it's become a cliché. But that doesn't mean it isn't true. Of the five hundred women I interviewed, nearly 80 percent mentioned competing with other women over physical appearance. Even among women who didn't primarily define themselves by their appearance, the topic of beauty almost invariably emerged as a painful area.

And no wonder. Everywhere we look, a barrage of media images encourages us to compare ourselves not only with each other but with the most beautiful women in the world, women who have made a full-time job of taking care of their skin, their bodies, their teeth. In a February 22, 2004, *New York Times Magazine* special issue, author Mary Tannen comments dryly in her article "Women on the Verge" on how the standards for beauty are rising:

> Helicopter into an Indian village in the mountains of Colombia, extract a sixty-year-old peasant, fly her to Manhattan and stand her next to a sixty-year-old event planner, and you will immediately see how modern urban society has changed the way we look. The peasant feels she has made herself presentable if she has washed her face and combed her hair. The event planner has found it necessary to have a chin implant, an eye tuck, and dermabrasion. The peasant is happy that she has enough teeth to chew her food. The event planner, thanks to her dentist, has all her teeth, which she has whitened regularly. Furthermore, when the event planner's daughter is sixty years old, she will judge her mother's improvements crude and rudimentary.

Tannen was trying to make a point about the punishing pace of cosmetic improvements, but she inadvertently illustrated the theme of female rivalry as well. The sixty-year-old event planner is relieved to win the competition with her peasant counterpart, but is already judged and found wanting by her daughter.

This endless cycle of competition—a contest that every woman must eventually lose—is echoed poignantly by Samantha, a third wife who at age fifty is now competing not only with other women but also with her younger self:

> I look at pictures from twenty years ago, and I can't stand it. I hate myself today. So I hate anyone and everyone who has it better.

Samantha's impossible contest is far from unique. Elsewhere in *The New York Times Magazine*, in a photo spread entitled "It's All in the Genes," movie star Natasha Richardson admits, "My feeling beautiful has always been linked to being five pounds less." Although Richardson is younger than Samantha, she, too, has entered a competition that by definition she can never win. Just as Samantha will never match the beauty of her younger self, so Richardson will never attain beauty in the present tense, only in some unreachable future when she is "five pounds less." Their dilemmas remind me of the White Queen's statement to Alice in Wonderland: Jam yesterday, and jam tomorrow, but never jam (or beauty) today.

In the relentless competition over beauty, plastic surgery becomes an obvious option, but even there, the stakes keep getting higher. In an April 15, 2003, edition of the *The Wall Street Journal*, Jennifer Saranow reports that by forty-five, many women have already had work done on their face, neck, and eyes. Now, she says, they're doing their hands. Likewise, in another *New York Times Magazine* article, Daphne Merkin asks Upper East Side plastic surgeon Gerald H. Pitman whether cosmetic surgery is addictive. "He stares at me as if I were being obtuse," Merkin writes. "'Is alcohol addictive,' he replies; it is an assertion, not a question."

My own interviews with plastic surgeons confirm that women can become "plastic surgery junkies" driven by an obsessive belief that winning the looks competition will somehow gain them the husband, career, or self they desire. Yet thanks to the She's Had Work Done syndrome, even women who have undergone plastic surgery are not necessarily safe from their female rivals, who are apt to follow any admiring comment with a contemptuous whisper: "Don't you think she's had some work done?"

Sometimes women feel frantic to have surgery before the aging process kicks in. "Women have to watch out," one of my savviest friends warns me, "or they'll have procedures too late and everyone younger will be way ahead."

On the other hand, sometimes women have their plastic surgery too early, or find that, for medical reasons, it simply doesn't work. Susanna, a fifty-two-year-old florist, reports:

> I am a breast cancer survivor. I had a face-lift the year before my surgery and it didn't hold because my estrogen plummeted. I am not a jealous person, but I felt that my friends who took hormones were doing better and looking years younger than I was. Then the hormone studies came out and I felt almost vindicated. There had been a period when it was the rage to take these pills and I wasn't in on it. Now the pills have been reexamined and I feel better about it. I feel we are all on a par. We all are sagging and hellish looking, and have to find other means to preserve ourselves.

It's not only faces and hands that women seek to resculpt. New trends in plastic surgery include Beverly Hills plastic surgeon Dr. Lloyd Krieger's "indented" tummy tuck. For $7,000 to $10,000, Dr. Krieger will not only cut along the bikini line to remove excess belly fat but will also cinch the waist muscles to create an hourglass shape. He's developed this procedure, explains Stephanie Kang in an August 6, 2004, *Wall Street Journal* article, because the new fashions call for a cinched-in waist. As women compete with each other to measure up, they reach for any weapon they can, even the surgeon's knife.

Modeling agencies have also felt the pressures of this new look, Kang reports, shifting from their classic 35-24-36 requirement to a curvier look of 35-24-38. The slightly larger hips are designed to make the waist look smaller. Imagine the competition at the modeling agencies, where two extra inches of flesh can make the difference between getting or not getting a prize job. As I peruse the pages of magazines and newspapers, looking for stories about female beauty, I've begun to have the feeling that no aspect of a woman's life or body is exempt. A headline in the August 31, 2004, edition of *The New York Times* proclaims that "In the relentless pursuit of fashion, feet pay the price."

Journalist Lorraine Kreahling reports that fashionable shoes are creating a host of health problems for women, from pain in the back, neck, and knees to nerve damage and arthritis. Virtually all bunion surgery is done on women, according to Dr. Gary Jolly, president of the American College of Foot and Ankle Surgeons. And, Kreahling notes, the very latest trend in cosmetic surgery focuses on the feet, as women have their toes straightened, shortened, or even removed in order to provide a better fit for high-style footwear.

Even more chilling is a September 27, 2004, *New York* magazine article by Laurie Abraham, reporting on the trend for pregnant women to worry about restricting their weight and maintaining their figures. Abraham's article begins with a look at Margot Tenenbaum, a popular, happily married, and successful, size-eight woman who went into paroxysms of dismay when she contrasted her own early eight-pound weight gain during pregnancy with a friend's report that she had never worn maternity clothes because she had been too nauseous to eat. The article then cites a 2003 Johns Hopkins study finding that 21 percent of well-educated, affluent, Baltimore-area pregnant women reported engaging in various types of "weight-restrictive behavior," including fasts before their doctor's visits.

Many of the women I spoke with expressed mixed feelings about their own pregnancies. For example, Gabriella, a forty-three-year-old sales executive for a large company, expected that her pregnancies would win her points in the never-ending contest among her fellow suburban wives. Instead of being envied, however, she actually lost status:

> I was pregnant four times in my late twenties and early thirties. No one seemed the least bit jealous of me, because my friends, who were gorgeous, were out partying and meeting different guys. It really bothered me how sexy and glamorous these free-spirited women were. I lost confidence in my own body, and I became jealous of these women who looked so great. I'm ashamed to say that I didn't think about how lucky I

was to have these children but about how I looked like a bag of potatoes while my friends looked unbelievable.

Mount Sinai maternal-fetal-medicine specialist Larry Rand, M.D. witnessed so many new mothers distressed by this issue that he has begun a study into the association between mild postpartum depression and pregnancy weight gain. "I don't want to feed into the culture of 'You must be skinny,'" Rand told Abraham in her *New York* article. "But I have a lot of empathy for what it feels like to lug around too much weight. If we lived in a world where nobody gave a crap . . . but we don't."

Clearly, many people do care about women's weight gain during and after pregnancy, if the media frenzy around Gwyneth Paltrow's 2004 delivery is any indication. The thirty-two-year-old Paltrow emerged from her pregnancy in such good shape that gossips suggested she'd stayed in the hospital a few extra weeks. A *Us Weekly* article featured pictures of Paltrow one week after delivery, wearing two girdles at the same time—"All the Hollywood girls do it," the actress told *USA Today*—as well as photos of the star in a low-cut dress. "How about them apples!" a caption comments, with an arrow pointing to Paltrow's swelling breasts. The remark becomes even cruder when you realize it's a pun on the name of Paltrow's daughter, Apple. Paltrow's breasts are bigger because she was pregnant and then breast-fed her baby; but *Us Weekly* turns her female experience into a dirty joke, even, perhaps, a covert attempt at becoming sexier. I don't know for whom we should feel more sympathy—Paltrow, forced to account for every bodily change, or the rest of us, put in the impossible position of competing with her.

Mired in Competition

For many of the women I interviewed, winning the beauty contest wasn't only a matter of status but of survival. These women felt that everything they had achieved in their lives somehow depended on their looks, and specifically, on being judged as prettier than other women.

Ironically, these beauty contests may do as much harm to the winners as they do to the losers. "The prettiest girl is always the popular girl, from grade school on," comments psychologist Jo League. "It is trickiest for . . . the beauties because there is little chance to establish one's self. . . ."

League's insight is echoed by the famous statement by French philosopher Simone de Beauvoir that adolescence is when girls stop being and start seeming. Beauvoir points out that the condition of womanhood in our culture is *to appear*, to be looked at, to present oneself to the male gaze. I would add that when girls and women struggle to look as men wish them to look, they inevitably end up competing with one another.

Rachel, for example, a thirty-eight-year-old banker, felt that her marriage of three years rested on her husband's perception of her as "the prettiest thing around," a perception that relied in turn on the absence of other attractive females:

I do not want any pretty woman around since I am married. . . . I believe it is smart to guard what is yours. I have seen so many unhappy endings. I am willing to have pretty, smart women as friends, if only they are attached. If my pretty friend is married, I feel okay. I know that marriage is no guarantee, but it would be overkill to worry about married women. I have to have some semblance of normalcy even when I am feeling threatened and jealous.

I think the reason I am so deliberate about this is because it is hard work to grow older and look good, to please a man. . . . I have canceled plans when I have heard that a certain woman will be there, and I have asked the hostess to move us to another table if there is a gorgeous single woman scheduled to sit with us. I have tried to get my husband's attention when I see a pretty woman walking down the street. I am not exactly proud of this, but I also know that it is necessary. It is difficult enough to measure up to photos in magazines of young perfect women. I do not need someone like that in the flesh.

Joan, at age fifty-four, agrees that pretty women are to be avoided, not only because they threaten her relationship but also because they challenge her sense of self. Notice the lengths she has gone to set up her life in a way that keeps her jealousy at bay:

I could never live in a big city where women are very glamorous. I learned this when I was in graduate school in Chicago and I found it intimidating. There were chic women at every corner, so I live in a small town. In this small place, I am the one who is chic. . . . I am the big deal.

For Joan, it's not enough that she avoid jealousy of others. She wants other women to be jealous of her:

I work hard at my reputation and my personal style, and am involved with every local event. I suspect that women are jealous of me, so my plan has worked. . . . Growing old here is easier than in a city where I would be jealous of all those younger women who would breeze by me.

Samantha, too, feels that the beauty contest has different rules in different locales:

Some places are more superficial than others. I find that when I am in southern California or Miami, I am more worried about how I look and how old I seem to people. In those environments, I become very insecure, and I don't like to see the young women parading around. When I get back to the northeast, I relax and I feel more like myself.

For Hanna, a forty-year-old middle-management executive, looks are important for yet another reason. She views her appearance as crucial to her career, and she sees both as fields of female competition:

I have done very well in the corporate world because of how I look. I know that being pretty is a big part of getting somewhere for women. And I know that this applies to work and in interpersonal relationships.

Even though I have been a good friend to two of my female friends, I know that they envy me my life and especially my looks. If I didn't look so good, maybe they would be more forgiving. None of this is said, but it is understood. . . .

. . . I am always aware of how I look and present myself and that I am politically correct, according to the magazines I read, in terms of how I dress. I know I need this. So my girlfriends who are heavier and believe that is why they are so miserable, or they just aren't pretty, really suffer. They hate me instead of trying to lose weight, somehow fixing what is wrong with them. And maybe if this one girlfriend in particular would stop talking about getting her nose fixed and just do it, if she would stop complaining about needing to diet and just lose weight, she would be happier with herself.

I suppose I am unkind about it, because I am spoiled, but there is a premium in our society on being an attractive woman. The higher I have climbed in the corporate ladder, the more it has mattered to me that I am appreciated for my ability. But I always have it mixed in with how I look. I have my own maintenance to consider on a continual basis and then I have this edge on other women, which is what happens when you are the prettier one.

It's bad enough that Hanna feels the need to win approval from the men who judge her as prettier and reward her accordingly. But clearly, her entry into the beauty contest comes at a price. Not only does she confuse her looks and her worth—a confusion that must grow more painful as Hanna grows older—but she must also perpetually mistrust the other women who she believes are her rivals. Even when she wins the beauty contest, she must justify her anxieties, regret the envy she faces, and struggle with a nagging sense of guilt that somehow her victory is responsible for her friends' defeat.

Maggie, too, has mixed feelings about her looks as she turns forty-nine. A former beauty, the middle-aged Maggie has begun to question the role that her appearance has played in her life. As a child, she recalls, her looks opened doors for her:

> I learned early on that I was worth looking at. I was the favorite child, niece, grandchild, and student. I was more popular than my two sisters, and my older brothers took me with them to parties when I was only thirteen because it made them look good.
>
> We grew up in a small town in the Midwest and I knew I had to get out of there. I began as a model and later I tried acting. I fit in with the right crowd because of how I looked, and I could get away with anything. . . . I could cut a movie line, I could sweet-talk the conductor on a train or the man behind the counter at the airport. I would hail a cab and two would screech to a halt for me.
>
> It was a fine way to operate as long as it lasted. When I married in 1980, I knew I was the prize, and I really thought I had it all. . . . I felt superior to other women. There wasn't a competition: I was beyond it.

Still, as Maggie remembers her youth, she paid a price for relying on her looks:

> I never made close women friends in the same field because we were too competitive. I think I disliked being one of many beautiful women, and I didn't last long as a model. It was only when I was winning that I really enjoyed it. I remember that at parties women would eye me up and down, but not come near me.

Only when Maggie began to lose her looks did she begin to make friends—and to feel the envy of which she had always been the target:

> Now, all these years later, I have women friends because I have gained weight and I am above average but no young beauty. Women are nicer

to me, which means that I am no longer anything special to look at. I have begun to look at beautiful women and feel what women must have felt about me at one time. They are the ones who will have it all, because their looks rule. They can win out over any ordinary woman.

If Rachel, Hanna, and Maggie are the beauty contest's ambivalent winners, Jeanette, the thirty-nine-year-old office manager whom we met in Chapter 3, has always felt like the sore loser. Not until she got cosmetic surgery did she feel qualified to compete. First, she explains, she compensated for not being pretty enough by being "witty and clever, having good clothes, good hair." But in the end, it was by physically altering her features that she felt as though she had leveled the playing field, even if her victory, too, came at a price:

Having a nose job and a chin job is both liberating and also makes a woman into a victim. I knew that I became prettier, but it has taken me years to believe it, and I suffered from low self-esteem before I could be changed and made prettier. I will always identify with the wallflower, the one who isn't pretty enough to be invited out on the dance floor. That is who I really am because of how I was as a young girl. I believed that my nose, which was long and bumpy, kept me from being considered pretty. I imagined that girls, then young women, and finally women, would say to each other, "Gee, Jeannette could be so attractive if only she didn't have that nose." And I began to wonder if I had to always think that way. It is amazing to me that I could simply pay to look better, that it is within our power, if we just make some money and put it aside for ourselves.

Sometimes, when women achieve a long-awaited goal, they manage to opt out of the beauty contest. An August 21, 2002, *New York Times* interview with Marissa Jaret Winokur, the young, heavy star of Broadway's hit *Hairspray* reveals that she has come to be proud of her body. "I always wear tight clothes," she told reporter Robin Pogrebin. "I don't want . . . to cover up my body." But, adds Winokur, she has lots of reasons to feel good about herself. "If I didn't have a boyfriend," she cautions, "if I hadn't had a career, I don't know how I would be. . . . I might have dyed my hair blond and lost fifty pounds."

A woman who followed Winokur's "road not taken" was Nella. After being overweight for most of her life, Nella lost sixty pounds at the age of thirty-six. She also lost most of her friends:

> I knew I had to do something when I could no longer look at myself in the light and I hated thin women. Slowly but steadily I began to lose weight. At first I had a few friends at the Weight Watchers meetings and at the gym that I joined. But as I got thinner, I noticed that they were whispering about me. . . . My closest friend at Weight Watchers stopped calling me, and then no one asked me out from the group of women at work. When I had to buy new clothes, my best friend from high school stopped complimenting me. She liked me fat because from the time we were fifteen, she always got the guys. One day I was actually thinner than two women at work. That was when the male sales reps started talking to me more than they had to. I felt like a new person: . . . I could look at myself naked in the light! I was okay with thin women finally. I laughed more, and I smiled more and got more clients. I highlighted my hair. About this time I met my future husband, but my friends were not happy for me. They were the opposite.

On the other hand, Merrill, a forty-year-old partner in her husband's business, found that she lost friends as she *gained* weight, because her friends envied her new comfort with herself:

> I have been overweight since my second wedding anniversary. Before that I was thin—for me—because that was how one got the man. My mother and grandmother insisted that I diet and that I go to a junior college, and then get a job. They had it all planned for me, I would be an

administrative assistant, I would be thin, and I would get the boss. Then my troubles would be over.

I did get the job, and the boss, but I didn't stay thin. My husband never seemed to care, and that . . . gave me some kind of encouragement. And later, my two boys thought that I was the prettiest soccer mom around. What more could I want?

. . . I am not ashamed of my appearance at all. I know that women whisper about me, that my weight is unhealthy, that I have such a pretty face if only I'd lose weight. I can sniff out women who are jealous of me because I am okay with who I am. . . . My mother recently suggested that I lose weight to keep my husband since there are so many pretty, thin single women around. But I doubt that I will, because this is me.

Despite her apparent self-confidence, Merrill still has not escaped the beauty contest. "Mostly, I feel good about myself," she concludes, but she can't resist one final burst of rivalry: "I have only a few lines on my face compared to my thinner contemporaries."

Youth Versus Age

One of the key frontiers in the never-ending beauty contest is the boundary between youth and age. Stereotypically, of course, the younger a woman is, the more likely she is to win the contest—sometimes literally. A November 14, 2004, *New York Times* "Oscar Watch" proclaimed that "the babe factor" gives younger actresses the edge in what is supposed to be a competition based purely on talent. Since 1990, though, only one woman over fifty has won an acting Oscar, and that was for Best Supporting Actress (Judi Dench, who won for *Shakespeare in Love*, in 1999). The then-seventy-two-year-old Lauren Bacall was nominated for Best Supporting Actress in *The Mirror Has Two Faces* in 1997, but lost out to the much younger Juliette Binoche (*The English Patient*), while eighty-seven-year-old Gloria Stuart, nominated for *Titanic* in 1998, was defeated by Kim Basinger (*L.A. Confidential*).

Still, in the world of the perpetual beauty contest, *youth* and *age* are relative terms. *Marie Claire*, a fashion magazine that appeals to women of a variety of ages, featured a makeover story entitled "How Much Younger Can You Look in a Week?" with the chilling subtitle "Age-Proof Your Looks." The woman concerned about looking younger is "Jackie," who is all of thirty-six. For a total cost of $4,933 and 6.5 hours spent in doctors' offices, Jackie tried eight age-proofing techniques: a new skin-care regimen, microdermabrasion, botox, restylane, tooth bleaching, brow shaping, a dietary shift away from carbs, and an image consultation to help her choose the right methods. When asked "Was it worth it?" Jackie reported that she'd gotten more compliments, including one from a makeup artist who thought she'd had a face-lift. "The whole process has been really rejuvenating," she concluded. Thus, while Jackie might be the object of envy for women in their forties, fifties, and above, she herself is concerned about "rejuvenating," presumably the better to compete with women in their teens and twenties.

When I interviewed cosmetic dermatologist Dr. Michele Anzilotti, she confirmed that Jackie's case was hardly unique. "What I see in my practice is . . . young women in their early thirties, wanting to have restylane or collagen injections," she told me. "These women are very aware of what aging does to their skin, and they want a jump start. It is not only preventive but makes them feel confident in a competitive world."

The competition extends even to women who have strong bonds, such as mothers and daughters. Deirdre, a forty-five-year-old real estate agent, describes how the perpetual beauty contest passes from generation to generation:

> I think I became competitive with my daughter once she began to look so amazingly sexy and beautiful. I saw myself withering as she flourished. I remember when my breasts looked like hers, and I see men my age and boys her age and everyone in between, watching her. I barely

remember a time when I was in her place. But I was—it was so long ago!

I look not only at my daughter but at her friends and at the attention they get from men and women alike. I look at their hair, skin, faces, bodies, and I really am envious. I regret my age and the choices I've made. I feel that there are not as many chances left and I can't seem to appreciate the parts of my life that are good, that come with being mature.

Of course, older women don't compete only with younger women. They also compete with one another. Mary, a sixty-five-year-old socialite, feels that plastic surgery is the newest region for the contests she and her friends have known since their teenage years:

I never thought I was the prettiest, but maybe my friends were envious of my lifestyle and that I had a wealthy husband. I say this because of how women sometimes acted toward me. I remember not thinking I was pretty, but knowing I looked good enough. Then it occurred to me, years later, that it could be that I was that pretty and that was why I could sometimes feel another woman's envy. Maybe it was a combination of all that I had: looks, money, a wardrobe.

It was not until my forties that I began to doubt myself because then I was becoming wrinkled. That was different from thinking someone else was prettier or that I wasn't pretty enough. This was very upsetting, and so I had a face-lift at fifty. I remember reading about Betty Ford having a face-lift and deciding that I could do it one day, and I did.

. . . Not as many women were doing it as today and all of my friends came to visit. I thought they were coming to cheer me up during my recovery, but they came out of curiosity. I was the first of my friends to do this and everyone wanted to see what it required. Then they all had face-lifts because mine had worked out.

Over time, we all compared our plastic surgery: whose looked real, whose looked fake, whose had lasted, whose had fallen, who needed one and hadn't done it. I think it was the next phase of women outdoing each other.

Anna, a fifty-year-old platinum blonde, also has friends who compete with her over such antiaging techniques as plastic surgery and hair coloring:

> I think one of the tricks of aging well is to lighten your hair. But my friends who are also blond by a hairdresser's wand seem angry that I've gone *so* blond. I can't believe this—after all, they can do it, too. I'm not stopping them. I don't own this hair color. I just like it and it makes me feel good, alive and peppy. . . .
>
> I have lightened my hair every year since I was in eleventh grade. I knew I was pretty when I started it, and at my age, it still sets me apart. I love having blond hair, but it hasn't stopped there. I have had a face-lift, and I get botox and glycolic peels. I know that I look good for my age, and that is my goal. Now my friends envy me, more than ever, because not only do I look good but I tell everyone how old I am. That makes them uncomfortable, I guess, because they are not shouting out their age.

At age forty-nine, Patti, who owns her own retail store, is hardly shouting *her* age. In fact, she is just beginning to contemplate her own face-lift. This is an action she considers necessary because of the unending beauty contest in which she has enrolled, a contest that requires her to compete against her friends, her daughter, and women in the media:

> I am convinced that twenty-five years ago, my mother and my aunts did not feel as I do about getting older. I look in the mirror, I read *People* magazine, my nubile daughter walks by, and I feel like disappearing.
>
> Had I lived in another era, it wouldn't be this painful. But today I have little choice but to take some action. If I don't, then I'll be looking like a hag compared to my friends, who have all done something. The worst thing is, I don't even know what I'm supposed to look like because everyone has had something done already. Who can I compare myself to? I'm

behind my friends, my so-called friends, and all the movie stars. I have to
do something and do it soon.

Even if cosmetic surgery allows for a temporary victory, no one can
stay a winner forever. "Unfortunately women feel judged more by what
is on the outside than the inside. Their identity is wrapped up by the
external," remarks Dr. Donald Cohen, a therapist whose practice includes midlife issues. "There is nothing wrong with preserving beauty,
but not to the point where women of a certain age lose their perspective."

On the other hand, according to psychotherapist and social worker
Seth Shulman, younger women may also envy older women. "For
younger women, the successes that older women have achieved, that of
mother, wife, and career, can be daunting. The identity of the younger
woman, even in her early twenties, is not fully formed. For this reason,
younger women can be envious of the older woman's history, experience, confidence, and wisdom."

This scenario plays out in the Julia Stiles/Stockard Channing film
The Business of Strangers. While Channing's character, Julie, has a high-
powered career for which she has worked her entire adult life, Stiles's
character, Paula, is just starting out as Channing's new assistant. Paula
is sent from the home office to another city, where she botches her
boss's presentation by arriving late with the presentation materials.
Later the two women, essentially strangers, spend a toxic evening together where they play a game of wits, uncovering each other's weaknesses and fears.

"I bet you had to eat a lot of shit to get where you are," the younger
woman says to the older.

"It was my choice. Nobody forced me," the older woman replies.

"Still, can't be easy, though," says the younger woman, egging her
on.

"Everybody eats shit. It's just a question of degree," the older woman
insists.

Counters the younger woman, "Or how much you can take?" Clearly, the younger woman is the one who envies the older, deliberately attempting to destroy her rather than learn from her.

A less deadly version of younger women envying their elders appears on the *Gilmore Girls*. When teenage Rory starts to date, she looks at her thirtyish mother in despair. "How do you always know how to do—that?" she asks Lorelai. Somehow, Lorelai has mastered the secret skills of putting together a sexy outfit, flirting, and generally holding a man's attention, secrets that the young and inexperienced Rory sees as out of reach until her mother reassures Rory that eventually, she, too, will have access to this feminine knowledge. In the world of the *Gilmore Girls*, at least one mother is happy to initiate her daughter into the secrets of womanhood, while the daughter appreciates her mother's guidance.

Other American media present the youth-age competition as a contest that the older woman can rarely win. The classic movie *All About Eve*, for example, begins as Eve, a young, plain actress (Anne Baxter) envies the glamourous, successful Margo (Bette Davis), who is just about to turn forty. The scheming Eve plots to take Margo's career, her friends, and eventually her man. In the end, Margo is triumphant, but only because she has agreed to cede much of the field to Eve. The younger actress's victory may be hollow—although she gets the Broadway role she wants, she'll be forever blackmailed by the George Sanders character—but she *has* won the prize she sought, while Margo's happiness is based on letting the younger woman steal her professional success as she herself settles down with the man she loves.

Even though several decades have passed since *All About Eve*, the pattern in many U.S movies and TV shows remains the same. Older women are almost invariably portrayed as washed up, contemptible, or evil. Particularly when they compete against younger, more beautiful rivals, older women are expected to relinquish their triumphs or face a humiliating defeat.

Beauty As a Sign of Worth

When Cinderella competes against her two ugly stepsisters, she's not only engaged in a beauty contest. The fairy tale makes clear that Cinderella's beauty is the sign of her pure heart and kind nature. People often confuse physical attributes with job competence, moral virtue, and other desirable qualities. For example, the Hamermesh-Biddle study, "Beauty and the Labor Market," has shown that someone perceived as attractive in the workforce usually nets a 5–10 percent increase in earnings over the plainer folk. And the women I interviewed seemed to agree that, in others' eyes, at least, beauty represented more than simply a pretty face and a nice figure; that it was, in fact, empowering.

Thus, forty-seven-year-old Jennifer feels strongly that both her good looks and her youthful appearance have been important to her success as a talent scout who is reentering the labor market:

> I was very careful at work not to let my coworkers know my age. I had been out of the workplace for several years and I didn't want to be ostracized. I was even afraid that my age could cost me my job because I work in the entertainment industry. I have done whatever makes me look younger. I don't know if I would have plastic surgery if I wasn't in this job, but I imagine that I would, maybe for dating purposes. I have had a nip and tuck and it definitely makes me look younger, and that makes me more confident. I like looking young for my age, who wouldn't? And lately I've been dating younger men who I meet at work-related events. That's refreshing, too, so I'm sort of having this new lease on life.
>
> But I'm always worried about my age. And I do wonder how the other women at work would treat me if they knew I was over forty-five. I think they might be more competitive with me then, or they'd push me to the side. I know it would change things somehow and so I avoid this happening. The truth is, I do envy them their age, because even with plastic surgery, you can't become thirty again.

As we saw with the Academy Awards, artistic and professional prizes often are awarded to younger, prettier women, suggesting that their beauty somehow enhances their abilities. A May 27, 2004, article in *The New York Times* by reporter Anne Midgette describes the controversy over the February 2004 recital of violinist Lara St. John. The musician first achieved notoriety in 1996, when the cover of her first album, *Bach Works for Violin Solo,* featured the then-twenty-four-year-old musician nude from the waist up, her violin demurely covering her naked breasts. That album sold more than thirty thousand copies, "big stuff for a classical music recording," as Midgette comments. But when St. John appeared in a simple navy blue silk gown at age thirty-two, the *Toronto Star* reviewer John Terauds wrote that she led not with her music but with her appearance. Terauds praises St. John's music but attacks her dress and style by describing her as "almost matronly . . . in a wrinkled pigeon-colored number that had to be one of the ugliest frocks to see stage lights this season."

While St. John was harshly criticized for her sexy album cover, she was equally criticized for what Terauds saw as her dowdy appearance. "I'm damned if I do and damned if I don't," she told Midgette, whose article details other examples of female musicians who make the most of their beauty and sex appeal. Although many classical purists view a female artist's good looks as somehow making her less serious, there is no doubt that the general public is eager to patronize concerts by attractive performers.

As with all types of female competition, the perpetual beauty contest is fueled by a basic scarcity, what I call the not enough pie syndrome. If there were enough rewards to go around—enough solo violin recitals, good men, high-powered jobs—I believe that female rivalry would be far less sharp. But because women have so little access to the goals they seek, they are forced to compete for a tiny slice of the pie, a situation that cannot help but breed the virulent competitions we have observed.

The competition continues even among the highest-ranked contestants, as demonstrated by the media-fueled rumors concerning Jennifer Aniston's supposed competition with Angelina Jolie over Aniston's estranged husband, Brad Pitt. Pitt supposedly split with Aniston after he spent time with Jolie on the set of *Mr. and Mrs. Smith*, a film in which Jolie and Pitt are romantically paired. The January 31, 2005, issue of *Us Weekly* was quick to capitalize on the gossip by comparing the two actresses in an article detailing the women's heights, earnings, number of marriages, family backgrounds—and how much nudity each has revealed on-screen. Ordinary women would imagine that *both* Aniston and Jolie could be prom queens, but apparently, there's room at the top for only one.

I was also reminded of the not-enough-pie syndrome when I read the December 12, 2004, *New York Times* article intriguingly entitled "Neptune's Daughters and the Ultimate Job Tryout." At a Chelsea nightclub known as the Coral Room, young women are hired to play mermaids and dance in the club's ten-thousand-gallon aquarium. The article described the cutthroat competition for the mermaid gig, which is in such demand that the club's owner gets hundreds of calls, letters, and Internet photos from applicants seeking to fill the half dozen positions.

To be allowed to audition, a woman must be attractive, sexy, and a good swimmer. But with so many would-be sirens, the owner can afford to be selective. In this case, mere beauty is not enough; the mermaids must appeal to male fantasies as well. Thus the article by John Freeman Gill quotes a young man at the bar as he watches one of the auditioners. "She's not a mermaid," the man insists. "You think of a mermaid as the thing you can't obtain."

Jam yesterday, and jam tomorrow, but never jam today. Not only are we engaged in a perpetual beauty contest that we can never permanently win, we must also convey to the men who desire us that they can never fully have us, even as our beauty is supposed to make us more desirable than ever.

Prizes and Penalties

In perhaps no other form of female rivalry is the price more obvious than in the perpetual beauty contest. By definition, any woman who wins the contest today must expect to lose it—if not tomorrow, then the day after, or the day after that. Pinning one's self-esteem to how we look dooms us to certain defeat, for in a world in which beauty is bound up inextricably with youth, the only way to frustrate a rival's victory is literally to die before she has taken your crown.

It can be difficult to see the true nature of the perpetual beauty contest, for we undergo a continual barrage of mixed messages about our looks. On the one hand, plastic surgery and ever-improved cosmetic procedures seem to offer the promise of liberation, assuring us that we'll feel better about ourselves when we look better, younger, more alive. On the other hand, once we accept that looking better signifies nothing beyond a transient physical condition, we are caught forever in an endless quest for youth and beauty, to feel, as Natasha Richardson does, that looking good always means being "five pounds less," or to envy, as Samantha does, a younger self to which we can never return.

As we have seen, defeat is not even the greatest price we pay for competing over looks. In the perpetual beauty contest, victory can bring penalties as great as defeat, for as we become preoccupied with our looks, we grow uncertain about our other attributes. Perhaps we, too, come to value appearance over all other qualities—wisdom, intelligence, skill, kindness. Or maybe we begin to doubt whether any other attribute we have is visible, or even whether it exists at all.

The perpetual beauty contest may be more fraught for women than any other province, as can be seen by the fact that virtually every story in this chapter is a cautionary tale. Women seem to pay a price both for losing the contest and for (temporarily) taking home the prize. Here, as elsewhere, tripping the prom queen can bring no more than a short-lived triumph, for in agreeing to the terms of the perpetual beauty contest, we are ensuring our own destiny of being forever judged and found wanting.

5

Magical Theft:
Envy over Relationships

From young girls on the playground to seventy-year-old women, there is one thing women share: the sense that we have to vie for the right friend, the right life—and the right man. Nowhere does female rivalry come to the surface more sharply than when two women are competing over the same guy. It's a cliché, but it's true: some 40 percent of the women I interviewed said that another woman—often a sister, a colleague, or a best friend—had tried to steal their man.

For example, Letitia, a twenty-three-year-old assistant manager of a retail store, felt betrayed by her best friend, Denise. The two women's closeness made Denise's effort to steal Letitia's boyfriend all the more painful:

> Our mothers brought us here from Jamaica together when we were six, and we were raised as sisters. We decided to attend the same college and I got a scholarship, but Denise did not. I think that was the first time that she was envious of me.
>
> Then I met a guy, Charles, who was from Jamaica, who I really

liked. . . . I couldn't wait to introduce him to Denise. That's how naïve I was. When the three of us met that first time, I knew I was going to have a problem. I saw how she wanted him and that she was no longer the same about me. She would call me and ask how he was; she would stop by his apartment.

I knew my mother would not approve, but I no longer considered Denise my close friend. Maybe if we hadn't known one another and were just two pretty women and Charles had met us each on his own, to choose, it would have been easier for me, a fairer situation. But to think that Denise and I were like sisters, and now she was trying to take my guy was too much.

In the end I let her go. I told her to get away and stay away. I had this part-time job with a promise from my boss for a full-time job after graduation, and I had a boyfriend I cared about. I had to keep my eye on this. . . . So I told my boyfriend that I saw what was going on. He agreed that she was coming on to him. I asked him who he wanted and he said me. "I don't talk to Denise," he told me. "Let her go find her own man and not take somebody else's."

But women didn't only tell me about friends stealing their boyfriends. Sometimes, a woman confessed, she herself was the thief. For example, thirty-five-year-old Gretchen, a married interior designer living in the Southwest, was not only willing to seduce her friends' boyfriends, she seemed specifically to target the guys who were attached to women she knew:

> I was never the prettiest, or the smartest, but I knew how to get what I wanted. In ninth grade I started with my friend Eileen, who I purposely convinced to break up with her boyfriend. . . . Then I went after him. I saw that Eileen was devastated, but I paid her no mind. I did it because I couldn't stand that she had him and that she looked the way she did, which was why she had him. So I had to get her guy to ruin her and also to prove that I was worthy of the same guy as Eileen.

It was twisted even then, when we were fourteen, and I doubt it gave me much satisfaction. It might have worked for a few days, and then I began to wonder what I would do after Ben and I were no longer making out in movie theaters. I realized I'd lost a girlfriend who had been a good friend, but that wasn't what bothered me the most. What bothered me most was that she was right: Ben was boring and a lousy kisser. She had said all that to me and I had ignored it, but she was right. Eileen, my best friend from kindergarten to ninth grade, never spoke to me again. Not that this stopped me.

I did the same thing to my friend in college with her boyfriend, and the price to pay was higher: I was kicked out of our sorority and iced for a few months. But this boyfriend lasted for a year. I felt less guilty with the college guy, probably because it is like murder: once you've done it, you can do it the second time more easily.

I found my husband the same way. . . . My friend from work and I were at a party three years ago, and she saw this guy and told me she thought he was cute, and I said nothing. But I did go across the room to talk to him when she went to the bathroom, and later, when she saw me leave with him, she gave me a look. I explained to her that he had wanted to talk to me. In a way, this was the cleanest I've come in these deceits. This time, she was jealous of me, because I married the man at the party.

Reviewing Gretchen's interview, I'm struck by how much more interested she seems to be in winning the competition with her women friends than in actually getting the guy. Her first rivalry, with her friend Eileen, was focused on her envy of Eileen's looks and her need to prove herself as Eileen's equal. The boy—"boring" and "a lousy kisser"—was hardly the prize she sought. Revenge against Eileen, and clear superiority to her, was far more important. Her subsequent relationships all seem to be as much symbols of triumph over a woman friend as they are about fulfilling relationships with a male partner.

If the competition doesn't spill over into actual "stealing," women often seem to be involved in a rivalry whose prize is the guy but whose focus is the girlfriend. Consider these three diverse examples that yet have something very much in common:

Sally, thirty-three, a specialist in market research:

Janet and I were both single for years, and we would get together and complain about the lack of good men. Then she met this man and married him very quickly. . . . She quit her job, moved to this brand-new house, and began a whole new life with a husband and baby.

I felt so left behind I couldn't stand it. I didn't even want to talk to her on the phone. I couldn't bear her happiness.

I began to avoid her, but really, if Janet had not married and become pregnant, I would not have felt so denied a baby and husband. It was her new life and her happiness, the fact that she had moved on, that made me so crazy and jealous. . . . Somehow, Janet had won after all these years of being together, through all these parts of our lives.

Felicity, thirty-six, divorced for three years, presently engaged:

I thought my husband, Ted, and I were just starting a life together, but he had an affair and wanted a divorce. Our only son was four. . . . Then I began to date John, someone at work, but he was married. We became serious, and I told him he had to make a decision. I was too jealous of his wife—because she was his wife—to care about his feelings. So I stooped as low as my ex-husband's new wife had, and broke up someone's marriage in order to land the man.

I really empathized with Ted's wife the whole time it was happening. Suddenly I saw how she must have hated me for being there when she wanted to be there. She was not jealous of me personally, I think, but of the position I was in. And that is exactly how I felt about John's wife. . . . Who knows what pain *she'll* cause now, to get what she deserves?

Adele, forty-five, married with two children:

I had a friend with whom I worked out, and we decided to go out with our husbands. . . . I immediately knew that she was making a play for

Roger. I distanced myself from her, but one day I saw her sitting with
Roger and some other people at our health club. She had these gorgeous legs and displayed them to perfection. A week later, Roger's secretary, who is loyal to me, said that this woman called at the office. That
was it. I called her and told her to stay away. I probably even threatened
her. I told Roger that if he ever spoke to this woman again, I would be
gone.

To me, the most fascinating aspect of each of these stories is the extent to which the women, ostensibly fighting over a man, are also involved with each other. As Sally comments perceptively, "It was *her*
new life and her happiness . . . that made me so crazy and jealous. . . ."
The actual baby and husband seemed less important to Sally than winning the competition with her friend.

Likewise, when Felicity began dating a married man, she began to
identify with the woman who had dated *her* husband. Even Adele, so
possessive of her marriage, makes a point of confronting the woman
who seems interested in her husband rather than focusing solely on the
marital relationship. It's enough to make one wonder which is more important, the husband or the girlfriend?

Divorce attorney Amy Reisen, whom I interviewed for this project,
told me that scorned wives often focus on the wives-to-be. "These
women think they will feel better if they lunge after the new women.
And since men usually leave for someone else, I see these feelings of
jealousy and revenge often. How could a pregnant wife who finds a gift
charged to Cartier for the new girlfriend not be jealous?"

The movie *My Best Friend's Wedding* plays with the problematic connection between women who are battling for the same man. The character portrayed by Julia Roberts is an independent journalist, happy,
carefree, and single. Then, a male friend announces his engagement,
and she suddenly feels certain that she has missed her chance at a full
life. She flies to Chicago to attend the man's wedding, hoping to sabotage his relationship with fiancée Cameron Diaz. But the Diaz character

is so innocent and likable that the Roberts character begins to feel ashamed. Throughout the movie, she seems far more interested in her competition with Diaz than in her own wishes and desires, with her feelings for the man she supposedly loves running a distant third. If we substitute "fiancée" for "wife," Felicity's words might have been spoken by Roberts's character: "I was too jealous of his wife—because she was his wife—to care about his feelings."

For an even more dramatic illustration of how women compete for men while relating to each other, we have only to look at the popular ABC reality show *The Bachelor*. In the first season, Alex Michel, an extremely eligible thirty-one-year-old bachelor, was introduced to twenty-five women from whom he was to choose his mate. To the producers' credit, the women came from diverse backgrounds, although Alex himself hailed from a "good family" and had attended Harvard and Stanford.

Over the several weeks that the show aired, the female contestants underwent the thrill of competition and the humiliation of defeat, as one by one, Alex discarded the women he found less attractive. Alex was the prize, but the show's focus was on how the women related to one another. They roomed together, ate together, and engaged jointly in the show's various activities. If we imagine the program being constructed differently—say, with Alex traveling to different cities each week to meet individual candidates—we see how much of the show's appeal lies in the way that women competed directly with one another.

Yet, although competition was encouraged—was, in fact, the whole point—the women also knew that looking mean, catty, or unkind would cost them points with viewers. In *My Best Friend's Wedding*, the Diaz character was portrayed not only as uncompetitive but also unaware that a competition even existed, just like Melanie Griffith's character in *Working Girl*. Likewise, in *The Bachelor*, women were literally encouraged to compete against one another, even as they tried to look as though their real focus was on their feelings for a man.

Both the movies and the TV show are dramatic illustrations of how women's competition over relationships brings women closer together even as it keeps them permanently apart. Any athlete will tell you that you are much closer to your competitors than to anyone else—they are the ones against whom you measure yourself, and only they can truly understand you. Yet since we women are not allowed to compete openly and are rarely praised for our competitive natures—not even in an open contest like *The Bachelor*—we have difficulty dropping the rivalry when it no longer serves us. Consider the poignant story of Valerie, a forty-year-old interior designer who is presently engaged:

> When my childhood girlfriend, Marcie, got married about six years ago, I did not go to the wedding. I knew that it was an unkind thing to do, but I knew no other way out. . . . Marcie was in a position that I not only envied but wondered if I'd ever get there myself. I really didn't want to see her walk down the aisle, or have the joy that brides have. I couldn't wish her any ill so I simply moved away from the scene itself. . . .
>
> I told Marcie that I had to be at a business conference and that it was so important for work that I couldn't miss it. This was a half truth because I could have given up the conference for her wedding. . . . There have been times since then when I have regretted this action. . . .
>
> I felt lousy that day, knowing I had less than she did and that her life was an improvement over mine. As friendly as we are, that wasn't easy for me to handle. Marcie's wedding made me remember how when we were kids, she always got the cutest boy's attention. Then she had the most dates in college. . . . Then we were on an even playing field because we both were single for a long period of time. In the end she won this round, too, and I admit, I had trouble dealing with it.

Had Valerie been able to confront her envy more fully, she might have been able to cope with it. Had she felt more empowered in her own life, she might not have felt so envious in the first place. As Seth Shulman, psychotherapist, suggests, female jealousy connects to a woman's sense of being unable to meet the wide variety of demands she currently faces. This stresses how women can be envious on all levels, because of the hardships and frustration that they encounter in every domain. Ironically, the very gains of feminism have created pressure on women to "have it all," a pressure that fosters female rivalry even as it promotes the myth of female friendship. "Women struggle to balance a marriage, children, and career," he says. "Some do better at it than others, and they are envied by those who feel inadequate. This can affect their friends and even their sisters."

While I agree that social pressures play a significant role in women's envy over relationships, I think the problem goes deeper. In my view, this kind of envy strikes at the core of female identities.

Proving Ourselves Through One Another

What fascinates me about women envying one another's relationships is the way it links women even while appearing to divide them. In many of the interviews I conducted, women suggested that the need to steal another woman's man was motivated not only by desire for the man, but also—and maybe more urgently—by envy of a particular woman. It's almost as though we think stealing that woman's man will make us resemble that woman. If we imagine that our rival has a better life than we do, then we may feel on some unconscious level that taking what belongs to her will give us some of her "magic." The man himself is less important than the possibility he offers, that of making us the envied woman's equal, of becoming as powerful and wonderful as she is.

This theme shows up in a number of fairy tales, in which a magic ring, cloak, or wand has the ability to give the owner supernatural powers. Often, a fairy-tale hero or heroine will steal the magic talisman from a witch, giant, or wizard, winning fame, fortune, and perhaps love as a result. Or a handkerchief dipped in blood is the talisman, as in the Grimm fairy tale "The Goose Girl." In this tale, a princess is betrayed by her lady-in-waiting on her way to meet the prince she is supposed to marry. Having lost her mother's handkerchief, the princess is no longer protected by that special female magic, so the lady-in-waiting is able to force the princess to trade places with her. Ultimately, the princess reveals her true identity and marries the prince, but the tale haunts us with its suggestion that taking something from a powerful figure, whether handkerchief or prince, seems to empower us to have a better life of our own.

Certainly Alice, a thirty-three-year-old emergency-room nurse, seems to endow her college friend, Ellen, with a similar kind of magic. Alice then tries to steal the magic by using the pretty and popular Ellen as "bait": When Ellen is around, the men flock to her, and Alice has a better chance of snagging a boyfriend. At the same time, Alice is desperate to protect herself against the competition that Ellen seems to pose, certain that any man will prefer Ellen over her.

Ellen was much prettier and more popular than I was. My way of dealing with Ellen was to use her when it benefited me and to try to hide her when her presence would not work in my favor. I don't know how I figured this out, but I knew instinctively that I couldn't have her around when I was first dating a guy or when my older cousin would visit with his friends. I believed that Ellen would lessen my chances of getting . . . a boyfriend. I assuaged any guilt for my poor behavior by convincing myself that Ellen didn't need me to meet a guy. . . .

One time when my cousin and his friend were coming to visit, I purposely lied to Ellen and said that I had to study in the library. I thought she had plans that wouldn't cross with mine, but I actually ran into her in the restaurant and I was caught in the lie. When Ellen confronted me the next day, I told her that I was protecting myself and that I liked my cousin's friend. I remember that she was astonished and didn't understand my fear that she would appeal to this guy. She was simply hurt by my actions.

. . . I have been this way with other female friends since that episode. I believe that one can't be too careful. I know that I operate in a rather paranoid world, where another woman seems empowered to destroy my chances of success with a guy, and so I preempt the situation. Today I am engaged, and I don't know how I will be once I am married, and if marriage will make me more secure. Right now, I do not intend to invite anyone too sexy or attractive to the wedding, and I have chosen my bridal party with this in mind.

Alice is on the verge of getting married. But instead of focusing on the wedded bliss she anticipates with her husband, her antennae are out for any possible female challenge. She believes that another woman's beauty or sex appeal has such magical power that even on her wedding day, it could destroy her husband's feelings for her, instantly creating an attraction to another woman that supersedes his commitment to Alice. It seems to me that Alice lives in a frightening fairy-tale world in which other females have a kind of magic talisman, enabling them to sneak into Alice's territory and steal *her* most precious possession.

I've found various versions of magical thinking in a number of plays, movies, and TV shows that deal with women stealing each other's husbands and/or boyfriends. Man thieving is the central topic of Clare Boothe Luce's classic play *The Women* (later a movie whose screenplay was also written by a woman, Anita Loos). As in many of the stories we have seen, the men themselves pale in importance compared to the women—indeed, the men are never even seen. Although the women talk constantly of their husbands, fiancés, and gentlemen friends, the cast is entirely female.

The plot revolves around innocent, lovely Mary (played in the film version by Norma Shearer), who temporarily loses her husband to Crystal, a conniving shopgirl (Joan Crawford). Mary's best friend, Sylvia (Rosalind Russell) is cynical and slightly dangerous as she tries to convince Mary to fight for her man, insisting that the world is a jungle in which no woman can ever trust another female. Yet in the world of *The Women*, written before it was commonplace for middle- and upper-class

women to combine work and family, women are socialites and debu-
tantes who spend time at bridge parties, hairdressers, department stores,
and exercise classes. It is this female world that nearly destroys Mary
while also toughening her up. By the end of the play, she has learned
how to be just as devious as Crystal, coming up with an elaborate un-
derhanded plot to steal back her man. In a famous curtain line, she
waves her newly painted fingernails in the face of her astonished friend.
"Jungle red, Sylvia," she crows.

In Luce's world, women had access to few professional jobs or independent sources of income, and men were indeed the key to women's
power. Stealing a man might therefore seem as good a route to upward
mobility as any other.

Contemporary television echoes the notion that competing for a
man might bring secondary gains. In the early episodes of the contemporary TV series *Desperate Housewives*, two suburban matrons battle it out,
desperately, for the one single man in the neighborhood. Not only does
Edie (Nicollette Sheridan) have designs on the man that Susan (Teri
Hatcher) wants, she also tried to seduce Susan's former husband when
the marriage was in place. While male companionship is at a premium in
this suburban world, there is also the possibility that Edie might want a
married woman's husband not because she desires the man per se but because of what "possessing" that man seems to offer her. An upscale marriage, even today, can offer a life of leisure, stylish dresses, and social
events. As psychologist Eleanor Schuker reminds us in her essay "The
Blinded Eye," "Envy is both social and intrapsychic. . . . To the extent
that a woman feels she lacks agency and power, she envies anyone whom
she imagines has these." And, to the extent that agency and power seem
available through a man, it's a logical next step to try to attain another
woman's power by taking her man.

In similar fashion, Iris, a forty-four-year-old shopkeeper, stresses
that she envies not her friends' relationships but rather the lifestyles
that these relationships seem to enable:

I find myself caught up in my friends' lives in terms of things. . . . I think this must be because I don't have children and I have a lot of freedom. It seems unfair to me that I can't have a certain kind of life. . . .

I know that I am very jealous of my friends for their things. They are a bit jealous of me because Rick, my husband, travels so much for business. No one seems to want their husbands around these days, and when we are out for lunch and my three best friends are talking about their clothes and vacations, I remind them that at least I don't have to kowtow to my husband, since he's rarely around.

This is little consolation though, since they have such better lives than I do. We are all in our early forties and we've been at these marriages for some time, so no one talks about how great their husbands are anymore. We talk about how we live, what we have, what money can buy. . . .

If I am with any of these friends, they will rush home to cook dinner for their husbands and kids. Or the babysitter is leaving and they have to get back. I don't want any of that. I just wish I had their wardrobes and cars; some of them have nice houses and cleaning help. I resent that Rick can't do it for me and that their husbands can. No one works full-time in this group, so it really is about the husbands and how they do. It gets to me when they have the life of Riley and I don't. I'm not close to anyone in particular anymore, probably because of how jealous I've become.

Cecily, a married thirty-five-year-old caterer with one son, describes the other side of the coin, revealing how it feels to be the target of her friends' envy. Again, Cecily's husband and marriage seem less important to her friends than the material advantages that her relationship brings.

For years, Jared and I lived in a simple little house in the middle of our simple little town, and no one paid us any attention. My friends were buying large homes and moving away; some were purchasing second homes. Many of them pegged me as a poor girl who didn't deserve anything better than what we had.

Then my catering business took off and my husband's toy business began to expand . . . and we bought this estate, because we could and we wanted to. When my friend Ellie came to the house for the first time, she said to her husband, "Why does Cecily have all this? It's making me sick that she has this, and I have less now. She's outdone me." . . . To me this friend had everything, and I thought she would be happy for me. Then the next week she heard that I was hired to cater the biggest affair in our town. She actually called to complain to me about my success and about my house. That was when I realized I could never trust this friend again, that the good feelings, if there ever were any, were only there when I had less. This woman was not really my friend, after all.

Divorce Envy

Sometimes it's the lack of a relationship that women envy in each other. Clementine, for example, a forty-year-old real estate agent, felt for a time that her superior marriage had enabled her to win the competition with her childhood friend, Lori. Then Lori's divorce threw Clementine into sudden doubt about her own life:

Lori told me she was getting a divorce from Jim, her husband of nine years, and I knew I wanted one, too. She and I had both gotten married within a year of each other, and both of us had our daughters on our second anniversaries. . . . I had married the more successful guy and I seemed to live a better life. . . . I thought that Lori married just to be safe and to escape the single world that was tired and old. I warned her that she would get tired of life with Jim, and I thought somehow that I was in a different position.

It turned out that my husband, Joshua, was really cruel to me, and Lori did tire of her life. She confided in me that she was having an affair. That was when I first felt envious. . . . Her affair sounded like a great escape . . . a way to get through a marriage.

I never met anyone with whom I could have a secret life, but Lori used her lover as a springboard to divorce. I knew that I had to divorce, too. I couldn't imagine the life on the other side of it, but Lori understood what was ahead. It took all of my courage, but I did divorce Joshua. I was envious of Lori during my divorce because she was one step ahead. While Josh and I were thrashing it out, she was already legally divorced with a decent settlement and had taken back her maiden name.

Then I finally was divorced, but I didn't do as well as Lori did in terms of finances, and it seemed that Joshua tortured me much more than Jim tortured her. Lori was dating someone by then, and had tossed out her first lover. I couldn't find anyone to meet and while I was relieved to be divorced, I was jealous of Lori's new life.

It took me a while to find my way after the divorce. Then Lori met someone else, and he was great. They are getting married, while I am wondering if I really care about the man who I see on a steady basis. It seems to me that Lori is always there before me, even in these trying situations.

As with the other women we have heard from in this chapter, Clementine seems far more preoccupied with Lori than with either her husband or her new boyfriend. When she evaluates her life, she looks not to her own relationships or to herself and her own goals but rather to her friend. If she's ahead of Lori, her life must be successful; if she's behind, her life is a failure. The specifics of Lori's situation—whether she is married, single, dating, or in love—seem to make little difference; nor does Clementine seem to care about her own relationship status. Winning the relationship competition—that is, achieving the relationship she wants with Lori—is her main concern.

Tara, on the other hand, found that her friends had mixed responses to her divorce. A twenty-seven-year-old woman with two small sons, Tara felt that her friends reacted with interest and sympathy, but only at first:

My friends loved me during my divorce. They wanted to meet me to hear all the gory details. They asked how I was going to survive, if Sam had left me for another woman. Once their curiosity was satisfied, they let me go. Two of my supposed friends who were single even tried to date my ex-husband. And my married friends were afraid I'd steal their men.

Tara goes on to explain that her friends' rivalry stemmed from their initial envy of her marriage itself:

Enough women in my culture do not marry their partners that it was a big deal when I had a real wedding. Then my divorce came and I guess they felt I got what I deserved: for being so high and mighty as to have a regular wedding and a real husband, a real father to my children.

For Tara, her divorce was the occasion when her friends showed their true colors, a revelation that made her question all her previous assumptions about female friendship.

What hurt me most was that no one really cared about me. I was like a phenomenon. First they wanted to catch whatever I had that got me married, then they wanted to run away from me so no one would walk out on them, like it was some disease that worked either way.

I don't even trust my sisters, only my mother now. My one sister who has been alone with four little kids for six years always resented me because I had a husband and a house for my children. Now that I'm in no better shape than she is, she tries to be nice, but I always smelled her jealousy and I don't bother with her much.

I just wonder why women can't be kinder going up and kinder going down. I was always looking for good women friends, for my sisters to act like sisters, but after my divorce, I gave up. I know that everyone is worried about herself and her chances of getting a better life. That doesn't leave much room for friends, since everyone wants the same thing.

In Tara's words—"they wanted to catch whatever I had that got me married"—are echoes of the magical thinking we saw earlier. Tara's friends seem to think that both her marriage and her divorce were special qualities, whether positive or negative, that they had the ability to either steal or "catch."

Tara's story also suggests the prevailing theme of not enough pie. If there are only a few chances of getting a better life, women are forced to compete with one another for those rare opportunities. Either they'll be trying to steal a woman's good luck or crowing over her bad luck, but neither response provides a basis for friendship.

"Women deal with divorce and remarriage as a second chance," remarks Dr. Ronnie Burak. "It is a different stage for them and they are out for themselves this time around, in order to get it right. A best friend might feel left behind."

Indeed, Alyssa, a fifty-seven-year-old schoolteacher, resents the friends who appear to have a better situation:

> I can't stand that my two best friends—one who is divorced and the other who is widowed—have found new men. Even though Ellie, my friend who is widowed, has been through a lot, ever since she met a man, it's been hard for me to watch her happiness.

Part of the problem, Alyssa explains, is simply her own loneliness. She actually has been abandoned by Ellie, at least to some extent:

> We used to go to movies together and play cards, but now she is always with him. Since they've been together, if they see anyone, it will be his friends, or their children.

But Alyssa is also responding to the new difference in the two women's status:

> Ellie is considering moving in with her boyfriend, and that makes me envious. I would like to have a man who would want me to move in with him, and it's not happening. So even though I don't have any financial worries and my children are good to me, I am lonely, and I see that my

two best friends aren't willing to spend as much time with me as they used to. My other best friend got married right after her divorce and she has a whole new life. They travel, and they don't see old friends either. They are almost like teenagers when they are together, so I try to avoid them as much as possible.

Losing these two friends to their new lives has really put a hole in my schedule. I find myself alone doing things I used to do with them. It used to be fun to look for guys together, but I didn't find one and they both did.

Again, we see the other side of the coin in my interview with Barb, a woman who fears her divorced friends. While Tara was hurt at the way her married girlfriends dropped her, and Alyssa envied her divorced friends' happiness, Barb, a thirty-three-year-old mother of three, insists that divorced women know no bounds in their efforts to steal other women's men:

Since I have three kids, I hear about divorces a lot, in each of my children's classes, and I watch my back. It's all about what it takes to be happy. If it takes getting some other wife's husband, the rationale is that the women weren't friends, their kids just happened to be in the same class or hockey league or something. It's as if once this woman is no longer married, it's a free-for-all for her since her life has changed. So I stay away from any of the mothers at school who are getting divorced. It's just too harsh a world, and women can be ruthless. I can't take any risks, and any single mother, even if she is my friend, is a risk as far as I'm concerned. . . .

The mothers who have great careers are the most scary because they are probably ruthless at work. So if one of those mothers gets divorced, I'm sure to keep it to myself and not let my husband know. Especially since my husband is successful, and successful women like to be with successful men. . . .

I remember my single days and how we were all like vultures when it came to a cute guy at a party or a bar. I know that nothing is sacred and that while women pretend they are your friend, it isn't really so. In a way, a woman who is divorced is less afraid of rocking the boat. She already did something that was a nightmare—she ended up divorced with little kids. Now it is her turn to get back, if her husband dumped her, or to simply shop for a new husband if she dumped her husband.

I know this sounds like I'm paranoid, but I know what goes on in the minds of these women. I've sat at enough coffees while the kids are in rehearsals or at an after-school activity to know that young mothers are very worried about themselves. . . . So they have no respect for the other mothers, their supposed "friends."

Bethany offers a different perspective on the way divorce can become the expression of female rivalry. Now age forty-eight and single, with two college-age sons, Bethany discovered three years before I interviewed her that her husband at the time was having an affair with a divorced colleague:

I had a similar job, as an accountant at another accounting firm, so I was astonished. After all, didn't I have all of the prestige that she had? Wasn't I working full-time and raising our kids? Didn't I have a master's in business too? . . . We even had the same first name. I couldn't believe it.

Because the colleague resembled Bethany in so many ways, and yet seemed to be preferable to her, Bethany began to question her own identity:

She wasn't younger or prettier, she was just who he preferred. This made me feel like our competition was more to the point. This woman had to have my husband, and I couldn't win. We were automatically jealous of each other and yet we were equals. I know I can't compete with some gorgeous blonde who is fifteen years my junior, but why did he choose . . . a partner . . . who is so similar to me?

Bethany had three significant responses to her husband's choice. First, she felt that with no obvious distinguishing markers—looks, age, status—there was no basis for her husband to choose. The other woman was "just who he preferred." It's almost as though Bethany was so used to defining herself in terms of her ability to compete with other women that when neither woman has any obvious competitive advantage, she assumes that both women must be identical and is astonished that her husband would go to the trouble of favoring one over the other.

Second, without the markers, Bethany is at a loss in knowing *how* to compete. She can't pull rank against a younger, less experienced woman, or bemoan her disadvantage at having to compete with a "gorgeous blonde." If the only basis for her husband's choice is "who he preferred," then there's really nothing Bethany can do to fight for her man, let alone to triumph over a female competitor. The man's preference takes precedence over the women's rivalry, leaving Bethany feeling more hurt, more disempowered, than if she'd been engaged in a more obvious contest.

Third, the similarities between Bethany and the other woman led Bethany to expect a kind of solidarity, or at least some mutual sympathy. And when the other woman put her own needs ahead of Bethany's, Bethany felt betrayed, even by a woman she had never met:

> We both know how hard it was to land our jobs at these firms, and how hard it is to hold on as you get older. We shared a very similar experience. . . . So his having to have her made me feel worse than ever. It just made me realize that there are not enough men to go around, like there aren't enough jobs out there.

Although I would probably agree with Bethany that there aren't enough men to go around, I'm struck by how she keeps trying to change the story back into one of female rivalry. No, she insists, this isn't the tale of a husband who fell in love with another woman and chose to leave his wife. Instead, it's the story of a predatory divorcée who stole a husband from a woman with whom she should have had more sympathy. The woman, not the man, is seen as the active player in the story, a player who might have behaved better had there been enough men to go around.

Therefore no matter which side of the rivalry she ends up on—winner, loser, thief, victim—a woman who competes over relationships lives in a world ruled by women. Although men seem to be the ultimate prize in this world, they have very little to say about how events actually unfold. To hear the rivals tell it, all the work, all the decisions, and all the outcomes are determined by how far a woman is willing to go in her efforts to steal or keep her husband. Hence the effort to protect the precious man from contact with desirable women, or even from hearing the latest news of a divorce. ". . . If one of those mothers gets divorced, I'm sure to keep it to myself," Barb remarks. "Especially since my husband is successful, and successful women like to be with successful men. . . ." The husband's choice, whether he would rather be with Barb or someone else, is not nearly as important in this scenario as whether Barb can mobilize herself to guard her property.

I can see why women, feeling desperate to win the mates and jobs that are in such short supply, would create this myth of their own power. Because in real life, of course, men make their own decisions about whom to stay with, and they may very well choose younger, prettier women as their first wives get older. This has been a common theme in our patriarchal society, where aging works against women even as it favors many men, who often become richer, more powerful, and more prestigious as they get older. This imbalance of social power gives men far more relationship choices than women, as well as vastly greater access to prestige, money, and the most desirable jobs. It can be comforting to pretend that these powerful males are really just pawns or sexual fools, at the mercy of any clever woman who decides to set her sights on a new target.

The price we pay for such a myth, however, is twofold. First, it shifts our focus from the need to create a more equitable distribution of resources onto our resentment of other women. Instead of asking why there aren't more good men and good jobs, we vent our frustration on our fellow females.

Second, in competing with other women, we deprive ourselves of the very people who might be able to join with us to change these unhappy conditions, let alone the people who can comfort and support us as we try to build our own lives. As I reread the voices in this chapter, I was saddened to see how many of them concluded that they no longer trusted any women—colleague, neighbor, friend, even sister. Men were unpredictable and elusive, but women, it seemed, were the sole enemy, the only gender with whom we battle it out.

Even in the area of fashion, traditionally viewed as women's efforts to attract men, we seem to focus on each other. In an August 2004 opinion column in *Harper's Bazaar*, "Do You Dress for Men or Women?" journalist Sarah Sands argues that women in fact dress for other women, who are far more critical than any man could ever be. An *Elle* article by Christine Lennon, "Free for All," chronicling the insults Lennon receives from other women who mock her profession as fashion writer, asserts in a tag line that "dressing well . . . is always the best revenge." In fashion, as in everywhere else, female rivalry keeps us divided and weak, even as it also links us in a never-ending competition.

6

Snow Queens and Soccer Moms: Envy over Children

When thirty-seven-year-old Shawna told me about her lifelong contest with her childhood friend, Jill, I was not surprised to hear that the two girls competed for grades, guys, and friends, as we saw in Chapter 3. Nor was it unusual that as adults the two women competed over relationships, status, and money. But with remarkable frankness, Shawna went on to explain that the two women also competed over every aspect of mothering, starting with who got pregnant first:

> Jill and I had our first children within six months of one another. During the pregnancy, we would laugh about who had gained more weight, who had better maternity clothes. But we weren't really laughing, we were competing.
>
> Jill's son was born first, which made her triumphant. Then we competed over who was the cuter kid, whose mother or mother-in-law fussed more over her grandchild, who had better sitters and more free time. The first birthday parties for each of our babies were like showdowns.
>
> From that time on, if I got pregnant, Jill had to get pregnant. We

each have three children, but I have two girls and one boy, which annoys her, since she has only boys. Anyway, that lessens the competition between the kids. Now we compete over who does the most: more car pools, more PTA meetings, the most volunteer meetings at the school—is it Jill, or is it me? Ahead of us is a competition over which kid gets into what college, marries who, lands what job. It's how it works with us, and it's been like this since kindergarten.

It's not surprising that a society that still considers mothering an integral part of female identity would encourage women to compete over children: fertile versus infertile, mothers versus childless women, working mothers versus soccer moms, mothers of high-achieving kids versus mothers whose kids are average or troubled. Yet the very society that insists on measuring a woman by her children's accomplishments also neglects a mother's actual needs, failing to provide adequate day care, health care, and other vital resources to support the work of mothering.

As a result, women compete in all aspects of this charged issue. First, their sense of womanhood is at stake: who wants to be judged in her role as mother or to face the stigma of admitting that she doesn't want children? Second, mothering in our culture is a classic example of "not enough pie": not enough support either for choosing to be a mother or for deciding not to be one.

Competition over mothering becomes particularly painful when it involves close friends. Christine, a thirty-eight-year-old magazine editor living in Florida, was beginning her fourth attempt at in vitro fertilization just as her best friend, Alicia, had become pregnant for the third time. The two women had served as maid or matron of honor at each other's weddings, and they had been close since childhood. Yet the difference in their childbearing experiences created a rift that led Christina to become cruel and competitive:

I had no more energy or time to listen to Alicia as she droned on and on about her children. . . . It was hard for me to see her with her children . . . she just popped them out in four years' time. . . . When she called to tell me she was pregnant with her third, I said to her, "Not again." I was that jealous and that sorry for myself.

For Christine, the sense of having lost a contest was all the sharper because of the twinning syndrome that I spoke of in Chapter 1. She and Alicia had married within three weeks of each other, participating in each other's weddings. Then Alicia went on to become pregnant with relative ease, while Christine began a nightmarish round of visits to fertility specialists. An experience that would have been painful under any circumstances became well-nigh unbearable as Christine compared herself to her friend:

I blame myself for marrying late. . . . Then I look at Alicia, who also married late, and it's been a breeze for her. I love her children, but they remind me of what I can't have.

Christine's anguished sense of being left behind was so sharp that Alicia's suggestion to adopt was viewed not as an attempt to help but as an effort to vaunt her own victory:

I was offended that she, Miss Fertile Myrtle, thinks adoption is a solution. She knows that I want to be pregnant and . . . that I need to get on with my life. . . .

While I'm happy for her, I can't believe what I've been denied every time I see her. I don't want to give up, and seeing her makes me realize how far behind I am. I am jealous of every young mother in theory, but in fact, it is Alicia's children and her life that makes me most upset because she and I are best friends.

Christine's point couldn't be clearer: her friend Alicia somehow owed it to her to struggle with the same problems and suffer from the same losses. If it were only children that Christine envied, she would feel no differently toward Alicia than toward any other mother. But because Alicia was her best friend and therefore supposed to mirror Christine exactly, Alicia's motherhood feels like a betrayal. As a result, the friendship is waning:

> My marriage seems more taxed every time that I talk with Alicia on the phone. So I'm pulling away, even though we live in the same town.

As we saw in Chapter 1, one of the later episodes of *Sex and the City* offered a fictional version of the same problem: Charlotte, unable to have a child, deals poorly at first with Miranda's pregnancy. Charlotte feels as though Miranda has pilfered something that rightfully belonged to her. This illogical response is possible because Charlotte defines her own identity primarily by comparing herself to her women friends. If Miranda has a baby and Charlotte wants one, Miranda must somehow have taken Charlotte's child.

As Christine and Shawna both testify, women can have trouble seeing themselves as separate beings whose destinies are not inextricably linked to their best friends' lives. If you and your friend share an identity, that friend becoming pregnant or having a more accomplished child suggests that she stole that prize from you. Only when you see yourselves as separate can you distinguish between her good fortune and your bad luck.

Widening Options, Deepening Envy

Ironically, as with many of the issues explored in this book, competition among women has intensified as their horizons have broadened. Until the nineteenth century, as historian Gerda Lerner reminds us in *The Creation of a Feminist Consciousness*, ". . . the choice of remaining single was only a choice of one kind of dependency over another." While married women were dependent on their husbands for support, single women "might choose celibacy and the religious life, in which case they depended on their superior and the male clergy." Although some widows could have relatively independent lives, thanks to their control of the income and property their husbands had left behind, being married was really the only viable option for women. Motherhood, in particular, was the most important means of cementing a husband's loyalty.

Today single women have a wide range of options for economic self-sufficiency, as do mothers, married and single. Most women of child-bearing age are working: the U.S. Department of Labor, Women's Bureau reports that over 74 percent of women between the ages of twenty-five and thirty-four and 77 percent of women between the ages of thirty-five and forty-four are in the workforce, while 71 percent of the female population is composed of working mothers with children under eighteen.

Generally, the rapid entry of women into the workforce has had enormous consequences for every sector of society. While this trend has enabled a new potential for female solidarity, it has also caused the possibilities for women's rivalry to grow significantly. Now that women appear to have more choices about marriage, child rearing, and lifestyle, they face more judgments about those choices: from society at large, from one another, and from themselves.

These judgments are all the more painful because of society's mixed messages about motherhood. As pioneering feminist Betty Friedan put it in her classic work, *The Feminine Mystique*, mothering is an occupation both "reviled and revered." As a result, this quintessential female experience inspires women to struggle with feelings of incompetence, guilt, and self-doubt—feelings that are only exacerbated when women compare themselves unfavorably to one another.

For Lola, at age seventy-eight, her status as a childless woman is an ongoing struggle.

I have spent my entire life explaining how I was married but had no children. I was always envious of my friends who had children, and their

family life. It isn't that I didn't find my way, but that this has always been hanging over me.

When Lola's friends' children grew older, Lola experienced a reprieve. But her relief proved to be short-lived:

As my closest friends' children grew up, I sort of escaped this feeling. . . . Then there was this mad scramble for who would do what with their lives. Once again, I was the odd person, because by then some of my friends had remarried and had stepchildren. Those who liked their stepchildren would hold it over those who did not. I saw they were the lucky ones, but I didn't even have a stepchild to try to love. Again, I was cheated.

Lola's second-class status was all the more painful to her because in other areas of female competition, she had been a winner, not a loser:

As a young woman, my friends were jealous of me because I was pretty and I married a very handsome man. Then, as everyone's lives became concerned with children, no one was jealous of me anymore.

As with Christine, it's not clear which Lola regrets more: the actual relationships of which she's been deprived—no children or stepchildren "to love"—or her loss of status. Both seem painful in a world that increasingly isolates women as they become older, rendering them economically and socially dependent on children and stepchildren for both financial support and emotional ties. To a woman facing a bleak, isolated, and perhaps impoverished old age, the feeling that she's "behind" or "less than" her friends is adding insult to injury. And in this context, the expanded range of choices that our society seems to offer women can appear as a cruel joke.

On the other hand, now that women are allowed, and even expected, to succeed professionally and to have active sexual lives, women with children may well find themselves envying their childless friends. Gabriella, the forty-three-year-old marketing executive whom we first met in Chapter 4, expresses anguish when she looks back on her experience with her four pregnancies in her late twenties and early thirties.

> My husband and I lived in a young, hip part of the city. We were young and maybe cool, but having kids definitely set me apart from the other women . . . who were gorgeous . . . out partying and meeting different guys. They didn't even want a steady boyfriend, and there I was: I had a husband and one child, and three more ahead of me.
>
> It was very hard for me in terms of my body image. I knew, rationally, that being pregnant changes you and that you might not bounce back, but you can come back. I'd always had a good figure and so I knew, intellectually, that I would again. But it . . . really bothered me. These women wore miniskirts, tube tops, and were half-naked while I was in maternity clothes.
>
> If I hadn't met these women, I doubt I would have been so obsessed with losing the weight after each baby was born. I went on crazy diets and worked out like mad to get my former body back. To this day I blame my pregnancies for anything wrong with my body—sagging breasts, a stretched-out stomach—the things you can't fix by a diet or at the gym. I never had the years that other woman had to be sexy and free. I was breast-feeding when they were in string bikinis. I sometimes wonder if we're all caught up, now that we're older.

Likewise, Antoinette, a thirty-six-year-old full-time mother and former ER nurse, recalls feeling envious of childless women while she was pregnant and "fat":

> I was at a friend's husband's fortieth birthday party when I was pregnant with my third child, and it was a really glamorous affair. I looked like an elephant, and all the couples were dancing and partying. The women were in tight-fitting short skirts. I felt so conspicuous—out of the loop. It

wasn't that no one else had been through this. But no one else was pregnant at that time. . . . I really thought my husband was watching the other women, sort of checking them out, but that wasn't my main concern. I was thinking more about how I would look after this pregnancy, would I ever get my body back in shape? Wasn't I thinner and more attractive than most of the women at the party when I *wasn't* pregnant? So instead of being so excited about this third child, I was preoccupied with feeling that I was unchic and unattractive with my friends at a party.

As recently as fifty years ago, our society expected working-class, middle-class, and upper-class women alike to bear children and be stay-at-home mothers. In such a narrow scope, women competed over children, husbands, and houses, but at least they had the satisfaction of knowing where they stood.

Today, women have many more choices, and many more opportunities for anxiety. Instead of "winning" in one domain, they're now expected to triumph in several. The social change that would provide subsidized day care and flex time, enabling women to more easily balance motherhood and a career, has yet to be made. Even when a woman succeeds at the vital task of raising children, she can easily feel as though she's failing somewhere else. If a colleague or friend manages better in this delicate balance, it becomes another form of rivalry.

From June Cleaver to Debra Barone: Mothers on TV

As we consider women's struggles with choices around motherhood, we can see society's ambivalence reflected in popular culture. In the 1950s and 1960s, for example, virtually every woman on television was a mother, with June Cleaver, Harriet Nelson, and Donna Reed offering iconic versions of the stay-at-home mom.

Significantly, during the 1960s—a decade when fewer children were living in households headed by a single woman and the nuclear family seemed to be a cornerstone of our society—only one single mother appeared on television: Julia. The short-lived show of the same name aired briefly in 1968, starring Diahann Carroll as a widowed mother working as a nurse and raising her young son. Significant, too, was the fact that Carroll was African-American, the first black woman to star in her own sitcom. If you compared *Julia* with the rest of TV fare, you had the impression that white mothers were always married and staying home, while the lone black woman was a single, working mom.

In the 1970s, a few childless working women began to make their appearance. It's hard to recall now how radical *The Mary Tyler Moore Show* was when it debuted on September 19, 1970. Mary—originally supposed to be a divorcée, rewritten as a woman whose engagement had been broken—takes off for the big city and tries to get a job. Her efforts to survive as a single working woman look almost archetypal in retrospect. She is the only woman in her office except for a recurring character, Sue Ann Nivens (played by Betty White), who, despite being a childless professional, hosts the *Happy Housewife* show at Mary's station. Back home, Mary has a best friend, Rhoda (Valerie Harper), also a single woman, and a smug landlady, Phyllis (Cloris Leachman), who continually reminds the "single girls" of her own superior status as wife and mother. The premise of the show is how unusual it was for Mary to try to make it as a single woman, with no man or marriage anywhere in sight. ("Girl, you're gonna make it on your own," promised the famous theme song as Mary triumphantly threw her hat into the air.) Mary wasn't compared unfavorably to married women or mothers; instead, she and Rhoda were portrayed as an entirely different species, operating under a whole new set of rules and standards.

As women entered the workforce, TV changed as well. In 1976, Linda Lavin began starring in the long-running sitcom *Alice*, in which she played a white single mother. The show was based on Martin Scorsese's 1974 movie, *Alice Doesn't Live Here Anymore*, about a woman who flees with her young son, trying to escape an abusive husband. In the TV show, Alice is motivated by her husband's death, rather than his abuse, but in both versions of her story, she ends up working in a diner outside of Phoenix. Part of the TV show's popularity rested in its then-unusual portrait of the female solidarity that Alice shared with the other waitresses, feisty Flo and naïve Vera. Although in true sitcom style each female character was made to be quite different from the others, the women more often bonded than competed over their differences. While Alice was the only one raising a child, she never seemed to make the others feel they were defective on that account; nor did she envy them their "freedom." All three women were more preoccupied with earning a living than with mutual competition, banding together against their gruff but lovable male boss.

It wasn't only single mothers who worked on TV, however. Many of the most famous and successful 1980s sitcoms featured married women, both black and white, who held down full-time jobs while raising families. Working moms were positively portrayed on such long-running comedies as *Family Matters*, *Roseanne*, *Family Ties*, and *The Cosby Show*. The women on the first two shows had blue-collar jobs, while *Family Ties* and *The Cosby Show* featured an architect and a high-powered attorney. But all four women seemed to balance work and home without trauma (and without the help of a nanny, maid, or housekeeper).

As the 1980s ended, though, TV began to glorify the stay-at-home mom once again, comparing her favorably to both working mothers and childless women. The contrast is striking. In *Roseanne*, episodes featuring the married Roseanne and her childless sister, Jackie, usually avoided making judgments about either woman. Each had simply made different choices and was now living with different results. Moreover, as the successful sitcom went into multiple seasons, the women's roles began to change: Jackie chose to marry and have a child, while Roseanne's children grew up and left home. The show was remarkably committed to presenting both women's choices in an even-handed way, showing that neither motherhood nor childlessness is a static condition.

But other TV shows were not so tolerant. On the hour-long show *thirtysomething* (1987–1991), virtually every professional married woman left the workforce to stay home with her children, while single women uniformly expressed anxiety over both their singleness and their childlessness. Two decades earlier, Mary and Rhoda had seemed carefree and excited about their independent lives. Now on *thirtysomething* Ellin and Melissa agonized constantly over their loneliness and sense of failure.

Thirtysomething also began to portray female rivalry in a new and more painful way. The show's first episode set the tone. Hope, a former writer, has chosen to stay home with her infant daughter, but her single, childless best friend can't accept that Hope has moved into a new life. Each woman fears being abandoned by the other now that their choices are no longer the same.

Thirtysomething almost always came down on the side of stay-at-home moms, who were shown to be happier, healthier, and more satisfied than working women once they gave up their careers and focused on parenting. In the 1990s and early twenty-first century, TV trends went much further, portraying stay-at-home moms whose premothering work lives seemed unimaginable. This included Debra on *Everybody Loves Raymond* and the two sisters on *Yes, Dear*, not to mention Marge in the animated show *The Simpsons*. Watching these modern mothers as they take their kids to the playground and nag their husbands to be more helpful around the house, you might almost think the women's movement had never happened, except for the new license it seems to have given women to complain about their husbands.

Perhaps television has finally come full circle, though, with the character played by Felicity Huffman on the hour-long show *Desperate Housewives*. In that show's premiere in the fall of 2004, the Huffman character is portrayed as miserable and frustrated for having given up her career in order to stay at home with her four bratty children. At the grocery store, disheveled and distraught, she runs into a serene, beautifully dressed, and childless former colleague.

Although the colleague clearly prefers her own life path, she prompts Huffman to express the standard platitudes about the joys of motherhood. Huffman glances over at her sons, who are wreaking havoc in the cereal aisle. Clearly visible on her face is the wish to say that leaving her job was the worst mistake of her life. Instead she is forced to smile ruefully and, crushed by the weight of society's expectations, agree that being a mother is the best job of all.

I had never before seen a TV mother express such regret for her choice to stay at home with her children. And as I considered this scene, I could not help but think again that some of the rivalry over children that I'd heard about in my interviews stemmed from women's regrets about how limited their choices are. After all, motherhood is not the right option for everyone, and even those of us who are delighted to be parents are often deeply frustrated both by the sacrifices we've had to make and by society's mixed messages. But instead of directing our resentment where it belongs, once again, we turn our anger on other women, seeing them as rivals, victors, or competitors, and diverting ourselves from more useful efforts to improve conditions for us all.

As Sherill, a thirty-four-year-old medical-lab technician, explains it, having children is a bond at work and also a source of rivalry:

> I've been at this job for eleven years, and three of us have had kids since I got here. In some ways . . . we can talk about our lives, about how hard it is to have a job and little kids. But it always comes down to who is a better mother, who does more, and who secretly feels trapped. No one at the lab would dare admit that. Still, I do feel trapped at times.

Roberta, a forty-year-old hairstylist, has made a different choice, but faces the same rivalry. Having chosen to work part-time so as to be more available to her daughters, she has encountered envious criticism from her female friends:

> I knew not to listen to any of my girlfriends when it came to my situation at work. . . . The fact that I'd been at this job so long that I could cut my

hours and keep the position bothered them. Most of us work, and we all feel guilty, but I did something about it. I was able to work from eight-thirty to three. Why don't my friends follow my lead? Instead they're angry at me, angry at the stay-at-home moms they know. . . .

Making Motherhood a Full-time Job

Historically, as numerous scholars have pointed out, the actual raising of children never occupied a woman's entire attention. With their children strapped to their back or clustering around their feet, peasant women worked long hours doing household labors that were vital to their families' survival—tending livestock, growing food, making clothes, and engaging in other subsistence tasks. The suburban housewife of the '50s, freed from economic responsibilities and assisted by labor-saving devices, had far fewer demands on her day, although her infant or toddler still required supervision and running the household was part of the deal.

Today, especially among the middle and upper-middle classes, motherhood is seen as a job that requires great effort. Children need special courses, a plethora of educational activities, and a wide variety of clothes, toys, and related equipment. Many high-achieving mothers seem to transfer their ambition and drive from the workplace into the home, creating numerous child-centered tasks and then rating themselves on how well they accomplish them. As described by Lynn Schnurnberger in a June 2002 article in *More* magazine, "Suburban Supermoms," this new wave of FEMMS (Formerly Employed Mature Moms) are turning motherhood into a full-time profession. Schnurnberger suggests that these women are as zealous about shaping their child's world as they were about "pulling off a megadeal or a multimillion-dollar merger." Now they are expressing their ambition through school fairs and town charity events.

Deprived of company spreadsheets or an ever-growing résumé, these women look for other ways to measure their results, and their children's performances are often what they focus on. As Jackie, a first-time mother of twin sons and partner in a law firm, confesses, she was worried about her sons' acceptance at the best schools when they were infants.

> Already I was thinking of which Ivy League schools my sons would attend when they were just a few days old. I'd been in the work world for so long that I knew I had a lot of catching up to do: what preschool was best for them, what grade school, and would it be private? Or, since we live in a city, would the boys be eligible for a special program in a public school? If they did the public school, I'd have to get them in gear soon. Here I was thinking like this, and then I had to research it, and meet other mothers and learn from them at the same time that I'd have my sons competing with their kids for placement. I knew what was ahead, and I knew I'd enter the ring just like I had for all of my own success, determined to win.
>
> My two closest friends have just had babies . . . and I can see that it's going to be a shooting match there, too. Already we're talking about whose kid sleeps through the night. My one friend has a brother on the board of the most coveted school, so I guess the other friend and I will always whisper that her son was accepted based on that. I know we're just shifting gears here but remaining competitive. Now it's all about our babies, our children.

Similarly, Annette's three-year-old daughter is already being tutored and shown flash cards in order to do well in the preschool that will land her in the "right" grade school.

> I won't have my daughter, Brianna, fall behind. In fact, she has to be ahead. My sister's daughter is four months older than Brianna and walked at ten months. Brianna didn't walk until she was a year and seems to be a late bloomer, which bothers me. In fact, it makes me crazy. So I've gotten Brianna to read words on sight, and I feel like we're getting somewhere. I've also stopped listening to my sister when she boasts about her

daughter. It's better for me to think of Brianna's future and get that set, which is competitive enough. But a few days ago, my sister called to say her daughter is doing programs for preschoolers on the computer. Now I have to find out about these programs. I will ask Brianna's nanny, who tutors her when I'm at the office. She's been instructed to only use educational toys with Brianna and to read her books as much as possible.

Of course, children grow and learn at individual rates, often in fits and starts, and whether these enrichment programs are integral to life success or not, it's the mothers' emphasis on them that is troubling. It seems to me that the mothers' competition is less about ensuring their children's growth than about affirming their own worth, and winning the new contest for "Best Mom."

Nevertheless, women often view their competitiveness as a helpful motivational tool, especially if they believe their children are not doing well. Suki, for example, a fifty-two-year-old dental hygienist, is frustrated with her twenty-five-year-old adult child who seems to be having difficulty growing up. Her son hasn't yet decided upon a career and has never held a full-time job; recently, he moved back home to make ends meet. Seeing that her friends are in the same boat both relieves Suki and goads her on to new efforts:

I look around and see my friends going crazy with their twenty-eight- and thirty-year-old kids, and I don't feel like as much of a loser with my twenty-five-year-old. I think we're in a race to get our children somewhere, finally, but watching my friends suffer kind of helps me out. It gets me going. If someone's son gets a job, I work harder on my own children.

Suki's words make it clear how invested she is in her children's achievements. She doesn't speak of helping or advising her offspring, but of "working harder" on them, as though her work, not theirs, would determine the quality of their lives. In a world where mothers take their children's accomplishments so personally, is it any wonder that children have a hard time growing up?

The sixty-four-year-old Mira, a former public relations executive, also sees her children's accomplishments as extensions of herself. Although she has backed off from more direct competition with other mothers and grandmothers, she explains that it's only because she now feels more dependent upon her former rivals:

> I'm a socially competitive mother with my friends and their children. I have been like that my entire life and the only reason I've mellowed is out of necessity. . . . This is how I've operated for years. I only back off when I know I've said enough, or I'd go on and on about them. I don't go too far because I really need my friends.

With unusual honesty, Mira acknowledges that boasting about her children says less about her feelings for them than about her own need for glory. Consequently, her grown children aren't even pleased to hear her bragging:

> I doubt my adult children appreciate me pushing their children's accomplishments at my friends. I doubt that my daughter-in-law cares if I boast about her. I used to dislike her, but she's a good mother and the kids are great. She's also a judge and I like that. So today we get along. She's proved herself.

Mira's terse phrase implies a world in which every woman has to prove herself to someone. The daughter-in-law can't be loved simply because she's a kind person or because she makes Mira's son happy. She has to prove herself through producing "great" kids and through her impressive career, giving Mira material she can use in competition with her friends.

The unfortunate part is that by competing through their children, mothers miss much-needed opportunities to draw on female bonding and support. Gina, age sixty-two, had a longtime best friend and coworker, Wilma, who might have provided some crucial comfort during Gina's struggles with her drug-addicted son, support that would have been particularly valuable to the widowed Gina. Yet because of their competitive relationship, Gina hid her troubles from her friend:

> I wouldn't tell Wilma that my son is a drug addict. We were so competitive about the kids since they were small that this would seem like defeat. We live in a small southwestern town where Wilma and I worked together in the high school cafeteria. Nothing mattered much except what your husband did and how your kids turned out. There wasn't much about our lives that had to do with our own glory. I was the best cook around and Wilma could bake up a storm, but our kids were the proof that we existed. And we competed about them all the time. I knew if my girls didn't marry the right boys that it would make me look bad. The women in town would talk about it.
>
> My girls came through for me. . . . My older daughter married into a wealthy family and lives in a big house. I look at my girls and I know they have a chance at something better than what I had, and I'm glad for them.
>
> I was always covering up for my son. He was a ne'er-do-well from the time he was in sixth grade. But Wilma's two sons have good jobs. One is an accountant and the other is in the service. My son never went to college and that was shameful to me.
>
> His problem is bad enough, but the fact that I can't get sympathy from Wilma because we've been showing our kids off to each other all these years is ridiculous. Still, I will not tell her because she will judge me and then remind me of how great her sons are. It would be salt on a wound. I'm dealing with this alone because I am a widow, but I know I have to keep it a secret from my best friend. I don't want her sympathy—not unless things get worse.

Single Mothers in the Ring

Single mothers are in an unusual position when it comes to competing over their children. On the one hand, they are at a disadvantage, almost by definition, when compared to married mothers or mothers with partners. On the other hand, their difficulties don't exempt them from envy, either as a perpetrator or as a target. When it comes to tripping the prom queen, single mothers can stick a foot into the aisle with the best of them.

Louisa, a forty-one-year-old single mother, describes the painful envy she feels for mothers who have partners:

> I was returning from a convention in Las Vegas with several people from my office. When we arrived at the airport I saw that a woman who works in my department was met at the baggage claim by her husband and two young children. . . . There was all this hugging and kissing at being reunited, as I stood there alone, waiting to meet the driver from the car service so I could get home to my son as soon as possible. But no one would be hugging me when I arrived. My nanny would nod and sigh with relief that her responsibilities would be lighter for a few weeks until my next trip, and my son would be asleep. I always wake him when I get back late at night, but there won't be anyone greeting me like the family at the airport. . . . It's something I wish I had.

Dana, at forty-nine, works as a producer for a radio host and is the single mother of two teenage girls. She describes her position as contradictory. On the one hand, she is envied for her success at work. On the other hand, she doubts that other women envy her personal life, despite society's general valuation of mothers over childless women:

> Every once in a while a single friend without kids will say to me, "At least you have those children." But usually women are still looking for the great job, the great husband, and then the perfect family. I only win on

two counts, work and kids, and that is where I am envied. Few envy me
the single-mother route.

Dorraine, a twenty-six-year-old African-American transit worker, acknowledges that few women in the mainstream community would envy
her single-mother status. But, she told me, women of her own background resent her small successes, in a pattern that began in childhood:

> My mother made sure that each of us went to college. But in our neigh-
> borhood, she was unusual and all the other women hated her for it. That
> made her not want to boast about us, but to keep it kind of quiet so it
> wasn't used against us. She had a difficult life, but she worked hard for
> her children.
>
> As a single mother who wants her children to do well, I also have to
> be careful. . . . I have never been on welfare as an adult woman, and for
> this I am envied. I don't tell my friends or coworkers about what I want
> for my boys. I stay quiet so they don't get jealous and don't gang up on
> me for wanting things that they consider outside my reach. Or worse yet,
> if one of the women at work hears that my son got a job after school,
> she'll send her son down there to try to take it away. I feel like my plans
> for my children can be taken from me by jealous women.

Like many other women I spoke with, Dorraine expected more from
the women who shared her situation. She discovered that these were
the very people most likely to envy her:

> At work, I have found that the women who are my race and religion are
> the ones who keep me from getting somewhere. It's as if they are afraid
> that I might outshine them, and so they won't even give me a chance. I
> have a boss who is female and from the same neighborhood. I expected
> her to be on my side, but she's too worried about herself. She would
> never try to help me. Instead she checks me out—my clothes, my hair, my
> sons. I might get as far as she has gone and she wouldn't like that.

Dorraine has come to understand that she is envied precisely because people can see themselves in her. Having done well, she seems to stand as a living reproach to others who have not achieved the same things, and as a threat to women who have accomplished more. Nevertheless, she insists that if she herself were more successful, she would be generous rather than envious:

> I know I wouldn't mind if a woman came along and wanted to get ahead. I would understand, especially if she had kids.

Sometimes the apparently more successful women nonetheless resent and compete with single mothers. Thirty-nine-year-old Lutetia, for example, expected to find sympathy and friendship from the married, professional mother whom she met when their children were in the same play group. Instead, she encountered a virulent envy:

> Cindy likes to talk about everyone in the class, especially about who is pretty. She analyzes one woman on a constant basis and tells me that the woman cares about her appearance more than she cares about her children. I find myself defending this woman.
>
> Last week we had a conversation in which Cindy insinuated that I am not attractive but old and tired. I said to her, "In my day, I used to be pretty." And she said to me, "Well, you have other good qualities." This was after I told her that I was lonely as a single mother and that I want to start dating and need to feel good about myself. Then she asked me if dating is what I really want to do. Meanwhile, she is married and financially secure through her husband.

Although it seems clear that Cindy is creating a competitive atmosphere with all the play group mothers, Lutetia also seems prone to envy and anxiety over her position relative to Cindy. As she considers Cindy's advantages, she feels resentful and demoralized:

I am a struggling musician. Cindy is also a performing artist but has a husband with a solid job. There is a huge difference. That has become another topic of discussion for us. She likes to tell me how her career is working out, how she is getting bookings. It makes me feel wretched.

Lutetia's experience with Cindy has led her to question her own role in the female rivalries that depress her:

I don't know why I thought that Cindy and her friends were on my side. When we were with the group of mothers last week, at Starbucks, she told all of us that "something good is happening with her work." Later, when we were alone together, with our daughters, I asked her what was happening. She knows it matters to me, since I am a performer, too.... She said, "Oh, I can't tell you. It would jinx it." I wonder why I find women like her who treat me like this, and then try to make them into my friends.

Lutetia and Cindy seemed to struggle with the dynamic that echoes throughout female rivalry: being like me is supportive; being more successful than I am is a betrayal. Whatever the more successful woman's motivations, whether she is gloating over her triumphs, simply enjoying them, or both, the less successful woman feels as though she has been denigrated, maybe even insulted. From her point of view, the resentment is justified: *How dare she rub my nose in her success?* she thinks. But from the more successful woman's point of view, the less successful woman is being a foulweather friend, supportive when things are hard but furious when life goes well. Witness this revealing anecdote by Jenna, a divorced single mother, age forty-two, about her ups and downs with former best friend, Shelley. When married, the two women had experienced a rift that almost ended their friendship. But for a time, their divorces seemed to reunite them:

During my divorce Shelley and I were as close as we were during high school. We both were worried about our sons and about selling our houses, making money, getting fair alimony, child support.

> Later, I began to date and Shelley didn't. . . . It was a nightmare for me, because she would encourage me to leave the boys with her overnight so I could be with my boyfriend, but once I actually came to pick them up, she hated me and was furious that I'd gone out. This caused a bigger rift than when we were competing over our lifestyles and our husbands doing well. And there was always, throughout the divorce and dating scene, the question of whose kids were brighter, cuter, more achieving.

As a result, Jenna reports, the possibility of healing the rift in their friendship evaporated. From her point of view, the relationship only worked when she and Shelley were both so miserable that they had to depend on each other's support. As soon as either woman found a little respite from her troubles, the competition started up again.

Monsters-in-law and Daughters-in-law

No chapter on competition over children would be complete without mention of the battle between in-laws. In my book on mothers-in-law and daughters-in-law, I described the many ways that two women, both in positions of power, engage in an ongoing rivalry. When I was doing the research for this book, I heard a similar story from Kathleen, a sixty-six-year-old mother of a son who lives with a woman thirteen years his senior. Kathleen's point of view is that only one woman can possess her son, and she wants it to be herself:

> I don't know why this woman, Andrea, had to have my son, Jack. They have been together for eight years and while Andrea has teenage children, she and my son are unable to have children. I feel that this relationship has kept my son from having a family of his own. I don't like that she keeps him from this and I have made that clear to Jack. Andrea has also made her feelings clear and so we are at an impasse. My belief is that Jack should be married and have young children. I am very proud of him: he is an accountant and makes a nice living. I think that Andrea saw

him coming—she had a husband who had trouble making ends meet, and she knew she would be financially sound with my son.

Since they have been together, he has stopped sending me plane tickets to visit him back home and he rarely even calls me. There is no question that Andrea has won, because we really can't share Jack—it won't work. But I won't let up, I won't stop trying to win him back. He was mine first, and I don't trust her motives one bit. I keep calling him at work and I pay no attention to her plans for him, just like she pays no attention to mine.

Clearly, Kathleen isn't prepared to give up sole ownership of her son, putting any daughter-in-law or girlfriend in the position of fighting her for Jack, whether she wants to or not. Either Andrea "wins" by having a relationship with Kathleen's son, or Kathleen "wins" by splitting up the couple. Given Kathleen's intransigence, no relationship with a daughter-in-law is even possible.

The Greek myth of Psyche and her mother-in-law, Aphrodite, recounts how the mother-in-law confronted the younger woman with a series of challenges. These were intended to discourage Psyche from being with Aphrodite's son, Cupid. After endangering Psyche's life with her demands, Aphrodite ultimately recognized that Psyche loved her son enough to warrant the mother-in-law's respect, but the resolution wasn't an easy one.

Of course, daughters-in-law also resent their mothers-in-law and envy the closeness that a husband shares with his mother. In some cases, a daughter-in-law will try to get her husband to cut ties with his family of origin or at least to make a clear commitment to putting her first. Once again, *Everybody Loves Raymond* is instructive, as both daughters-in-law on that program are in a continual battle with their intrusive, possessive mother-in-law. Inducing their infantilized husbands to show primary loyalty to their wives rather than their mother seems to be a full-time job that is never quite completed.

Ending the Mommy Wars

It has become clear to me that when women compete over their children, both they and their children lose. Instead of focusing on a unique bond with their children, competing mothers have their eye on other women. Just as women competing over a man lose focus on the man himself, so do women competing over their offspring end up shifting their attention from the children, who are supposedly so important, to the female rivals who absorb more of their emotional lives. Decisions are made not on the basis of the children's good but because a particular school, program, or achievement seems to offer opportunities for outdoing a rival.

And, once again, women lose out on the potential support and assistance they might get from other women in the same boat. If mothers can't turn to each other for help, to whom can they turn? The loneliness of being an isolated mother is indescribable, and the pain of losing friends over child-based rivalry is severe indeed. Thus, Cathy, a forty-six-year-old mother, describes her regrets over how competing with other mothers cost her friendships that she valued, but lost.

> I admit I've lost some and won some in my competition with other mothers. But my ambition for my children has always come first, and with that comes a competition with other mothers. They're just as ambitious for their kids, and so my job has been to compete with the other mothers and to teach my kids to be competitive with their friends, classmates, teammates. That's how it works. I wasn't going to compromise any of my children's chances at being number one for a friendship.
>
> I had one girlfriend and we were very close, and competitive since we're both in the same field. We did everything together with our kids, and we were not so nice about the other mothers and their children, quite frankly. But in the end, I encouraged my son to join the wrestling team and to squeeze her son out for the same category. I wouldn't have even considered wrestling as a sport if it hadn't been for this friend. She

really believed her son would get a sports scholarship to college, so when this happened, it hurt her son's chances. And for that, we aren't friends anymore.

I regret it, and I also know that my son gained an advantage. But the lesson was learned, because this happened with my oldest son, and I wouldn't make the same mistake with the other boys and their friends, and a girlfriend/mother, I wouldn't do it the same way again. At the time, it seemed worth the risk—in retrospect, it wasn't.

So long as women continue to make children the pawns in their contests with female rivals, both mothers and children will suffer. And we'll end up raising a new generation that values competition above all else. Finding a way past the mommy wars into a lasting peace is of prime importance for mothers, children, and all the rest of us.

7

Working Girls and Bossy Women: Envy on the Job

Maureen, thirty-two, is an internist in an all-female practice:
I see that Lillian, my boss, who is in her fifties, is envious and jealous of me. I think that she keeps important work from me because she is afraid that I will get the credit for doing a good job. She leaves me to figure things out for myself when it would be so much easier for her to simply tell me how she has done it in the past. I know that it wasn't easy to get here and that twenty years ago it must have been even rougher. But I am so willing to learn from her and so eager to get the benefits of her expertise. It's a shame it has to be this way.

Robin, forty-three, is a banking executive:
Maybe I am paranoid, but I don't trust the young women who my boss brings into the company. . . . I don't appreciate younger women clouding my vision. Everything I have in my career I earned the hard way. I don't need these young women who look better and sexier threatening my security. Maybe they think they have something to offer, but they should

be threatened by me, too. It's enough that I have to worry about two coworkers who are my age, but now we are bringing in young women and I have this urge to distance myself.

Tori, forty-five, has been in sales for twenty years:
There is this mentality where women are jealous on every level, and then we are competing for clients. If you make money, if you have a good marriage, if you wear nice clothes, if you are younger, and most of all, if you are good at work, the other women sort of hate you. Nothing is said, but it can be felt. . . . Because this office is filled with women, it becomes even harder to compete and to win. I am not like this at home or with my friends, but I separate myself completely when it comes to work.

Although the stereotypes about catty women have focused most often on relationships, the women in my interviews were highly concerned about work as well. In my study I found that 70 percent of women of assorted ages felt a keen competition with other women at work. Older women feared the younger, prettier women who came into their offices; younger women felt that the older, more established women resented them and held them back. Women bosses felt undermined by their female employees; female employees felt singled out unfairly by their women bosses. And women of all ages and levels felt that other women, whether underlings, supervisors, or CEOs, competed with them at every turn, judging them not only on their work performance but also on their looks, style of dress, marital/dating status, children's success (or lack thereof), and general demeanor.

For example, Becky, a thirty-year-old employee at an Internet company in northern California, had worked at the job for only six weeks before finding that competition among the female employees extended to virtually every detail of their lives:

One woman at work who has chronic colitis competes with anyone else who isn't feeling well. If a coworker has a headache, cramps, or is exhausted, this woman carries on as if she is dying. Also, she's heavy, and she is mean to anyone who is thin. If you gain weight, she'll be nicer. There is one person who is really pretty at work and this woman is so jealous of her. She says nasty things to her, really insulting. . . .

Another woman lives with her parents although she's thirty-four years old, and she's jealous of everyone else's life. Actually, the woman with colitis and the woman who lives with her parents are best friends.

Then the women who are married make the single women jealous, and the one who has a baby is the luckiest of all. We're all wishing we could be her. But she's depressed after having a baby. So all of us resent that she has a one-year-old baby and she's depressed? How dare she be that way!

No one cares so much about a career, but we don't like if someone gets a raise—that makes everyone crazy. . . . And everyone watches the clock. If you leave early, they talk about you and if you leave late, they talk about you. . . . Everyone e-mails at work about each other, writing things like, "Isn't her shirt too tight?" "Don't you think it sounds like her boyfriend isn't into her anymore?" Who has the worst illness, who is married longest, who is sickest—these are the women at work.

I heard complaints like Becky's from women in a wide range of professions and industries. Nurses told me that when someone on the floor gets pregnant, the other nurses make her life miserable. Lawyers talked about firms in which only one woman could make partner, setting up fierce competition among the female associates. Women in finance told me about competing for clients. Women in academia complained about competing for tenure. Although many of the women in my interviews had once expected to find help from female colleagues, virtually all of them reported bad experiences. Here's Aggie, a thirty-six-year-old bank officer in a southern city who has spent the last eleven years working herself up from teller to her present position:

Women are nice here, and some of us have been together for quite some
time. But there is no team effort between us. If one of us should pitch in
more—say, a customer comes in and needs to get some paperwork done
and I'm so busy that I need someone else to fill in—it doesn't happen. . . .
Instead there is this constant dumping. I see certain women just sitting
back and not pulling their weight. Then if I call them on it, they'll be vin-
dictive. You'd think because we're minority women at this branch that
we'd hang together, but that isn't how it is.

Aggie is especially frustrated because she feels her female coworkers
treat each other far worse than the men treat either the women or each
other:

The women are more passive-aggressive, while the men just say it like it
is. . . . This is an ongoing battle at the bank. Some days I handle it better
than others, but it's always a part of my day.

Lauren, the forty-two-year-old president of a nonprofit company,
has little trouble with colleagues or employees but is frustrated by how
threatened her female board members seem to be by her ambition, her
achievement, and her life as a single working woman:

The women can be very catty and unkind. It astonishes me that at a
board level, I will do better with the men than with the women. I find
that men on the boards are more interested in the facts and figures and
more focused on the business at hand.

The women on boards, primarily, have not worked, and they are
more interested in the dynamics of who said what. . . . They don't look
at me the same way they would if I were a man. There is a pretense
among female board members that there is a story behind the story. So
the male board members are more supportive of me, while the women
are not as open toward me. These women do not cut me any slack and

I have to prove myself. They are hanging me until I prove myself wor-
thy. . . .

Unlike mine, their power doesn't come from any personal achievement, and so there is a resentment and a jealousy toward me. It is almost
as if my position at this nonprofit reflects on their own lives and what
they haven't done for themselves. Because I am single, it makes me even
more of a threat. If I were married, these women might be more friendly.

The Taboo Against Ambitious Women

To some extent, I see women's rivalry on the job as yet another symp-
tom of how women are set up to compete for insufficient resources. If
only a few positions are earmarked for working women, we will naturally compete with each other for those prizes. Remember Theresa, the
lawyer we met in Chapter 1? She and two other associates at her predominantly male firm were all competing for the single slot reserved for
a female partner. Had the women been part of the general pool of
competitors—several associates, each with an equal chance to get one
of the limited number of partner positions—their "grudge match"
might have been diffused. But with only one female-partner slot, the
women were unable to extend their competition to the men. As a result, the specifically female focus of their rivalry intensified.

But what about the women who envy coworkers with whom they're
not in direct competition? Why do so many women refuse to mentor
younger colleagues, as Maureen described, even when the younger
women are clearly not in line for the older women's position? Why do
so many female employees give their women bosses a hard time, as
many high-level women complained to me, resenting women's supervision and reading female authority as bitchiness rather than strength?
Why are so many female bosses harder on their women employees than
on the men, as I also heard repeatedly, so that women supervisors treat
male employees with respect while approaching women workers with
contempt?

After I'd heard dozens of female complaints against bosses, coworkers, and underlings, I began to think that too many women have bought in to the notion that a woman's place is always at the bottom, never at the top. As a result, they feel threatened by any woman who dares to break the mold. Even when women are not directly in competition with one another, they seem to resent a woman who does well. Then, when a woman has succeeded, she may fear—often with good reason—that other women will try to undermine her, and so she may try to make a preemptive strike. In our youth-oriented culture, she might worry about a younger coworker coming to take her job, as Robin does. Or, having struggled so hard to get where she is, she may simply want to distance herself as far as possible from other, less successful women. In this way, she reminds herself and her male superiors that she is an exceptional woman, very different from the "mommy trackers" and less ambitious women who stereotypically make up the rest of the female workforce.

Beyond fearing rivalry from others, though, ambitious women may also have difficulty acknowledging their own desire for the power that has traditionally been reserved for men. Seeing other high-achieving women do what they have done or would like to do is threatening, and so they undermine those women who remind them of their own forbidden wishes.

This theory is supported by the work of psychiatrist and science writer Anna Fels, whose book, *Necessary Dreams: Ambition in Women's Changing Lives*, explores how high-achieving women struggle within our culture. As Fels describes this syndrome, "[female] ambition necessarily implied egotism, selfishness, self-aggrandizement, or the manipulative use of others for one's own ends."

If women's ambition is seen in such thoroughly negative terms, how can women ever openly aspire to achieve? Apparently an ambitious woman is single-minded and focused in a society where these qualities are reserved for men.

If women are not allowed to be ambitious, they will naturally have a difficult time coping with openly power-hungry female colleagues, supervisors, and employees. In fact, they may go further, channeling their dangerous desires for success into resentment of other women, competing with other females on a variety of seemingly minor issues. Maybe it's safer to compete for the position of "sickest" or "most un-happy," as women do in Becky's office, than to openly aspire for the job of company president or the status of being the office's top sales rep.

We've already seen that women have been given not one but two double binds where competition is concerned:

1. **Play to win, but look as though you're not competing.** In *Working Girl, My Best Friend's Wedding, The Apprentice,* and *The Bachelor,* women who are openly ambitious are punished, while women who win without seeming to try are rewarded. Strik-ingly, it doesn't matter whether we're talking about competing for a man or a job (or, in the case of *Working Girl,* both), the rules are the same, which makes for a very disabling message for women at work. In most of America, the workplace *is* a compet-itive arena. For a woman to succeed on the job, she must be comfortable competing to an extent that the culture generally doesn't permit.

2. **Compete only against other women, never against men, but don't admit that, either.** In these EEOC-managed times, companies aren't supposed to have jobs that are specifically slot-ted for women. Yet often "everyone knows" about the informal quota system in which women are allowed only a handful of partnerships, a token number of executive positions, or a few specially reserved faculty positions. Thus, women who compete with each other may be responding to the ways that companies and institutions often put the two genders on different tracks. Sadly, this intragender competition cuts us off from the very

coworkers who should be our natural allies on such issues as equal pay, promotions for women, child care and family leave, sexual harassment, and other workplace concerns.

Clearly, part of the problem of female rivalry could be solved if women felt free to compete against men. But if we believe the movies, women who compete with men on the job are almost always punished when it comes to romance. The classic example, of course, is *Adam's Rib*, in which Katharine Hepburn plays a defense lawyer going up against her DA husband, portrayed by Hepburn's real-life romantic partner, Spencer Tracy. The couple's professional competition is rewritten as a romantic tiff, and when Tracy triumphs by using Hepburn's own tactics against her, he demonstrates not only that he's a better lawyer than she is but also that he's a better husband than the other, weaker man who had begun to pursue her. Although Hepburn's character wins the trial, Tracy's character gains the moral victory, an outcome that both characters greet with relief. While this film was released in 1949, it offers a message that continues into the twenty-first century: men and women may enjoy competing for a while, but both sexes will be happier if the men win.

In another Hepburn film, *Pat and Mike*, Hepburn plays a female athlete, who you might think would be allowed her competitive spirit. But, like Melanie Griffith in *Working Girl* and Julia Roberts in *My Best Friend's Wedding*, Hepburn's character doesn't really *want* to compete but must be encouraged to do so by her male coach (again played by Spencer Tracy), who also falls in love with her. Unlike real women athletes, and unlike Hepburn herself, the character is portrayed as an unwilling competitor who comes into her own only at the urging of a loving, supportive man.

What we have, then, is a situation in which women are not allowed to compete for power and success in a culture that increasingly values those qualities. Is it any wonder that women sublimate their competitive urges into rivalry with other women, focusing not on the "male" prizes of money and power but on the "female" territory of looks and behavior?

Thus, *New York Times* columnist Maureen Dowd, cited in an editorial in the September 2004 issue of *W* magazine, points out that professional women in Washington, D.C., are judged relentlessly for their appearance. "If you are a woman in Washington and dress well, you are suspect," the article quotes Dowd as saying. "It means you are not spending enough time studying the Law of the Sea Treaty."

Likewise, "Beauty Politic," an *Elle* article by Ana Marie Cox, notes that Washington, D.C., women are notoriously style deficient, and asks querulously, ". . . are Washington women style ignorant or just style agnostic? Are they too absorbed in the intricacies of Beltway politics to care about beauty or simply too busy to do anything about it?"

Granted, *Elle* is a woman's magazine that is supposed to emphasize looks and glamour. Yet comparable men's magazines, such as *Esquire* or *GQ*, seem able to send a different message to its male readership: when men are out for power, what they wear is less important than what they do. Women aren't allowed a similar luxury. They have to compete on both grounds, professional and sartorial, even if, as in the 1970s, they do their best to imitate male attire and dress in jackets and ties.

On the Job: Secret Enemies

Psychologist Dr. Ronnie Burak sums up another problem: "The tradeoff for women is success versus connecting," she explains. "To succeed in a friendship with another woman, a woman has to show her vulnerability." But to be successful, a woman has to be tough. Apparently a woman can either have friends or succeed, but not both.

This was a conflict about which many of the women I interviewed spoke, often with great poignancy, regret, or self-criticism. Giselle, a thirty-nine-year-old woman working in a predominantly female sales office, ruefully acknowledged that if she has to choose between being liked and winning, she'll go for the professional victory every time:

> I think it is the fear of losing that pushes me. That is why I am so driven at work and I take whatever opportunity I can. I see how difficult it is for women, but at the same time, I also know I'm part of the game. I want to be liked, but I also need to be ahead and stay ahead. . . . When an opportunity presents itself in my office, which is mostly comprised of women, I know I have to get there or it will be gone. And the more successful I become, the more I have to jump in, ahead of the others. . . .

Ashley, a forty-three-year-old midwestern surgeon, believes that she herself has worked out the success-friendship contradiction but that virtually none of her colleagues has done so. According to Ashley, women in medicine only pretend to want friendship and connection. When push comes to shove, female physicians will step all over each other to get ahead:

> Maybe it's because being a surgeon is so macho that the women surgeons I know treat each other so horribly. . . . I haven't seen much good go on between the women, and I can't imagine that it will improve anytime soon. Each year another woman appears on the scene and at first I think, "Wow, this is great, the more women, the better off we all will be." But that isn't the case. What happens is that we act like we care about one another and we all meet for drinks, once a month, to talk about how tough the male discrimination is. But it's a sham. . . .
>
> At the last meeting, one of the women was complaining about a male surgeon in her division. She said that he wasn't really capable and that a woman with such low standards would never have a job at this hospital. One of the other women doctors actually reported her remarks to the department. The doctor was chastised and asked to apologize,

and it became an ordeal. I wasn't surprised. I knew that my female peers were there more to get information about other doctors than they were to help one another succeed.

Ashley considers the female rivalry she has experienced as something that goes far beyond the general level of competition in the medical profession:

There are those who will say that it's just too competitive in our field, and that is why we can't really be supportive. But I think it goes deeper than that. I think that women are so rivalrous that they don't ever want to see another female surgeon do well or get an interesting case. They want to undermine each other, even at drinks, after work, where we are getting together to be a support system. So much for female bonding. . . .

Ashley's bleak view of women in medicine is supported by the portrait painted on *E.R.*, one of TV's most popular medical programs. Although the *E.R.* writers try to create happy endings for women, in which females overcome their rivalry to find common ground, the show is also honest in depicting the gender-based competition that takes place at all levels of the profession. In "Providers," an episode that first aired on January 27, 2004, for example, a young nurse living with a doctor feels envious of an attractive resident who develops a crush on the same man. The two women eventually bond over their common sorrow at a patient's horrible fate, but not before the nurse expresses her envy and resentment of the female doctor, whose greater education and higher status seem to give her an advantage.

In the same episode, difficulties continue for the character of Dr. Susan Lewis, recently made head of the emergency room. As a female boss, she finds it hard to exert her authority over both male and female underlings, who tend to ignore her or trade on their previous friendship rather than give her the respect due to her position. Susan's difficulties are intensified because of the resentment of an even higher-placed woman, Dr. Kerry Weaver, the prototypical "bitchy" female boss whom everyone fears and dislikes. Kerry tries to whip Susan into shape as an effective supervisor, while Susan struggles with her own dislike of Kerry as well as her need to properly manage her staff. The men on the program tend to shrug off Susan's efforts to take charge, while the women, who are used to treating her as a friend, resent her "bossiness" more than either Kerry's or a man's. Thus, women in authority are shown to struggle between two unacceptable alternatives: being nice and ineffectual, or being strident and disliked.

My research shows that whether women choose connection or success, they experience a certain amount of conflict, even in a predominantly female workplace. Elyana, a fifty-five-year-old managing agent of an all-female North Carolina real-estate agency with forty employees describes the tensions that result:

We have both a competitive atmosphere and one where women are friends. Not a day goes by that there isn't some kind of crisis in the office. Either with a deal falling apart and the woman crushed; or with a deal going forward and most of the other brokers jealous; or with a family crisis, like a kid getting caught with marijuana in his pocket at school, in which case we all rally around the poor mother and forget our competitive natures.

No one is here in this business . . . because it is the job of our dreams. . . . We are here because . . . our husbands lost their jobs or stopped making enough money to support us and our kids; or if a husband walks out on us or drops dead; or if we are bored to tears chauffeuring our kids to school . . . and thought this was at least something we could master fast. Whatever our story, once you get to this company, you better play hardball.

Despite her position as supervisor, Elyana herself is desperate to be liked. She says she's used to inducing women to be her friends even in situations where she seems to triumph over them:

My need is to get the women to like me. . . . I've always won at that even
when . . . it's . . . hard. . . . I won the beauty pageant in my hometown
and I was the one every boy invited to the prom. I had guys lined up and
my mother told me I could just choose one, but why? Why not a few? So
if women hated me in high school for that, they hate me now. It doesn't
matter that I'm in my midfifties; it matters that I still look good. I walked
by a work area yesterday where three women were sitting and over-
heard one say to the other, about me, "Can you stand it? She not only
looks the same, she looks better." I'd be offended, but those women
would say the same thing to my face.

Elyana may be winning the competition, but in her view, every
woman in the office is equally involved in rivalry, not just professionally
but with regard to looks, children, and every other domain:

We're all doing the best we can to take care of ourselves, to age well, to
be in shape. We have to get our kids into college—another [reason] . . .
that everyone in this office will snicker at everyone else—and then married off, I suppose. Plus we have to sell real estate. It's competitive everywhere I turn.

Men, who are allowed to be openly competitive, also seem to have
more leeway making friends, even at work. Because their rivalry extends only to professional matters and not to personal issues, there's
more room for friendship and collegiality. Women, like the teenage
girls Rachel Simmons described in Chapter 2, are supposed to be continually "nice." Their need to suppress conflict and insist on being
"friends forever" actually gets in the way of developing good relationships with colleagues, who never know when the mask of friendship
will drop.

Thus, Beth, fifty-one, felt betrayed when a longtime colleague
whom she considered a friend engaged in a seemingly needless act that
hurt Beth's own chances for promotion:

Everyone is very nice at the school where I teach. But I know that one of my supposed friends was responsible for my not getting the position I wanted. This woman and I have taught together at this private school for the past fourteen years. I know that she . . . is ambitious, yet she is also very generous with new staff, especially young women. . . . Now she is the head of the middle school, but I have heard that she discouraged my application to be head of the lower school. I'm surprised and hurt, because she and I began together and both of us have mentored younger women at work. . . . Why would a friend not support me?

In a world where older women are undervalued, a woman in her fifties in a position of power feels she must guard her territory. Beth's colleague seems to feel that two women in the same age bracket in high positions—heads of the middle school and the lower school—will be too much. Her job may seem more secure if she knows she is the only woman at the top.

Matilde, a dancer in her twenties, doesn't have to wonder about why female performers compete with one another. She knows the answer: there simply aren't enough jobs to go around. The same scarcity that created a kind of friendship among fellow dancers also creates an intense rivalry:

In college we began to support each other because there was so little external support, so our support had to come from within. I would go to auditions where there were sixty women and five men. The men got all the roles and the women hung together while a handful were picked. . . .

But as much as we hung together, we couldn't all be friends after a while because of our profession. Some of us were cutting it, and others were beginning to realize that it was time to find other jobs. As reality hit, there was more competition and less being together. For the women who were very close, when one was picked and the best friend wasn't, it was a deal-breaker.

Sometimes, Matilde reports, it was the rejected friend who moved away from the more successful dancer, unable to tolerate her friend's achievement. Sometimes, the successful dancer lost touch with her struggling friend, out of guilt, anxiety, or simply divergent life paths. Either way, women who could have been supportive friends with a passionate shared interest became rivals and competitors instead.

Matilde's insights are echoed in Anne Wennerstrand's essay, "Advice for Grown-up Dancers: Toxic Envy: Two-Stepping with the Green Monster." Female dancers don't feel in charge of their destiny, Wennerstrand reports, and as a result, they feel hopeless. Their hopelessness soon leads to envying other dancers, with "jealous, competitive feelings" of the women who are their rivals.

This conflict between connecting and competing finds its way as well into the weekly online advice column, "About Professionalism, Etiquette and Problems in the Workplace: Ask Sue," by Sue Morem, operating on the site www.careerknowhow.com. In a spring 2003 column, a woman writes in about jealous coworkers who "have created and spread rumors" about her, including the innuendo that she has slept her way to the top. This woman is younger than most of the women in her office and has indeed advanced quickly.

Sue's answer acknowledges how common female envy is on the job. She tells the woman that her colleagues seem "petty and jealous" and suggests, "Perhaps they are disappointed with their own careers and aren't able to be happy for anyone who may be achieving more than they have." Although Sue suggests that the woman speak to her coworkers directly, she admits that such efforts are likely to be "futile."

In some cases, women become so tired of the tension between connecting and competing that they simply choose to work in an all-male environment. At age thirty-five, Alicia is the only female server in a famous northern California restaurant. She is willing to work at her demanding job, which requires running food up the stairs on heavy trays, because it frees her from the feminine competitiveness that marked her previous workplaces:

In my last job, in an office, I had a female employer who was okay but not actually fair. She was all right to me, but I saw how unkind she was to other women in the office. When someone told her off, it was long overdue. But I wanted out of there at that point; I'd had it. I opted for something completely different. . . .

I have come to appreciate working without women in the environment. Women don't like me, maybe. . . . I'd rather be in a chauvinistic place than with a bunch of women who are mean and unfair to you.

Alicia is quick to acknowledge her own competitive nature. She's an athlete who is willing to go all out on the field. In fact, she says, "the only women with whom I've had any connection at the workplace have been women who also are jocks." It's not competition she minds but the way that women treat each other, channeling what should be an open contest into more subtle rivalries.

Dominique, a woman in her midthirties, has also suffered from female rivalry even though she is in a virtually all-male profession. She drives a bus in a northeastern city, a job she has held for the past seven years:

This is the same as any other job, you have your friends, and there are people who are not your friends. And those women are against you.

There aren't many women bus drivers, so you'd think we'd stick together, but we don't. When I first came on this job, I thought, wow, there are only a handful of women and mostly we are the same race, and this could work out. We understand each other, I thought. But just because we understand each other doesn't mean we're there for each other. . . . Sometimes I feel closer to some of the women passengers who I'm driving than to my female coworkers.

There are all sorts of ways that we don't treat each other as we should. The schedule is sometimes hard for a woman, especially if she has kids, and no one steps up to help her out. That's a way that we make each other suffer. We all talk to our male boss, and we don't look out for each other. So it seems hopeless and unfriendly when we should be working together. If enough women talked to each other at the job, maybe one of us could get elevated to a supervisor.

Brenda, a fifty-three-year-old former police officer, encountered a similar rivalry during her eighteen years on the force:

There were so many problems being a woman on the police force twenty-five years ago. . . . Even though I won a lawsuit because of how women were laid off, the women did not hang together. If I wanted a promotion, I would talk to the men on the force; I would not bother with the women.

Meanwhile, the men were favored and got away with bad behavior, and that needed to be changed. The men in charge gave the twenty-five-pound trigger pullers to the women and twelve-pound trigger pullers to the men. That was the kind of bias women were up against in the '70s, and yet the women would not help each other. The women on the force in those days would act like little girls, because there was no other option.

In an encouraging note, Brenda reports that conditions for policewomen have changed, at least to some extent:

Today there are more women bosses, but they are against the other women. The problem is that women bosses aren't used to having any status, and they don't know how to act toward the women. Especially the old-time women, those who had been around back when I was working there. The old-timers don't know about equality, so they knock any and all women around. The younger women want camaraderie and equality. Not to say it will happen, but at least they believe in it.

Stealing on the Job

Just as women worry about other women stealing their boyfriends, so do they fear female colleagues stealing or otherwise undermining their positions. The ethics of on-the-job stealing are unclear. On the one hand, the workplace is a competitive stage, as shows like *The Apprentice* make clear. In this dog-eat-dog world, women are allowed, even encouraged, to engage in a little catfighting, although their serious professional contests may be trivialized as personal rivalry. On the other hand, women are expected, and expect themselves, to be "nice" and unselfish, and they look to other women to fulfill their ideas of friendship and female solidarity.

The problem is sharpened when women are specifically pitted against one another rather than against the larger employee pool. For example, an October 2004 article in *Fortune* magazine by Ann Harrington and Petra Bartosiewicz, entitled "Most Powerful Women in Business: Who's Up? Who's Down? And Is That a New No. 1?" focused on "the alpha females of American business, 2004." Although every woman in the article had by definition competed against numerous men to win her exalted position, the article spoke as though women were engaged in an all-female contest. The language betrayed the personal terms in which female professional competition is viewed: "Seven new women managed to *elbow their way to the table* . . ." [emphasis added]. The image is telling—you only elbow your way into an area where you're not wanted. Even when women compete against one another, they're pushing and shoving, like frantic buyers at a clothing sale.

A November 2004 article in *More* by Nancy Collins profiling the British prime minister's wife, Cherie Blair, likewise treats Blair as though she were operating in an all-female world. Although the article notes admiringly that Blair was recently ranked "the most powerful woman in Britain, twelfth in the world," she is once again compared only to other women. Entitled "The Real Cherie Blair" (even though professionally the woman goes by Cherie Booth), the article does not emphasize Blair/Booth's professional achievements but rather her ability to balance a high-powered legal career with being the mother of four children. It's hard to imagine any story about Tony Blair doing the same. Despite the description of Blair/Booth's work as a lawyer and human-rights activist, she is not compared to other high-powered figures in her field, nor even to her husband. Rather Blair/Booth is compared to everyday women, as though this were the most important ring in which she should compete.

The notion that women are competing primarily with each other exists even at the highest levels of U.S. business. In early 2005, Hewlett-Packard's board asked Carly Fiorina, the chief executive and one of the most successful women in America, to step down, in a move apparently initiated by another woman. George Anders's lead article in the *Wall Street Journal* on February 10, 2005, described Fiorina as one of "an alluring, controversial new breed of chief executive officers," and, significantly, as a loner rather than a team player. Perhaps her "go-it-alone" style was related to the efforts of Hewlett-Packard board member Patricia Dunn to oust her, as reported in a *Journal* article by Pui-Wing Tam. According to Tam, "Patricia Dunn, an H-P director since 1998 . . . is the vice chairman of Barclays Global Investors, H-P's third-largest institutional shareholder, and was the principal author of the board report." Although Dunn was clearly not alone in her wish to remove Fiorina from her top post, the woman-to-woman rivalry of this power struggle is striking.

If women are directed to compete against one another, they tend to fear their female coworkers while virtually ignoring the men. Elyse, a thirty-eight-year-old school principal who sees her profession as competitive, feels far less fear that men will threaten her job than that women will. Although she has already dismissed most of her female colleagues as unworthy competitors, she continues to be on the lookout for women who might take what she has:

There are not many women in my position, and most of the women at this school are teachers, not even heads of divisions. I know that they both respect me and are envious of my position. But I'm not worried about them because none of them is a contender for my title and I do an excellent job.

It was when my boss brought in a woman to interview last year for the assistant superintendent position that I was on guard. She was younger and quite accomplished already in the field of education.

Elyse responded immediately, seeing the situation as "It's her or me." If she was to keep her own job, she had to make sure this new woman was not hired:

I saw that she had some weaknesses, and I played them up at once. I told my boss, who wanted a woman in this job so that it would be politically correct, that she was not the right person. I did this even though it wasn't the truth. I didn't want her there. I wanted to be the only woman in power at the high school.

Ironically, society's very insistence on hiring more women—the "political correctness" that may have helped Elyse win her own position—now threatened her role as "the only woman in power":

My boss was set on bringing in a woman, and he found another qualified younger woman. She was also quite impressive, but I told him that she drank too much at a business lunch. I did this to cover myself—I didn't want a woman under me. In the end, he found a man and I'm so relieved. I suppose I was jealous of these women and didn't believe that we could work together. It was a matter of my anticipating a future where a woman could take my job . . . my taking the chance away before it could happen. In the end, they had to be jealous of me because they didn't get the job and I have a great job—an enviable job.

Fifty-one-year-old Augusta describes a similar dynamic from the opposite point of view. Recently returned to the workplace after ending a twenty-year marriage and newly equipped with a master's degree, she describes how the female head of her office felt threatened by her, and by most other women as well:

> The woman who offered me my job seemed so enthused about my brave reentry into the workplace after a tough time as a single mother. Now she is my worst enemy at the office. Yet she is kind to me compared to how she treats the other women who work with us, especially those who are ten or twelve years my junior. The only ones she bothers to be nice to are the twenty-five-year-olds because I think she figures at her age, sixty-three, she will be gone before they become a threat.

Augusta is particularly disappointed in the female rivalry she's encountered because she sees how easily female solidarity might have been established instead:

> This is a business where many women work together and so few men are around that we could all be friends and have a terrific time of it. I am absolutely astonished that this woman, my boss, turned out to be so worried about herself that she is unkind to each of us.

Dana, whom we met in Chapter 6, works as a radio producer, a profession in which she has often triumphed while other women fail. Although she doesn't believe that she is responsible for her colleagues' troubles, she understands that they see it that way:

> I was very lucky because I am in a male-dominated profession, and I have always done well. Several years ago, the company laid off a group of people, including a woman who I had worked with quite closely. . . . She compared herself to me the day she was asked to leave. She asked our boss if he thought that I was better than she was, and this got back to me. I had tried to help her and had actually looked out for her in a few instances. I knew that I was able to stay because I was a nicer person to

have around. Still I considered this woman my friend and at the same time, I always felt she was envious of me.

I was struck, rereading Dana's interview, to see that she stressed not her professional competence but her being "a nicer person to have around" as the reason for her success. Just like the heroines of *Working Girl*, *My Best Friend's Wedding*, and *Pat and Mike*, Dana must insist that she is not ambitious and that she has no interest in triumphing over another woman, even if she is competing with another woman for the same job. Regardless of circumstances, however, Dana feels she must focus on her willingness to help her rival ("I actually looked out for her in a few instances"), attributing her on-the-job victory to her personality, not her abilities. No wonder that she goes on to comment that, "although I have done quite well in this business, I am very insecure at work." If your workplace success rests on your personal qualities rather than on your competence, it is difficult to feel secure.

Dana is clear, though, that whoever wins or loses the workplace contest, all women are harmed by the endless rivalry:

I think that the workplace does this to women and then we do it to each other. Had I not chosen a profession where men rule, it might have been different. And I am not on the envious side but the one who is being envied. It can't feel good to be envious, but it makes me uneasy to be envied, too. It destroys the trust between women.

Betina, now forty-four, is also uneasy about being envied. To her surprise, it was her much younger assistant who saw Betina as enviable, echoing the classic movie *All About Eve*:

When I was thirty-nine, I hired an assistant who was twenty-two. The past five years with this assistant, Rafaela, have been quite a roller-coaster ride. Rafaela came to me from an excellent college but without any real skills. I taught her the business, all the nuances, and I gave her a promotion early in the game.

Betina expected to be rewarded for this show of female solidarity. Instead, she faced the younger woman's envy:

It was so odd to me that instead of being pleased I could see that she was jealous of me. I think that Rafaela resented my success and my looks—I am much thinner than she is. She resented that my husband was also successful. Not that we didn't work hard for it. My husband pointed out to me one day that I didn't need to take Rafaela under my wing because she begrudged me my looks, my body, my clothes, everything.

Finally, Betina found a way to disarm her assistant and diffuse her growing envy:

One day I confronted her and she admitted that it was my self-esteem that bothered her the most. She said she was jealous of that. Since then, Rafaela has found a boyfriend and a life. She has become happier with herself, and I have kept her on because I believe in her. And I don't want her to always be jealous of another woman. I want her to know that we can both do well and it's okay.

To Betina, the most disconcerting aspect of her relationship with Rafaela was the discovery that she could be the target of another woman's envy:

I never would have imagined that someone young and pretty would covet my life. I would only have thought that it could be the other way around. Here I was, approaching early menopause—and she wanted what *I* had?

Fifteen years younger than Betina, Ilana is only twenty-nine, but she is already discouraged about the extent to which she has been envied by her coworkers. For the past five years, Ilana reports, she has worked as the manager at a chiropractor's office, after having been the manager at a music store. Despite their obvious differences, the two jobs were similar in their climate of female rivalry:

> The theme was always to watch out for your back. I was just lucky that I became a manager in each of these places because there were always plenty of other young women who were coworkers. I don't think that I did anything special to deserve the position.

Like Dana, Ilana tries to diffuse other women's envy by insisting that she doesn't really want the prizes she gets, and she knows she doesn't deserve them. Certainly, she doesn't present herself as deliberately determined to succeed. Instead, as she explains it, her victory has almost nothing to do with her:

> With my first job, I was out of college and I'd worked there part-time for two years already. That was why I got promoted, because I'd put my time in. And I suspect that my college degree helped.

Despite her efforts at modesty, however, Ilana remains a target of female envy:

> There were a few other girls who worked with me, and two of them made it clear that they'd been passed over. The funny thing is, I thought these girls could be my friends. . . . Instead they were always mean to me. . . . I think they resented that I was overqualified, in a way. So I started worrying about my job and stopped worrying about making friends. I knew that they could undermine me and so I watched them closely.

When Ilana left the music store for a chiropractor's office, she discovered an even more competitive environment. Five chiropractors were engaged in a perpetual contest for more business, and their twelve female office workers picked up the spirit and competed with each other as well:

> If a chiropractor seemed to favor someone in the work pool, then the rest of us got jittery. I was always looking out to make sure I'd be okay. . . . If someone made one false move, everyone else would be happy instead of sympathetic. . . . The paperwork was where they could really blame each other, and so half of the time was spent trying to get a coworker—another woman—in trouble.

In this second job, Ilana was more willing to acknowledge her own role in her success. But this knowledge made her all the more fearful of her coworkers' envy:

> I got to be the office manager by doing a good job. Once I had that position, some of the other office workers became nasty. If I came in a few minutes late, if I ran to the bank and it took a while, they would try to use it against me.

Tired of the rivalry, Ilana is now looking for another job. But, she asks plaintively, "Will it be any better at the next place?"

Forty-one-year-old Sandra would say no. A stockbroker, Sandra describes her long-term conflict with a younger woman who finally did steal her job:

> This younger woman, Lydia, came to the brokerage firm where I worked. Her area of expertise was similar to mine and I could feel her watching me from the start. We were hired at different levels, and I had an excellent reputation and had been at this for ten years when Lydia arrived. But Lydia's arrival caused big problems for me. She tried to push me out. . . . I found work unpleasant once she had been there for a few months, really unpleasant. And the irony is that I was the one who

looked over her résumé and recommended that she be interviewed. I helped her get her job, and then she wanted mine!

Lydia made Sandra's life so unpleasant that, eventually, Sandra left the company, filled with resentment but resigned to the fact that she would never be able to defeat her rival:

I witnessed her every move. . . . After a while, I decided I couldn't stay at this firm, even after the years that I'd been there. After all the inroads I had made, I was the one who left to work elsewhere, because I could see how she operates, how she decided how to get me tossed aside. It all started because she saw what I had and she wanted it to be hers. Sometimes there are happy endings when two women are in the same field, but my experience was just the opposite. Now I envy her because she has my old job.

Maria, a thirty-seven-year-old executive at a nonprofit company, sees that conflicts among women at work are even sharper where race is concerned. A white woman, Maria tries to build solidarity with her African-American employees and colleagues, because she feels that she, too, is the victim of discrimination:

Absolutely I see that black women are hired at a lower level and not promoted. Even in my kind of work, where I try very hard to avoid such a situation. I have been in this business for sixteen years, and the changes come slowly. Yet I have made up my mind to hire minority women and to give them chances to move up the ladder. I believe this is the only solution to the problem. . . . As a white woman I have had to prove myself many times over, too. I am very aware of trying to help women in this field, and I sense a strong bias against me, not because of my race but because I want to hire other women to work for this agency.

Georgie, a thirty-four-year-old African-American woman, feels that both black and white women have treated her badly:

> I know that I don't compete against other black women or other women who are minorities. But I definitely feel that white women put me in my place. I have had several jobs over the past twelve years, and mostly I have answered to white women. I have worked as a nurse's aide, a chambermaid, and a nanny. I have spent many hours with white women and white employers. Although some of these women have been very kind, others act superior and are unfair. . . .

Georgie is currently working toward her teaching degree at a junior college, not so much to make more money but because she wants "to have some kind of power, some kind of authority." But her recent marriage and the birth of her child have made her "more sensitive than ever before to how minority women are treated":

> In my neighborhood I feel that I have some clout, but outside, on the street and working for white women, I feel that I have less. I have to fight for a job and then I hate the work, even if I beat someone else out for it. It is almost like all women are in the same boat, and then women who are minorities have it even worse. So we aren't even nice to each other. If there is a male boss, then we all feel it, and if it is a woman boss, she is usually white, and how she treats us depends completely on who she is.

"Not all of these women are the same," Georgie adds. "They might have some power but they didn't create the system, they are just a part of it, too." Yet she feels that in such a competitive system, she can count on neither female solidarity nor racial support.

Rivals or Colleagues?

Is there any hope for women achieving a true solidarity at the workplace? I believe there is, but only if women can see that they actually do share a common interest. I was fascinated by Susan Antilla's op-ed piece in the July 21, 2004, edition of *The New York Times,* "Money Talks, Women Don't." On the one hand, Antilla reported, a woman had won a landmark settlement in an EEOC suit against the investment firm of Morgan Stanley, which had to pay forty-three-year-old former saleswoman Allison Schieffelin $12 million in her 2001 lawsuit. In addition, a $40 million fund was established to facilitate claims by other female employees at Morgan Stanley and a $2 million diversity program was begun. On the other hand, Antilla comments, ". . . Morgan Stanley, and all of Wall Street, scored an even bigger win: the statistics remain under wraps." Antilla argues that Wall Street will make genuine changes in its treatment of women "only when its culture, and the hard numbers of compensation and promotion, are exposed in open court." For such disclosure to occur, Antilla explains, female employees will have to break the confidentiality obligations that securities firms impose on them, exposing the truth not only for their own sake but for those of all women workers.

When middle-class women first entered the workplace in large numbers in the 1970s, they felt an optimism about career possibilities for women, an optimism quickly turned into competition, jealousy, and envy. Once again, it seemed, women were competing not on a level playing field but only against one another. In the male-dominated workplace, women's rivalry extended to every aspect of their lives—not only job performance but also age, dress, looks, finances, children, and marital status. What at first seemed like a brave new world of job opportunities only cranked up an already painful competition. The limited positions available for women at the top rendered the rivalry even more fierce, making the few women who reached the pinnacle seem "different" and even more threatening to their fellow females. Like extraordinary beauty or having a spectacular husband, job success became another type of stigma for the woman seeking acceptance among her peers.

This unhealthy work environment, in which women feigned kindness and a lack of ambition, was remniscent of the "good-girl" culture of the 1950s and 1960s, despite the genuine opportunities that had opened up. The desire to "trip the prom queen" in the workplace thus puts us all in a double bind: unable to compete openly, yet dissatisfied with our lack of success. As with other aspects of female competition, the solution lies in working together for "more pie." When we join forces to improve conditions for all women, we will all benefit. If we continue to get sidetracked by female rivalry, all of us will eventually pay the price, either by achieving less than we might have or by becoming the target of envy, rivalry, and rage.

Part 3

Revolutionizing Rivalry

8

Dispelling the Demons: How to Spin Competition, Jealousy, and Envy in Our Favor

For many of the women I interviewed, female rivalry—their own or others'—seemed to play a hurtful, destructive role in their lives. It made them suspicious of other women, even as they doubted their own abilities to hold on to a man, keep a job, or enjoy a friendship. It drove them to look askance at their successes and to suffer more intensely from what they saw as their failures. For Gina, the widowed food-service worker with the drug-addicted son, rivalry over children cost her the support of her best friend at a particularly difficult time. For Valerie, who could not bear to attend her best friend's wedding, rivalry caused her to fail a friend, creating a burden of guilt that she continues to carry. Competition, envy, and jealousy would seem to be unhealthy forces in women's lives.

Jill, a forty-eight-year-old paralegal at a midsize Michigan law firm, is a prime example of a woman whose feelings of envy and jealousy appear to have isolated her from other women:

I don't want to live this life, single mom, working mother, stuck in the burbs. When someone from my old life calls and tells me that she and her husband are going away for vacation or that her husband just bought her a ring for a birthday gift, I think I'll puke. I expected things to be different at this point and it bothers me a lot.

My way of getting through it is to call no one and make no plans. I guess you could say I'm sorry for myself; I've even blown off a few blind dates. First I put an ad in the local paper and then I turned the guys down. I'm in a funk and my girlfriends sicken me, the ones who are happy.

Jill's misery isn't only because of her own feelings of envy, she assures me. It's also because her friends and family have isolated *her*:

All of my girlfriends are married, even though that seems hard to believe today, with such a high divorce rate. I'm not included very often in their plans because they are part of a couple and a divorced friend is a tag-along. . . . The weekends are the worst for me, when my kids are busy with their friends and with homework and my friends still have the life I had, and I'm all alone. My two sisters live on the East Coast and they wouldn't exactly understand anyway. They would never divorce, neither of them, and so they judge me and think I'm a loser. I can only imagine what they write about me in their e-mails to each other. I resent this treatment, so I can't count on family at all.

Jill realizes that she has the possibility to align with other single women. But she rejects the terms on which their solidarity is offered, which she sees as a sisterhood based on dependency and complaint:

I have met some single women at the gym, and all they want is for someone to take care of them. Preferably a man who has some money. I have no desire to sit with other women at a restaurant where there's an early-bird special and hear them moan about how hard it is to find a man and to get paid for part-time work. I've done it, and it's very depressing.

Likewise, Olivia, a forty-year-old office manager, struggles with rivalry at work. Having worked at the same job for fifteen years, she's never been able to win the respect or appreciation of her female boss, a situation she had come to accept. But when thirty-year-old Gwen was hired to assist that same boss, Olivia found herself overcome by envy:

> I've worked so hard to build this company up and to do the right thing for my boss. And it hasn't mattered to her. Now, suddenly, this Gwen, who is perfectly fine, is being treated with kid gloves by my boss. I wonder if it's because they went to the same college. Is it because of the greater age difference? Is it something I didn't do that Gwen does? I feel so small and unimportant. I don't want to be petty, and I like Gwen, but I resent her for the way she is being treated compared to the way I have been treated.

Olivia's competitive feelings are all the more painful because she sees so clearly how the situation might be different, companionable instead of rivalrous. Instead, she envies Gwen for getting better treatment from her boss, and she envies her boss for being the object of Gwen's admiration:

> A part of me says, "Why can't we all work together?" Both my boss and I could teach Gwen the ropes. But Gwen looks to my boss as a mentor and I don't know what she thinks of me. I find it all very hurtful.

For women like Jill and Olivia, female competition is a game at which they cannot win. First, they lose the actual contests—the single Jill feels inferior to her married friends; Olivia feels ignored by both Gwen and her boss. Moreover, their own feelings of rivalry make them feel grudging and small. Jill admits that she's "feeling sorry for herself" and "in a funk"; Olivia insists, with an obvious effort to overcome her own resentment, that Gwen is "perfectly fine." Clearly, beyond their frustration at "losing," they dislike the sense of being in a contest.

But what about the women who find competition energizing? What about the women whose rivalry with others, including other women, motivates them to higher levels of achievement? Or the women whose envy leads them to a more vigorous pursuit of their own life goals? What of those women whose jealousy sparks them to seek greater clarity about what they want and how far they're willing to go for it? Can we find new ways to spin these familiar feelings of rivalry in our favor?

Certainly Kara would say that we can. At age forty, she feels entitled to be competitive, and she's raising her daughters to feel the same way:

> I expect my daughters to be competitive like I have been, definitely with skiing, snowboarding, and quite seriously when it comes to squash. When I was younger, I played squash with the older women who were excellent players and now I play with younger women and I seem to be the older one. Both ways, I play to win. I will play squash with a woman who is a bit better than I am because I love the competition. Whether she is older or younger, I feel quite victorious if I can beat her, and that is my intention.

For Kara, competitiveness in sports is acceptable. Being competitive on the squash court allows her to choose where else she does, or does not, wish to engage in contests:

> I believe that my competition in sports translates into my life. But because I take out most of my aggressions on the squash court, I don't have to be like that in every part of my life. . . . Because I am so driven in my career . . . the only time I feel jealous is if I meet a woman who has gotten further ahead. I also feel encouraged by women who are winners, it makes me want to do better, as long as no one steps on my toes. This is what I tell my daughters, to go for the kill, don't let anyone get in their way, and do it because it betters them.

Kara has found a way to move past the simple equation of "competition=bad, cooperation=good." Instead, she's created an approach that allows her to use competition to improve her own performance, and to feel encouraged rather than threatened by her powerful competitors.

Likewise, Lucy, the thirty-five-year-old manager of a woman's bowling league, sees ways that competition can be good for women, but only if they approach it in the right way. Her motto is "Don't get envious, get your own life." When women can view rivalry in that spirit, she says, the competition is healthy. Likewise, when competition with another team brings teammates closer together, the contest has been a productive one. But when women draw the wrong conclusions from their envy, it can lead to unnecessary rivalry, backbiting, and petty behavior:

> The women will do mean things to one another. They are on the same team but they are not team players. I find myself on the phone making sure that some of the players are not with my A team because the A team can be so rotten to anyone who doesn't score well enough. . . . You should see how pressured it is when we're in a match. But it's the only time we all seem to be on the same side.

Unlike men, who restrict competition to specific spheres, women tend to globalize their rivalry, as Lucy explains:

> I think it goes beyond how they bowl, and it starts to be about whose husband makes what, and who has a better job . . . who has nicer kids. Only the women who stop moaning and gossiping do okay. Like this one woman who kept feeling she had less and finally got herself into night school, landed a better job, and forced her husband to do better at work. Now she doesn't envy anyone, she's at the top of the heap.

Despite her insights, Lucy herself is not exempt from envy:

> I must be too busy working on keeping this team together to be jealous of anyone, but I do know that the younger women who join are looking very fresh and full of life. I feel tired, with kids and work and a hus-

band . . . I just try to hold it all together. I don't want to be like the women on the team. I don't want everything to be a competition or filled with jealous moments.

Stella, a thirty-eight-year-old southern California store owner, has also found a vision of healthy competition through her participation in sports. She seeks strength and skill in her female tennis partners and feels heartened, not threatened, by their ability:

I like to play tennis with women who are very good and where it is an even match. I prefer these women to be smart, accomplished, and athletic, which is how I perceive myself. . . . It doesn't mean that I'm not competitive, but it's a positive kind of competition. . . . No one cheats or is impolite, or I won't play with them.

I like it best to play with someone who is a little better than I am because it makes me play better. So although I am competitive—and I was a tournament player when I was younger—I was never mean-spirited. . . .

To me, being in sports competition makes me more competitive with other women, but in a positive way. I sort of have an edge, a kind of toughness that keeps me away from the bad kind of competition between women and keeps me with real friends who I can trust. I respect my friends, and I think that they respect me. It's a wonderful edge for me to express my anguish and to have a constructive use of my anger by playing competitive tennis. It helps me have boundaries and gives me a way to deal with everything else without feeling upset. . . .

Likewise, Thea, at age forty-five, has been playing competitive tennis for ten years. She, too, feels that sports help women accept the healthy side of competition while continuing to be supportive of one another:

I see women in my tennis league who are kind to one another and others who are really mean. I find myself working hard for harmony because

I believe it is possible. The women who are easy-going and open minded . . . are a pleasure. They have made friends of every sort by being on this league, and they get a lot out of it.

By contrast, Thea says, women who are competitive off the court—those she calls "snobby" women—are uncooperative and difficult to work with:

The ones who are demanding think they are great players. They . . . do not work and have an easy life where money is no object. These women arrive late, cancel last minute, and are only nice to the other women who have a similar lifestyle.

Since I have been running my league for so long, I now keep the snobby women away from the other snobby women. I mix and match intentionally, and I ignore the pushy ones. I see that my plan works, also with the strong players supporting the women who want to become better, who really want to be good. The common theme of tennis is what makes it possible, and when I set it up so that they have to blend, they are forced to be decent about it.

As Thea points out, situations in which women are allowed to be honest about their competitive side can also allow them to be more cooperative, joining with other women against a common enemy. For such camaraderie to flourish, we must be honest about our rivalry, an honesty that many of us find difficult to achieve. But once we overcome the myths, the door is open for us to achieve true solidarity at last.

Clearly, the growing acceptance of female competitiveness in sports is one sign of progress for women in our culture. We've come a long way from the day when females athletes were primarily seen as petite gymnasts or girlish figure skaters. When Tonya Harding's involvement in an attack against Nancy Kerrigan hit the news in early 1994, much of the coverage focused on the shocking fact that Harding wanted so desperately to win. She was compared to the princesslike Kerrigan, who was generally portrayed as good-hearted, innocent, and decidedly uncompetitive. The hours of grueling work that Kerrigan had put into her career were ignored, while her sweet smile and reported kindness were seized upon by the press. Since Harding's rivalry had led her to a criminal act, the media often implied that a female competitive spirit was, by definition, pathological, with Kerrigan as the "good-girl" alternative.

Compare this saccharine and repressive view with the media's open appreciation of tennis players Venus and Serena Williams, who in 2002 were ranked number one and two, respectively, at the French Open. "Williams Sisters, in Their Own World, Don't Need an Opening Act," by George Vecsey in the September 8, 2002, New York Times, described the conflict each sister felt about being "cruel and calculating, as tennis players must be," even when "somebody you love is across the net." Coverage of the two sisters continues to stress both their willingness to engage in no-holds-barred competition and their deep love for each other. This positive view of female competition seems to me a definite step forward.

By the same token, singer Jennifer Lopez's support of the JLo Girls Team, an all-female soccer team, suggests a new appreciation for girls who play to win. Both camaraderie and competition are part of team sports, of course, and Lopez makes sure to stress both aspects of the experience, providing both her own team and other girls in the local league with special headbands made by her company. In a June 23, 2003, article by Jim O'Grady in The New York Times, Lopez is quoted as saying that the girls on her team had "team spirit, strong self-esteem, and a passion to become winners," an echo of the union of bonding plus striving that Lucy seeks to achieve with her bowling league.

The 2003 film Bend It Like Beckham portrays some of the conflicts that may ensue as girls try to become winners while coping with traditional female expectations. Both Jess, who is Indian, and Jules, who is Anglo, love to play soccer, and both girls play to win. They're able to support each other as fellow teammates, but clash as they begin to compete over the attentions of their male coach. Female friendship is sorely tested as the same competitive spirit that serves the two girls on the field interferes with their private relationship. Ultimately, though, the girls bond as athletes and as friends.

But outside of the coverage of women in sports, popular culture rarely portrays women's competitive natures in a positive light. Competitive women are almost always portrayed as mean at worst, a little crazy at best. The character of Monica on the TV show *Friends*, for example, evolved into a famously competitive person, so much so that she could be manipulated into doing virtually anything if another character framed it as a contest. Once, after a disastrous party, her boyfriend comforts her by saying that it may have been the worst party ever, a description upon which the distraught Monica eagerly seizes. "You mean," she says tremulously, "if there were a contest for worst party, *I* would win it?" Her competitive nature is portrayed as an aspect of her compulsive cleanliness and her relentless perfectionism, unpleasant characteristics that her friends tolerate.

Yet even Monica was rarely allowed to compete against the other women on the show; more often, her battles were with the men. Although she was occasionally shown pursuing her professional ambitions as a chef, her competitive nature was not portrayed as an admirable aspect of her high standards or as a trait with which we were expected to sympathize. In fact, when put in charge of a restaurant kitchen, she's such an ineffectual manager of the primarily male staff that she has to get her friend Joey to pretend to let her fire him, in order to scare the other workers. True, no character on *Friends* ever showed much ambition, or much talent for getting ahead—the laid-back, slacker aura of the show was part of its charm. But even the men on the show occasionally had to compete for jobs, promotions, or professional recognition. Monica's competitiveness was written as completely personal, and more than a little nuts.

Fictional Monica offers a sharp contrast to the real-life Kara, from earlier in this chapter, who sees competition as a motivating factor, something that induces her to play at the top of her game and to pursue her professional goals with increased vigor. Unlike the Katharine Hepburn character in *Pat and Mike*, Kara views competition as something that can enhance her identity, rather than diminish it. In so doing, she offers us another perspective on female rivalry.

Arenas of Competition:
Bedroom, Boardroom, Newsroom, Playing Field

As we've seen, one classic area for women to compete is through relationships. Stealing another woman's boyfriend or husband has traditionally been considered the ultimate victory, the final proof of being more attractive and desirable.

Clearly, the deliberate attempt to sabotage another woman's relationship is an aggressive act. Yet when I studied women who engaged in extramarital affairs in conjunction with my book *A Passion for More: Wives Reveal the Affairs That Make or Break Their Marriages*, I discovered that women more often sought sexual or emotional satisfaction *for themselves* rather than *against another*. Although some of the women I studied were prompted by rivalry with another female, particularly a friend or a sister, more were simply seeking a remedy for their own discontent. In some cases, a woman sought empowerment through a successful seduction, simply needing to know that she still had the capacity to attract a man or wanting the rush of controlling someone through her sexual power. In other cases, the woman was seeking a kind of sexual or emotional fulfillment, either because she wasn't getting it in her marriage or because she wanted to reassure herself that she had other options beyond her husband.

Interestingly, when women were not directly competing with other women—that is, when they weren't deliberately trying to steal another woman's man—their affairs may nevertheless have been motivated by competitiveness or envy. Seeing what they perceived as other women's satisfaction—sexual, emotional, and/or marital—they decided that they wanted to be equally satisfied and took unprecedented steps to become so. Thus, some women use competition and envy when it comes to marital infidelity. A friend's ability to find a lover may stir up her own feelings, and she then takes the risk for the anticipated reward.

Likewise, throughout my research for all my books, I found women who were impelled to go back to school, visit a fertility clinic, or get an advanced degree once they saw a female relative, friend, or colleague taking similar steps. Envying another woman became a force for growth, motivating women to "better themselves," as Kara might say, or to "get their own lives," as Lucy would put it.

Another positive use for competition is, of course, to achieve at work. Certainly women who feel comfortable competing in the professional arena have a definite edge over those who shy away from work-related contests. An article from *Elle*, "The Women of Court TV," describes the many female anchors and reporters on that network as both professionally competitive and personally cooperative. These women strive mightily for success even as they support each other. "I love working with women who aren't afraid to put it out there," says Lisa Bloom, cohost of *Trial Heat*. "We'll argue on the air, but when we get off we might hug each other."

Women have now been in journalism for several decades, but there are many other professions where women are scarce. A September 9, 2004, Associated Press article, "Women Make Inroads in Video Game Industry," reported on the small number of women in the virtually all-male preserve of electronic entertainment. Yet, although fewer than 10 percent of all game developers are women, the first Women's Game Conference was held in Austin, Texas, in September 2004, evidence of the increased female interest in the competitive world of gaming.

At this point, most women who enter the video-game industry are likely to find themselves competing with men. (The AP article cited Jennifer Canada, one of two women and ninety-eight men in Southern Methodist University's Guildhall School of Video Game Making.) However, the establishment of a women's conference for the industry suggests that female game designers will, at least for a time, turn to other women for support—and, perhaps, compete with other women as well.

Women in the boardroom are likewise pitted against each other, as every episode of *The Apprentice* reveals. Although the program ostensibly allows, indeed, encourages, women to compete with men as well as women, coverage of the show often focuses on "catfights" between the female participants, rating them on their looks and desirability as well as on their professional acumen.

As I was conducting research for this book, I found a remarkable balancing of on-the-job rivalry and support in the unlikely venue of a strip club when I spoke with Casey, a twenty-nine-year-old stripper in a southern city who planned to attend college in the fall. When the women at the club had difficulties, she reported, they were there to help each other out. But when one of the women did markedly better than the rest, envy took over:

> The women I've met are a strange group. There are a few veteran dancers, although by about thirty-five you are too old to do it anymore. The younger women learn from the old-timers, but once the younger ones become really popular, the older ones shun them.
>
> Every night we start out in the dressing room, helping each other. If someone forgets their makeup case or a pair of shoes, we all pitch in. There's a kind of friendly atmosphere, like we're all in it together. But as the night goes on and some girls are clearing a lot more dough than others, it gets intense. When we are ready to go home, there's all this tension in the air. That's when things fall apart. But the next night, we're all buddies again.

Although the women at Casey's club had trouble coping with each other's success, in the end, solidarity prevailed. Because the women needed each other so much, particularly in the face of the world's disapproval of their work, they found ways to make room for competition rather than let it sabotage their connection.

Another Track: Alternatives to the Perpetual Beauty Contest

I find it chilling to consider the extent to which women have become rivals on the basis of their looks. Fortunately, there are some more encouraging stories I have discovered, both in my interviews and in my research into the media, in which women have found new ways to aspire to their own standards of beauty. Perhaps competitiveness is still an issue to some extent, with women seeking to be "all that they can be" in the looks department. But at least there are instances where their self-image does not depend on having contempt for another's woman's looks, weight, or age, which frees women to value their own appearance, however close or far it may be from society's standard.

An October 3, 2004, *New York Times* article by Alexandra Jacobs, for example, tells the story of actress Jennifer Coolidge, "Queen of the Ugly Stepsisters," as the headline calls her. Although Coolidge did look for the "beautiful-girl" roles when she first began, she lost them, she believes, on account of lax grooming. "'But to be honest,' [Coolidge] added, 'a lot of those good-looking girl parts aren't very fun.'"

The article details Coolidge's adventurous sense of comedy, her self-confidence, and her sexual presence (despite being forty-two years old and having a plus-size body). It also mentions her thirty-four-year-old live-in boyfriend, who loves Coolidge both for her looks and for her comic flair. Although Coolidge told Jacobs that she would "like to play someone attractive next," the article makes it clear that she thoroughly enjoys her quirky character parts, including "Stifler's Mom," the sexy older woman in the *American Pie* movies who initiates one young teenage boy into the mysteries of sex.

Likewise, a July/August 2004 article in *AARP Magazine* by Nancy Griffin profiles the fifty-four-year-old Cybill Shepherd, who insists that she hasn't "had work done," enjoys her advancing age, and has decided "to liberate herself from the tyranny of diets." After gaining thirty pounds to play Martha Stewart in a TV movie, she decided to stay at her new weight, joking, "I'm ready for my Shelley Winters parts now." Ironically, she says, because she refused to "admit" to having had plastic surgery, she lost a yogurt commercial whose copy read "Well, okay, so I've had a few nips and tucks here and there."

Part of Shepherd's serenity comes from a new attitude toward her earlier breathtaking beauty, an appearance that seemed to have won her the love of director Peter Bogdanovich, in a famed Hollywood affair, as well as the plum parts that Bogdanovich went on to offer her. According to Griffin, Shepherd sees her beauty as also leading her to feel separate from others and emotionally stymied. "It's a kind of mask that I sit behind and watch people react to," Shepherd now says about her blond allure.

Both Coolidge and Shepherd work in an industry where women's looks are central to the kinds of work they get. Yet both women refuse to engage in female rivalry, at least publicly. Coolidge is a character actress who doesn't get to play the beautiful heroines, and Shepherd, once the prettiest girl in town, is now over the hill by Hollywood standards. But both women have developed alternate standards to those of the perpetual beauty contest, choosing instead to focus on their creativity and their artistic goals.

Strikingly, there are very few portraits of happy older women in popular culture, and many of those that exist seem to come from countries outside the U.S. The British film *Calendar Girls*, for example, is based on the real-life story of middle-aged women in a small British village who learned to appreciate their bodies by posing nude for a calendar used to raise funds for the local cancer center, where one of the women's husbands had recently died. Strikingly, the solidarity among the women turns into a bitter rivalry when the leader of the group is singled out by the media for undue attention. Eventually, though, the women overcome these divisions to reestablish their friendship.

The 2004 movie *Being Julia*, also a British production, forgoes female solidarity for an unabashed portrait of rivalry between women of different generations, but is one of the few films that portrays an unqualified victory for the older woman. Based on a novella by W. Somerset Maugham, *Being Julia* is set in 1930s London, where the fifty-something actress Julia is the toast of the town. When an ambitious young man falls in love with her, Julia feels reborn. Then, when he abandons her, she feels old and unloved, particularly after both her ex-lover and her husband seem smitten with the same young actress. But Julia's age and experience are on her side. Beautiful, desirable, and much better at manipulating events onstage than the younger woman, Julia manages to humiliate both her young rival and her ex-lover while winning back her husband's admiration. The treatment of her character, played by Annette Bening, is a striking contrast to Bening's role in the American-made *American Beauty*, in which her husband finds her shrewish and demanding, and prefers his idealized lust for one of his daughter's teenage friends. Although the Bening character in that film is allowed to have an affair with a man who finds her desirable (played by the handsome if smarmy Peter Gallagher), the film relentlessly mocks her sexuality and sets her in opposition to all the younger women in the film.

The negative portrayal of the aging woman, losing her looks and envying younger women, does not necessarily match reality. According to an October 2004 survey in *More* magazine, most women age forty to forty-four actually feel better about their looks than they did five years previously. The magazine, geared to older women, took a poll among 3,383 readers, revealing that of women under forty, only forty-two percent are pleased with their looks, compared to 64 percent of women age forty to forty-four.

However, *More*'s good news is qualified: only 45 percent of women at age fifty-five approve of their looks, and only 35 percent of women at age sixty. And *More* literally perpetuates the beauty contest with it's annual "40+ model search," in which women older than forty can win a contract with the Wilhelmina modeling agency, besides being featured in a special *More* article where they get to share their beauty secrets. Once again, I find myself torn between two responses: on the one hand, I applaud the notion that women over forty can be considered "spirited, gorgeous women," in the words of the article covering the magazine's fifth annual contest; on the other hand, I wonder why the "beauty contest" continues decade after decade for women, with no respite in sight.

So finally, it is to "real-life" women to whom I turn for hope, women like Jacqueline, who at age sixty feels that the beauty contest has finally ended, and with it, the envy and competitiveness that have marked so much of her life:

> It is odd how life turns out. The two women I envied most in high school are now working at the same office where I work. I remember in high school how these women were tall, thin blondes, and so popular! I was small and dark with curly hair and average legs. In those days I didn't know the blondes: they only hung out with each other and would not have talked to me. All the boys carried their books and their hair was long and silky.
>
> Today we all work together, and those two girls who were the cheerleaders in my high school and homecoming queen contenders, are now my best friends. . . .
>
> . . . I have done what I could cosmetically, but I also accept my fate, of aging. I think I am more accepting than those two blond friends. I've always colored my gray hair and I've bought the special antiaging creams and had a few face peels. But what I find is that being my age gives me a kind of freedom where I don't have to pretend anymore. It just doesn't matter now that we are all older, no one escaped the aging process. We are friends because we appreciate each other. I don't feel less anymore, and I'm no longer envious. Even if these two women are still blond, I know they go to the hairdresser just like I have to. And I'm sort of blond myself these days. We all have lines around our eyes, even after going to surgeons and dermatologists—some more than others. There is, at last, a common denominator.

Spinning Competition in Our Favor

How, then, can women make competition work for them rather than against them? Based on my research, here are some observations about ways that female rivalry can be made to have a positive spin:

1. *Acknowledge your own feelings of competition.* Nothing makes rivalry more intense than denying that it exists. As women, we're socialized to be "nice girls," shying away from the will to win and the desire to come out on top. Becoming aware of how much we want to be number one and perhaps even to triumph over beloved family members, friends, and colleagues can free us from the fervor of our competitive urges. Once we know how we feel, we can choose how to act, deciding whether to engage in a contest or let it go. If we don't realize how much we want to win, however, we are likely to channel those forbidden desires into resentment, criticism, and the kind of petty backbiting described both by Lucy and by Thea in this chapter. We'll find reasons to put down other women's clothes, relationships, or lifestyle while masking our own competitive natures.

2. *Don't be afraid of your envy and jealousy.* In these enlightened times, when women run for public office and seek corporate success, many of us have come to terms with our will to win. Our envy and particularly our jealousy may be harder feelings to cope with. These feelings are age-old and genderless; after all, it was the seventeenth-century French philosopher La Rochefoucauld who said, "In the misfortunes of our best friends we always find something not altogether displeasing to us." He was able to make a witty joke about the very human emotion of jealousy, but many women have a harder time admitting their own experience with this feeling. Speaking with hundreds of women, however, I've learned that those who deny their envy and jealousy most intensely are most likely to be sabotaged by it. These women either become extremely critical of other women or simply lapse into a stifling depression. Get to know your dark side—that's the only way to keep it from mastering you.

3. Find areas where you feel comfortable competing. Would you like to take up a sport, excel at a craft, move ahead at work, or engage in a competitive game such as bridge, poker, or chess? Choosing an outlet where you enjoy playing to win, whether you're competing against yourself, others, or both, can, as Kara, Stella, and others have explained, free you from rivalry in other areas of your life. There are many situations where you might compete with impunity: online sites enable you to play card games, board games, and fantasy games against strangers. A martial-arts class makes healthy competition part of the lesson, as do classes in tennis and golf. Running, weight-lifting, swimming, and other athletic activities can be done solo, with you competing against your own best performance. Or perhaps you'd like to go for a promotion, start your own business, or run for a political office. Finding places where competition is an integral part of the activity can help you grow more comfortable with it.

4. Notice when you become disapproving, resentful, or frustrated with others, particularly other women. Often, when we don't feel comfortable with our own competitiveness, envy, or jealousy, we sublimate our feelings into disparagement. It's the original dog-in-the-manger attitude: if we feel that we can't have a certain type of relationship, job, appearance, or lifestyle, we have to find reasons to deny it to every other woman we know. And if we can't actually undermine our rivals, we turn to sour grapes, insisting that we don't really want what she has, and finding reasons to fault her for having it. Next time you find yourself saying negative things about a sister, girlfriend, or female coworker, stop and ask yourself whether you are genuinely critical of this other woman or simply envious of her.

5. Use your envy and jealousy to motivate yourself. Treated properly, envy can become your new best friend, an unmistakable signal alerting you to your own deepest longings. If you dis-cover that you envy another woman's relationship, job, or ap-pearance, ask yourself what this response tells you about what *you* really want. Would you be happier if you lost weight, had a makeover, bought some new clothes? Are you seeking a more sexually or emotionally satisfying relationship? Do you need to start taking seriously your hope to have children, or to repair your relationship with the offspring you already have? Almost always, when we feel envious, there's something we can give ourselves or achieve on our own behalf, something we've been afraid to try for or even to admit we want. While jealousy is a darker emotion, even this troublesome feeling can inspire you toward a more vigorous effort to fulfill your heart's desire.

Coming to Terms with Competition

Although many of the interviews I have conducted for this book have painted a bleak portrait of female rivalry, some women have proven to be inspirational. Among these is forty-seven-year-old Anita, who offers a positive model for spinning competitiveness in our favor. "Being com-petitive is the only way to get ahead in life," Anita told me, adding that after a lifetime of competition, she has finally learned to compete in a healthy way:

I have been this way my entire life. I compete with myself, with my friends, with my sisters. The rest of my family is not like this, but I think I had such an unhappy childhood that winning something as silly as a spelling bee in grade school motivated me. So I became a competitive student and that won me scholarships. . . . After grad school I began my own business. Then I competed with other women in the same business to get ahead. I never considered men to be the competition, only other women who had a similar profile to mine.

I am a competitive sportswoman, and I am a competitive business-woman. I stopped competing for men years ago, when I met my future husband and knew I didn't want to play that game when it came to him. Because of this, I see my competitive streak as very healthy. I am competitive in the areas where I need to be. I know that some people view me as too competitive, but compared to women I know, who are competitive about everything—clothes, jewelry, men, kids, houses—I think I'm doing it for the right reasons.

Women who enjoy competition point the way for us to create new models. They make competition a flourishing part of their lives, while retaining the ability to stop the contest whenever it no longer serves them. Instead of tripping the prom queen, they are dancing to their own rhythm. And if part of the time they're out to win the dance contest, they're also finding new ways to enjoy the music.

9

Resisting the Urge to Merge

Among the most potent obstacles to female friendship are the three mistaken beliefs I identified in Chapter 1:

1. The Mommy Mystique suggests that our women friends should give us the kind of boundless, unconditional love that we hoped to get (and perhaps even did get) from our mothers— a level of total, unquestioning support that I believe is not possible, or even desirable, in any adult relationship. Numerous books, self-help programs, and talk shows have been devoted to the notion that a long-standing heterosexual relationship can become arduous. Partners won't always agree, and the common wisdom is that men and women should accept their differences.

No such healthy model exists in our culture for female friends, who are encouraged to believe that their relationship is the safe haven from all those gender-based difficulties. Then, when conflicts and frustrations arise with our friends, including feelings of rivalry, we're at a loss. Our girlfriends are supposed to make us feel good, not bad, so we either drop them, distance them, or settle into an uneasy coexistence with our troublesome emotions. The same applies when we realize that someone who we thought was a good friend envies *us*. Believing that true friends don't have bad feelings about each other, we have no resources or even any language to deal with the situation.

2. The Twinning Syndrome implies that our girlfriends should be just like us, sharing the same strengths, suffering through the same troubles, facing the same challenges. Thus, two single friends who share late-night popcorn and complaints about men may have difficulty negotiating the transition when one of them falls in love or starts dating regularly. Likewise, two friends who support each other through the ups and downs of married life may start to question the friendship when one of the women gets a divorce. If we need to think of our friends as twins, then a divergence of life paths may feel like a betrayal, and the opportunities for rivalry multiply. "You used to be like me, but now you have something I don't have" is the unspoken complaint.

3. Foul-Weather Friends describes the all-too-common pattern of women sticking together when they're all miserable, but turning on the friend who suddenly becomes happy. How many times has a woman felt punished by her girlfriends for losing weight, snagging a promotion, falling in love, or even leaving an unhappy marriage? The women in Becky's office, competing for the position of most miserable, are a perfect example. It's no accident that, as Becky perceptively points out, the woman with colitis and the one who still lives with her parents are best friends. Their bond is based on a common misery that would be threatened if either one became happier.

Thinking about the various models of female friendship reminded me of my own friend Lydia, an accomplished freelance journalist with a wide circle of acquaintances. Lydia is a single woman whose main interests are reading, writing, and politics, but she's created a remarkably diverse friendship network, including a stay-at-home mother of several children; a modern dancer who recently became a choreographer; and a union organizer who works with barely literate health-care workers.

Although Lydia can be a supportive friend, she's also one of the most competitive people I know. She tries to keep her envy under wraps, but I often detect a forlorn tone when the conversation turns to my husband, my children, or my career, in comparison to her single, childless, less secure life. She'll freely admit that she struggles with these feelings, however, prompting me to ask how she managed them with all of her other friends.

"Oh," she said breezily, "I compete with *you*, Susan, because we're so similar. I'm never going to have three kids, or a dancer's body, or a job that's more about bread-and-butter issues than about ideas. So with Melly and Shana and Janie, there's nothing to compete about. You're the one whose life I could have had, if only I hadn't had mine."

Still, I noted, she seemed remarkably comfortable admitting her envy of me and some of her other friends—a comfort that I found unusual, both personally and in terms of my research.

"Well," she said, "the big turning point for me was when I realized that female friendships weren't *supposed* to be easy. I'd always thought they were the refuge, you know, the place where you always felt good. And if you seemed to have something that I wanted, and I envied you, then I didn't feel good, so there must be a problem. It was a big relief when I finally understood that it was just as okay to have problems with a woman friend as with a guy."

Lydia and I went on to talk about our various experiences of female friendship. I realized, speaking with her, how often my own friendships with women had been based on expecting a kind of unconditional love untroubled by envy or jealousy. Ironically, most women, including my-self, are willing to accept the complexity of human emotions in our partnerships with men. But with our women friends, the bar is raised. It was in my conversations with Lydia, in fact, that I developed the three concepts with which I began this chapter. To me, this is a perfect ex-ample of how accepting the conflicts in our friendships with women can lead to not only deeper relationships but also richer lives.

Emerging from Merging: Valuing Separate Identities

Actually, friendships based in diversity are one thing the media does well, perhaps because nobody wants to watch a movie or a TV show in which two characters are fairly similar. On the comedy *Just Shoot Me!*, for example, which is set at a fashion magazine, would-be serious jour-nalist Maya Gallo (Laura San Giacomo) is portrayed as an uptight, po-litically correct, earnest woman. She would seem to be the perfect foil for the ditsy ex-model and fashion editor Nina van Horne (Wendie Malick), who is obsessed with clothes, men, drugs, and liquor. Clearly, each woman has access to a body of knowledge from which the other can benefit, though it is hard to imagine a real-life situation in which two such different women would not in fact be enormously threatened by each other. In their own sitcom way, however, the women demon-strate the liberating aspects of diversity. Once we stop expecting our women friends to be just like us and to want the same things we want, there is room for us to stop competing with them as well. Why would Maya even expect to be as well-dressed or as sexually free as Nina? How could Nina ever hope to be as smart and knowledgeable as Maya? Exist-ing within two different categories, competition becomes moot, and the women are free to learn from each other rather than resent each other.

Likewise, the show *Living Single*, which featured four African-American women living with or near each other in Brooklyn, made a great deal of the differences among the girlfriends: innocent Synclaire, ambitious Khadijah, fashion-conscious Regine, and cynical, sexy Max.

It was clear from the beginning that each of the women wanted separate things, needed different types of relationships, and faced her own personal challenges. In sitcom style, the women mocked one another, but were always there when a friend was down. Avoiding the foul-weather friends syndrome, however, the girlfriends also helped each other achieve their goals, both romantic and professional. Like *The Golden Girls*, an earlier sitcom featuring four older women living together in Miami, the humor of the program lay in the sharp contrasts between the characters, while the show's heart could be found in the deep love that the women shared.

Scrubs, a half-hour comedy that debuted in fall 2001, goes even further in its portrayal of female friendship, explicitly taking on the kinds of myths I have described. In one episode, Elliot, a female doctor, turns to a fellow woman physician for support in a battle with the hospital administration. Elliot's friend disagrees with Elliot professionally but finds ways to support her personally. The two women must negotiate a difficult situation in which they preserve both their professional integrity and their friendship, making room for both disagreement and solidarity. In another episode, Elliot realizes that she and her friend Carla, a nurse, have grown apart after Carla's marriage. Although the two women make plans every week, they never manage to keep them. The women discover that being friends takes work, just as marriage does, and that they have to make more of an effort to preserve their relationship now that their circumstances have changed. The show's message about female friendship is consistent: accepting the places where we differ, disagree, or just don't understand each other is the basis of a strong relationship.

Behind the scenes, though, the real-life sitcom actresses are portraying a far more simplistic version of female friendship. Reports on the close friendships of *Friends* cast members Jennifer Aniston and Courteney Cox Arquette, and of *Frasier* actresses Peri Gilpin and Jane Leeves, stress the women's similarities. True, the journey from being a relatively unknown actor to the star of a hit TV series would naturally be a bonding experience. But the focus of media coverage on these women is how similar they are, with the unlikely insistence that envy and competition form no part of their friendship. Rather than portraying the women's efforts to bond across their disparities and cope with their occasional rivalry, TV and magazine accounts suggest a conflict-free union between two sets of extremely successful and desirable women. Fans who read about these idealized relationships feel like failures when they and their girlfriends seem to fall short of the mark.

A frighteningly negative view of female merging is offered by the 1992 film, *Single White Female*. Jennifer Jason Leigh portrays an apparently normal young woman who answers an ad in the newspaper to become the roommate of another woman, played by Bridget Fonda. Soon the Leigh character is imitating her roommate's mannerisms. She borrows the other woman's clothes, gets a similar haircut, and even spends a wild night with her roommate's boyfriend. Rivalry shades into a full-scale appropriation of the other woman's identity—not simply envying what she has or even jealously wanting her dead because of it but actually seeking to become the rival who seems to have so much.

Although *Single White Female* was dismissed by critics as an over-the-top thriller, my own research suggests that this type of "identity theft" is not so uncommon among young women. A twenty-five-year-old woman, Rosie, described her experience with Pat, a college roommate:

> When Pat . . . tried to steal my boyfriend, I thought to myself, this has happened in high school, I know what to do with it. I told Jack that she wasn't a good person, and I told him that Pat was flirting with him, since he didn't seem to notice. But when Pat saw that Jack wanted to be with me, she took my book bag . . . my notebooks, and my stationery. She would sit at the computer and log on to my e-mail. . . . She sort of invaded my life. When I saw her at a football game wearing my rainslicker,

I freaked out. She had her hair in a high ponytail, just like I wear mine, and she was using my Burberry umbrella. . . . She was pretending she was me and I couldn't do anything about it. When the semester finished, I requested a room change. When I was packing, I noticed that pictures of my family were missing, as well as pictures of my two dogs. I sometimes wonder what would have worked better for Pat—to have succeeded in her play for Jack, or for her to have invaded my identity?

As we have witnessed in Chapters 2 and 5, women often endow their rivals with a kind of fairy-tale power, as though these supposedly successful females possessed the seemingly magical ability to achieve all of life's most important goals. Stealing a boyfriend—or a raincoat, an umbrella, an entire look—might seem to offer an envious woman the key to her own happiness. She is not interested in the actual man, let alone the specific appearance or fashion accessory. Rather, she thinks that by becoming more similar to her rival, she will endow herself with the extraordinary power she imagines her rival to have.

To me, this type of female identity theft speaks to the deep connection between rivalry and merging. The deep-seated jealousy that would inspire a woman to steal another woman's clothes, read her e-mail, and even walk off with her photo suggests that all women are fundamentally the same and that we are all competing for essentially the same things. Instead of recognizing that we are each unique human beings, rivalry taken to this extreme implies that we are all interchangeable. Your successful social life is not the product of your own personality, your specific efforts to be attractive and amusing, or even your own special look and sensibility. Rather, you have simply acquired some "goods"—a haircut, a photograph, a boyfriend. If I steal your "goods," I can have your life, and your success. I might as well be you.

Although twenty-year-old Mandy's experience hasn't been as dramatic as Rosie's, she, too, described jealous friends who seemed not only to envy her but to covet her identity:

I have gotten rid of my so-called best friend who wanted whatever I had, from my boyfriend to my blond hair. I was very careful not to choose a friend like that afterward. I learned to find friends who wanted to be close to me, not to have what I have.

Mandy sees her recognition of other women's envy as extremely liberating:

I'm glad I learned this lesson early because now I'll have true girlfriends for the rest of my life. I am able to tell who cares about me and who isn't sincere. I also know my worth as a friend, as a person. So I know how to treat people and how I should be treated.

Rosie and Mandy are both relatively young. But fifty-year-old Carla tells a similar story. For this extremely attractive woman, female envy implies that "women want to be me." So Carla has spent most of her life learning strategies for diverting or precluding female jealousy:

What I have learned to do is to win other women over. I want these envious women to know that I won't take anything that is theirs, that I really just hope for the friendship. . . . When I was younger, I didn't know what to do with how these supposed friends acted. Now that I've been around for a long time, I can face it. Then I can try to do something about it.

Interestingly, Carla sees that her strategies work differently in unique circumstances. When women accept their distinctions, they more easily deflect their envy. When they see each other as "all the same," they inevitably see Carla as a hated rival:

If I am in a diverse group at my office or in my religious class, then it is okay. Everyone has her own agenda, her own plan. But if I am in a competitive circle where everyone is looking for the same thing—a man, fi-

nancial security, beauty, brains, status—then I'm in trouble. Women in
that circle will hate me, no matter how hard I try to win them over.

Carla's perspective on female envy is striking. She perfectly cap-
tures the mixture of rivalry and merging—wanting both the other
woman's "possessions" and her identities—that I have been describing:

I see these women as driven by fear and greed, the same motivation that
drives people on Wall Street. These women fear what they don't have
and they covet it, too.

Moreover, Carla says, envious women are particularly vulnerable to
acting as foul-weather friends:

One of the most telling incidents was when I remarried and I ended up in
a good place. That was when I could really gauge who was my friend and
who didn't wish me happiness.

One new way in which women both bond and compete is that traditional female activity, knitting. In the first few years of the twenty-
first century, knitting groups for women of all ages became a trend that
spread quickly across the country, according to New York City resident
Debbie Stoller, founder of her city's "Stitch 'n' Bitch" knitting circle.
Knitting is now appealing to a younger, hipper crowd, according to her
book, *Stitch 'n Bitch: The Knitter's Handbook*. Women in their twenties
and thirties are discovering what their grandmothers had always
known: that knitting circles are a place where women can trade secrets
and become friends.

Yet even here, women must resist the urge to merge, or the bonding
quickly turns sour. One knitting expert in the Midwest told me that
"There are those women who befriend a fellow knitter, and those who

compete about everything, from life to the sweater they're knitting." If the women in a knitting group resemble each other as to age, type of job, and demographic background, competition appears to flourish. If they are a more diverse group, of various ages and lifestyles, they seem to allow each other more room for their individual strengths, even as they remain a close and supportive group.

Seeking Sisterhood, Finding Diversity

Throughout my research, I was amazed at the myriad ways that women found to compete. We've already seen how female envy manifests around appearance, relationships, children, and work. Although girls have traditionally been discouraged from being "too smart," forty-three-year-old Sela encountered enormous jealousy of her intelligence, as well:

> From first grade spelling bees to valedictorian of my high school class, I was always the smartest girl. And then I went to law school, where female students really disliked me because I was such a good student. I made law review; I was chosen by a few good law firms at a great starting salary. I married a classmate, and we juggled . . . our careers once we had one child. I hung in and had two more babies, made partner—and had only one female friend at the firm in ten years' time. There were other women, but no one seemed interested in being my friend.

Sela believes that as she became more successful in other domains—appearance, relationship, children—other women's envy increased accordingly:

> Since I managed to look good and have a husband and kids, I could actually feel other women being jealous of all of this.

The envy has grown to such a degree, Sela feels, that it has become a major source of pressure in her life:

The envy that coworkers have is amazing and unrelenting. My counterparts in other law firms also assess me, as do female bankers.

But, Sela wonders, since she and her fellow high achievers are all in
the same boat, why not create solidarity rather than rivalry?

My impression is that these other women's achievements and their intelligence are continually being tested and compared. Women like us have
spent our entire lives being the smart ones. Why not welcome it, why not
show off a little? But my equals in the work world do not want to share
the wealth. And the other women have always hated us for being so stu-
dious and for being rewarded for our efforts.

Rochelle, a half generation younger at age thirty-four, reports a similar experience:

I have stayed on the straight and narrow by always being smart. I grew
up in a neighborhood where being labeled a slut served you better than
being labeled brainy. While everyone judged everyone, being smart was
universally hated—by girls, boys, parents. Because, I think, it was so
threatening. It had nothing to do with being poor or uneducated, it had
to do with being blessed. There was no defense for being smart, so
everyone envied you, and as I got older, my friends were jealous.

As Rochelle grew up, the gap between her condition and that of
her friends widened, and the envy increased:

I had friends who at seventeen disappeared to have babies, or stuck
around and had babies. Either way, no one had much initiative. I hung in
and graduated high school and went on to college on a scholarship. I became a police detective and I waited to have kids. I married and divorced,
and remarried, but always I have been careful with my children and with
my job.

When Rochelle became one of the few women detectives on her local police force, she thought she would find at last the sisterhood she had always sought:

> There are few female detectives on the force, so it makes sense that we would work together. Not only that, but each of us has a story, like a divorce or being a single mom, or a victim of abuse, or something. Instead, the female supervisors are hard on us so we can't buddy up with each other. We are too busy watching our own backs. I thought I was finally with other women who would understand what it was like to be smarter than most girls throughout school, other women who had worked hard to get somewhere. But I have found it to be something else.

Rochelle never expected her life path to be easy. "It is hard to get ahead because I am smart and a minority female," she says frankly. But what hurts is that "Those who could help do not want to help." Most demoralizing of all is the hostility she experiences from other women like herself:

> If I walk into work dressed nicely, the other women look at me as if to say, "Who do you think you are?" I am starting to think that I will have to speak to a male superior to get somewhere, which is not what I ever expected.

Lori, forty-three, has battled unkind women in her new career as a teacher, after having purposely given up her first career as a medical assistant because the work environment was not conducive to friendships between women.

> Part of why I changed careers is to make friends in the workplace. I left a decent job at a hospital and earned my teaching degree. I'm tall and

fair and . . . teaching minority children. Many of the teachers are also minority women. I expected that they would welcome me and include me in drinks after work just because we all work together. Instead they made it clear that unless I did it their way, I couldn't be part of their clique. They wanted me to teach as they do, use only the books that they choose, and play by their rules. It became so unbearable that I had to file a report with the grievance committee about their treatment.

To Lori's surprise, her effort to assert her own opinion actually made it easier, not harder, to bond with her colleagues:

Ironically, my grievance won this group of women over and made the idea of friendship more likely. It was almost as though I had to prove that I wanted to be a part of their group but would still think for myself, that I wouldn't accept their meanness in order for things to improve. Now two women are becoming my friends, and I feel empowered. I actually stood up for myself and can have healthy friendships, too. I finally feel welcome, and I've learned about myself, how much I'd like to have friendships at work based on mutual respect and our differences.

Leanne, at age sixty-five, has what would appear to be a far more conventional life than Rochelle's or Lori's since hers encompasses marriage, children, a well-financed old age. She, too, has noticed both the twinning syndrome and the tendency to be foul-weather friends, leading her to describe friendship as "conditional":

When a few of my friends were widowed, they were actually jealous of me because my husband was still alive. These were friends who had known me and my husband when we were couples who would go out together. I would innocently invite them to dinner and they would come but hate me for having a husband when they no longer did. . . . When I had my first art show, a few years ago, my friends seemed jealous of that, too, of the fact that art has become such a part of my life.

I have begun to realize that I can't win by reaching out to my friends because they are jealous of my happiness. If instead I withdraw, they talk among themselves and are critical of me. So I pretend to care more than I do, because I know that if something happens to my husband, women friends matter.

Leanne's frustration with female envy is all the sharper because she knows how important her women friends are, and she imagines that they will soon be even more important:

My girlfriends sit in restaurants together, a group of five or six widows, and make a life for themselves. I'm in the couples world today, but there are no guarantees. Even if one friend is jealous of another because a man took her to dinner or her son is buying her a condo, we need each other. Or else we'd be totally alone.

Accepting Our Differences

Happily, in my research, I did find several examples of women who were able to overcome their rivalry and mend their broken friendships. Sometimes, however, the friendships seemed to founder when the women chose different lives and could only be mended when the women's lives were more similar.

Caitlin, for example, a forty-six-year-old designer who lives in a southern city, has ridden the ups and downs of her friendship with Michele. The two women met in the early 1980s at the nursery school attended by both their children. That the connection has prevailed all these years is testimony to their commitment to each other:

Michele and I met when our children were small, and our youngest children had not yet been born. We lived in the same neighborhood, and we rented houses for the same week at the same beach resort. That was enough to introduce our husbands and to become friends with children in tow.

We stayed friends until Michele moved across country and then we lost touch for several years. There was a bit of anger at that time and I didn't like the way that Michele left town. I think she knew but in retrospect neither of us handled it well. I felt abandoned because our lives were no longer parallel: she had left for another life. I was envious of her move, but too angry to care. . . .

So far, the story is familiar. Caitlin and Michele can be friends when their lives are "parallel," but when Michele asserts her difference by setting off on a new path, Caitlin feels envious and abandoned. However, their story doesn't end there:

We met a few years later at a party and it was as if no time had elapsed. But Michele still lived across the country and was only visiting for the weekend.

Then my husband became quite ill and died. A few months later Michele began divorce proceedings, and that was horrible. The good part was that she moved home. The two of us would spend Saturday nights with our eight children, huddled around my fireplace, wondering how our lives had turned out so unlike how we dreamed they would. Both of us had very good jobs at the same time and were dating. But it wasn't easy being single mothers with all these children, and we clung together in desperation half the time.

Once again, the two women find themselves on parallel tracks, so their friendship can resume. And once again, when their paths diverge, their friendship totters:

Michele moved in with a man, and my boyfriend broke up with me. Again, there was a schism, maybe based on envy and not being in the same place anymore.

To Caitlin and Michele's credit, however, the women were eventually able to overcome this second schism:

> Two years later, we found one another at a concert. Both of us had gotten hired, fired, and rehired during the last eight years. We have finally managed to put the bad stuff behind us.

Even with this happy ending, Caitlin admits that their friendship is still based on being alike. Now, instead of competing over relationships, they have moved on to rivalry over their children:

> Our children are like family to one another, and by now adults nominally, if not in behavior. We have a kind of competition about whose daughters will marry first that helps us get over how they seem to never grow up. That is our latest shared bond: our old, immature children. It's the similar experiences that keep us together.

Caitlin and Michele may very well go on into their old age as close friends, with their lives continuing to become ever more similar. My hope, however, is that women can begin to drop the need to bond over competition and similarity, and create new types of female friendship based on connectedness and difference. Perhaps the story of Terri and Nancy offers a more useful model. Terri, a forty-five-year-old artist, fell out with Nancy, her childhood best friend, but eventually, the two women were reunited:

> I can hardly remember what the quarrel was about now, but it certainly shook me up. I think that Nancy didn't approve of my lifestyle and was maybe jealous of it at the same time. My husband is in the entertainment business, and we were sort of jet-setting around during that period. I think Nancy thought I'd become superficial. She had continued in her job as a nurse practitioner, and I wasn't even working when the girls were little—I just went to dinners and luncheons and did things with the kids.

But Nancy and I had been trained together, we'd started our first jobs together. She must have thought I wasn't the same person anymore.

Of course, sometimes friends do grow apart. There might have
been a legitimate basis for Terri and Nancy to cool their friendship,
to seek other women whose interests were more similar. But even
though the two women went for years without speaking, Terri
couldn't let go:

I kept looking for Nancy in other friendships, trying to duplicate what we
had, and I couldn't. I missed her a lot. Then I was at the movies, two years
ago, and we ran into each other. Nancy acted as though nothing had happened. It was strange. I mean, she was the one who had left me and hadn't
returned my calls or acknowledged my Christmas cards or the birth of my
youngest child. I had been devastated—I even called her mother one time,
and she was nice but made it clear that she couldn't get involved. But then
after we ran into one another, Nancy called me and we spoke.

Terri found that her initial instincts had been right: "She thought
I'd lost myself to a slick existence. It was almost like I had to prove myself to my oldest friend to win her back." But, Terri reports, "I did win
her back, and now we get together all of the time. It's like family, we are
so close again."

The closeness, though, depends on Terri having learned to define
the relationship in a new way. "It's not like it used to be," she explains. "We don't have to be exactly alike. . . . We purposely keep it
light, and don't talk too much about our lifestyles. We go to the
movies together, or concerts, we work out together. So our friendship
is more activity-oriented than it used to be." By giving up on the
need to have an identical twin, a mommy, or a foul-weather friend,
Terri and Nancy were able to redefine their friendship in a more
adult and realistic way.

Another version of female bonding that offers the potential for true solidarity occurs in the workplace, where women can focus not on their personalities but on their dedication to a common goal. Sally, a forty-five-year-old employee at a southern California blood lab, told me that she and three coworkers have gotten along well during the twelve years Sally has worked in this all-female environment:

> It has always been a decent working relationship between the women here. . . . Since it's a small lab and a busy one, we don't have much time to get nasty to one another. . . . If a patient is unpleasant . . . we take turns giving her or him dirty looks. We have to protect each other—it's not a big place, but small, and it can get really crowded.

Sally is very well aware that her situation is unusual:

> I have friends who aren't happy with the other women at their jobs. They end up talking about it all the time. I listen, and I know I'm lucky.

In some degree, Sally believes, the racial bond as well as the gender bond contributes to her coworkers' unity. But as she continues to talk about her work, I sense that she thinks the nature of the work is more important than the type of women who do it:

> I am an African-American and so is Lennie, and the other two women are Asian. No one has a great sense of humor but we can smile on occasion. I always feel like someone who comes into our lab will go out with bad news, and that is disturbing, you can't deny that. Everyone has to get along because from early morning until evening, this place is swamped with people. We can't make any mistakes. We respect each other's job, and we do it right. I think this is hard work and I take it very seriously. We're not joking around, and we don't dump on the next person. We talk about our lives, but only along the way, because we always have a waiting room filled with people.

For Sally, the all-female lab is not a site of competition and back-biting. It is a place where the women employees enjoy a sense of satisfaction as they accomplish important work:

> There used to be a man who worked here instead of one of the women.
> I prefer to have all women: it feels like we have a kind of power, like we
> run a place that matters, that helps patients and doctors. Why not be
> with women for this? Why not work together?

Roll Over: Room for Each Other

How, then, can we resist the urge to merge, and develop healthier versions of female friendship? Here are some suggestions I've developed, based on my research:

1. Create realistic definitions of friendship. Much of the early women's movement focused on helping women overcome romantic notions of love and marriage that never really existed outside the pages of a fairy tale. Yet if we replace our romanticized vision of love with equally impossible ideals for friendship, we're condemning ourselves to another type of disillusionment. Understand that friends, no less than husbands, will have shortcomings. And the more intimate and important the relationship, the more their flaws will trouble us. It's good to expect a lot from friendship—I certainly always have. But unrealistic expectations of any relationship are a recipe for disappointment.

2. Cherish your friends' differences as well as their similarities. Too many of us expect to look into our friends' faces and see a mirror. We feel supported and affirmed when they share our tastes, preferences, and goals; we feel undermined and abandoned when they don't. It can be difficult to develop the

courage of our own convictions, to realize that you like motor-
cycles while your friend is more a carriage-ride-in-the-park type;
to enjoy a Merchant Ivory film while your friend would rather
watch an action film. And the higher the stakes, the more difficult it is to go it alone. Being the first in your group to have children can be a lonely experience; so can being the only one in
your group who hasn't had (or doesn't want) children. Yet part
of living a satisfying life is being willing to make the choices
that are right for each of us. Ask your friends for all the emotional support they're willing to offer—but don't expect them to
think, act, or choose the way you do.

**3. *Allow yourself to experience your own competitiveness,
envy, and even jealousy, and try not to judge yourself too
harshly.*** Maybe you're a quiet, reserved type while your friend has
always been able to walk into a bar and have her choice of guys at
a moment's notice. Perhaps you're still struggling with revising
your résumé while your girlfriend has already made partner at one
of the city's top law firms. Or maybe you envy your friend's happy
family life, her great boyfriend, or her size-0 figure. It's natural to
feel a pang or two as you hang back near the ladies' room or bang
out cover letter number 206. But becoming aware of your own
envy is the first step to mastering it. Acknowledging all the reasons you resent your friend frees you to remember why you love
her. Pay attention to your envious feelings, but keep them in
check. Remember, envy can lead us to self-fulfillment—if your
friend is moving to the big city and that's always been your dream,
too, her bold decision can cause you to take your own action. Being aware of jealous feelings likewise enables you to avoid situations that will trigger a harsh reaction. And when feeling either
envious or jealous, avoid conveying either criticism of your friend
or deprecation of yourself.

4. Keep the lines of communication open. This can be a tricky one. Many people take the instruction to share their feelings as carte blanche to engage in blaming, guilt-tripping, and manipulation. I once had a friend who confessed to envy every time I told her about something good that had happened to me. I soon got the message: my good fortune made her unhappy because of her own dire straits. I didn't exactly blame her, but I did wish she'd keep it to herself. So I'm not suggesting that you inform your friends about every little pang of envy. I am suggesting that if your sense of rivalry becomes a problem—or if you feel that someone's envy of you is getting out of control—that you find nonjudgmental, open, and caring ways to talk about what's going on. Choose wisely the frequency and manner of such conversations, but know that avoiding them altogether may pose a risk to even the strongest friendship.

5. "Don't get envious, get your own life." As I suggested in Chapter 8, and as Lucy suggests to her bowling teammates, the real value of rivalry is its power to put us in touch with our own desires. If you notice that a friend's life seems better than yours, ask yourself what you want in your own life that you're not getting. Do you really want exactly what your friend has? Or do you want your own version of it, or something else altogether? Maybe you don't want a steady boyfriend, but you would like to be dating more. Perhaps you aren't interested in imitating your friend's supercool fashion sense, but you would like to spice up your wardrobe just a bit. Or maybe your friend does have exactly the life that would make you happy, and you've simply never dared to go for it. If you know you can pursue your own hopes and dreams, you don't have to steal or envy hers. Instead, use your frustration to remind you that your own life is rich and full of possibility, and that only you can make those possibilities come true.

Two of the most inspiring interviews I conducted for this book focused on just such stories—women who moved from envy to self-empowerment. Kate, at age forty-four, struggled for a long time with her sense of inadequacy before she began to make the changes she needed:

> With my female friends, I feel all of these unmet expectations. I think this is because all of my friends are working and I'm not. I feel like I'm missing something but I never act on it. . . . I do a lot of volunteer work, but being on committees with women makes me feel like a stereotype. Nothing ever gets done, and women chatter away. I feel I was judged by my working friends because I've been a committee woman and a stay-at-home mom for years.
>
> Then, six months ago, I realized that I can do whatever I want. Maybe all these years that I led committee meetings made me sure of my capacities. I have to find my way, but I can only do that when I believe in myself. I'm ready to become a travel agent or a real estate agent, and to stop being so envious of the women who love what they do at work. I have to make it happen for myself, and this is the time. So strangely enough I feel better about myself than ever before. I can look any woman in the eye and befriend her now.

Jane, too, feels more confident in herself at age thirty-five, and so she has become less jealous:

> Maybe it was because I couldn't get to where I wanted to be that I was so jealous of my two smartest girlfriends. . . . But . . . suddenly, I am able to go out for drinks with Tyra and Julia and not feel on the outside, looking in. I don't grimace when they boast of their achievements. . . .
>
> Suddenly, things have become good for me. I've been promoted at

> work, and I met a great guy. I am finally seeing some results of my hard
> work in an ad agency, and I've tried very hard to be decent to the other
> women in the office. I'm also extending myself more to my friends than in
> the past. I no longer feel inadequate or stupid compared to Tyra and
> Julia—I feel more on a par. I see now that we are different, and that sort of
> lessens the competition. Maybe one day, one of them will actually envy me!

Although women like Kate and Jane were rare in my research, they did show up, suggesting a new approach to female rivalry. If we're aware of our feelings of jealousy and envy, we can work with them, rather than letting them rule us. If we're focused on ourselves and our own identities, we can put our energy into improving our own lives rather than envying others'. And if we accept that we and our friends are not identical, we can overcome some of the pain and frustration that come from wondering fruitlessly why our friends have things we seem to lack.

Bold Advances

Although the idea of "men are from Mars and women are from Venus" relates to heterosexual coupling, I appreciate the title of John Gray's popular book because it asks us to embrace differences in our loved ones. If only women could allow such diversity among their friends! One of the most painful stories I heard in the course of researching this book was the account of Desiree, who at forty-six fell in love with another woman. As she saw it, the discovery of her sexual interest in women led to the loss of both her husband and her best female friend:

> In the end I left my marriage to live with a woman. I felt I had to do it,
> and the idea of being married for the rest of my life and leading this con-
> ventional existence was like death to me.

Desiree's husband and her best friend were both "devastated," Desiree explains, and the two of them turned to each other for comfort. At first, Desiree didn't notice:

I was too preoccupied with getting my new life in order to stick around and pay much attention. I knew that in claiming my sexuality I would lose some friends, and I was willing to take that risk. I knew that my friends would talk about me and raise their eyebrows. Why not? I had been this housewife and mother for years. I had been someone who wanted a house with renovated bathrooms. I cared about window treatments. Then I realized that it wasn't who I was.

In Desiree's view, her best friend's betrayal was not in becoming close to Desiree's husband but in refusing to accept Desiree's true identity:

When I told my closest friend, she was astonished and definitely pulled away. She and my husband at the time would meet and talk about it. I was not jealous or envious—I doubt I cared. Then everyone dispersed. I don't have friends from before this happened. Instead, my life is divided. I suppose I don't belong with my old friends anymore, but I expected my closest friend to care enough about me, regardless of my sexual proclivity.

Now, Desiree reports, her friend has moved away, provoking mixed feelings of abandonment and relief:

This is better for me—I don't have to face the loss. And she wouldn't understand that this life of mine is right for me. We were too far apart for that.

Beneath the apparently calm words lurks a sense of sorrow that a close friend could accept Desiree only when their lives were similar. When Desiree discovered what really mattered to her, the friendship suffered.

Perhaps losing friends is natural as we grow and change. After all, a friendship based on common interests and beliefs may not be intended to survive one or another party's transformations. "The value in recognizing these emotions and learning how to deal with them positively is the key," remarks Antoinette Michaels, a relationship expert. "Each of us has her own strengths and weaknesses. It is how we face them and appreciate the friendship anyway that makes it work."

In this regard, I'm struck by the sunny portrait of female friendship in the film *Charlie's Angels*, in which three very dissimilar women make common cause in their battle to rid the world of evil. Surely their friendship wouldn't be so strong if it were based on traded confidences about bad boyfriends and family dramas? Being engaged in a shared activity, bonding over similar goals and dreams, offers another version of friendship than that of two similar women mirroring each other in all of their life stages.

Yet if a friendship can manage to survive life's long and winding road, how rich and welcoming it can come to seem! As I was finishing this manuscript, I had lunch with a friend who was in for the weekend from New Hampshire. Katrina, who is forty-seven, told me that one of the friends in her circle, Marni, had recently been diagnosed with stage-four breast cancer.

"We all felt helpless," Katrina said. "What could we do for her, knowing her situation? We decided that since a group of us love to knit, and since Marni's three daughters knit, that we would each knit a square for a quilt. I was put in charge of this project since I'm a professional knitter, and I asked each woman to contribute a square in her own style. The important thing was that Marni's twelve friends who live nearby, as well as her college friends and childhood friends, now scattered across the country, all be a part of this project. We ended up with twenty patches. I sewed the edges and lining of the blanket, making certain it was durable. Now Marni is wrapped in love for her chemo and to fight what is ahead. I feel that her friends are her inspiration, that it can make a difference, knowing we are there for her."

Although my own experience has thankfully not been so dramatic, I, too, have learned about the value of lasting friendship over the years.

Eleven years ago, when I divorced my first husband, I lost some friends and gained others. During this ordeal, I tended to gravitate to women who were widowed or divorced and to shy away from my happily married friends. I think there was an element of "misery loves company" in my choice of friends who felt, as I did, disenfranchised; and there was a measure of envy, perhaps even jealousy, in my difficulty with the friends whose lives reminded me constantly of what I had lost.

Over the years, some of my divorced and widowed friends remarried, or found great new jobs, or created another type of peace and happiness for themselves. I, too, moved on in my career and found a husband whom I consider a true partner. I wondered, sometimes, what became of the friends from my earlier life, but I allowed myself to lose touch with them nonetheless.

Recently I learned that an old friend was being honored by a charity, and I decided to attend to be a part of her special day. When she saw me walk through the door, she seemed genuinely pleased to see me. She called soon after and invited my husband and me to join her and her husband for dinner with another couple with whom I'd also lost touch. When I arrived at the dinner, my hostess was wearing a pair of earrings that I had given her fifteen years ago, while my other long-lost friend held up a purse that had been a group birthday gift that I had orchestrated nearly twenty years ago. I was so touched by their welcome. Whatever had transpired, I felt that I had somehow come home to a true version of "friends for life."

A Better Mirror

During the course of researching this book, I was happy to come across some women who were finding new forms of challenge and support in the midst of envy, jealousy, and competition. The stories they shared were a welcome reminder that when women help each other, both parties benefit.

In some cases, these new bonds were starting with our first female connection, the relationship between mothers and daughters. When daughters and mothers were allowed to embrace their differences rather than compete, their connection affirmed both the mother's achievement and the daughter's natural wish to try another path.

Faith, for example, a forty-seven-year-old high school teacher, told me how much she respected her mother's values, even as she described her own ability to go beyond her mother and achieve a happiness that her mother had been denied:

> My parents were too liberal and too ahead of their time. My mother's
> best friend and her daughter, who was my best friend, were not our reli-

gion or race. At my school, where my mom was a secretary, everyone talked about her because of this. . . . I believed in everything my mom stood for but I couldn't put it into action. . . .

It wasn't until I got a scholarship to a city college that I realized that my mom and I just lived in the wrong place. Our friendship with a black family in the '60s fueled my desire to get ahead. I didn't want to be like my mother, stuck in some crummy town, dreaming of a fairer world. I put my liberal way of thinking and my energy into my work. I was like my mother, but took it a step further.

Likewise, Lavinda is able to respect her mother's achievements while asserting that she herself has her own sense of contentment. At age thirty, Lavinda has worked in airport security for the past five years. She prefers to keep her colleagues at arm's length, as opposed to her mother, who had many close friends at work. About her mother's situation, she says simply, "I don't want that kind of job. I respect my mom for working where she does, but it wouldn't be my first choice. I'm very happy the way things are for each of us." Both Faith and Lavinda have forged relationships allowing for mutual respect and different personal choices. By choosing separate paths, the women avoid comparisons with their mothers, accepting that each woman has what is best for her.

Celebrity women may also model this healthy type of mother-daughter bond. For example, Naomi Judd and her daughter Wynonna are both country music singers, but Naomi's other daughter, Ashley, is an actress. The Judds seem to allow ample room for daughters either to follow in their mother's footsteps or to choose an alternate route to success and self-expression. They are an excellent example of how a bond that makes room for diversity is healthier than one that demands "a perfect mirror."

Mothers who seek to have their daughters mirror them exactly may also feel the need to be everything for their children. Seeing herself as her daughter's only adult guide puts a mother under enormous pressure to avoid every possible false move. After all, her daughter depends on her to get it right.

More healthy choices emerge when a mother and daughter broaden their sights and allow each other to be singular while making room for other adult women to play a role in the daughter's upbringing. In such a scenario, everyone has more freedom to choose for herself. Mothers are freed from the need either to compete with or merge with their daughters, while daughters are empowered to make their own decisions without feeling as though they are commenting on their mothers' lives.

Helena, a twenty-four-year-old political aide, has found herself recently able to appreciate her mother's achievements, both because of her own recent entry into the workplace and because her mentor has broadened the field for her. Now that Helena's mother is no longer her only role model, Helena has a new freedom to value her mother without feeling as though she's compromised her own individuality:

> My mother worked as a civil rights lawyer for my entire life. I resented the energy that went into her work. My friends and I would roll our eyes about some of her cases. . . . Until I graduated from college and began to work, it was easy to bash my mother and her friends. . . .
>
> Now I am sorry that I was like that, because I didn't give her any credit. She has helped me in my pursuit of a career and has been a real teacher, telling me when to push, when to pull back, how much of it is up to me to make it happen.
>
> My mentor, a professor from college, is also advising me, and I listen to both of these women with great respect. Ever since I began my job two years ago, my mother and my former professor are the ones to look to, and I take each of their advice.

Likewise, Betts, a thirty-four-year-old publicist, has benefited from the wider field of choice she enjoys by having both a mother and a mentor. And Betts appreciates her mother's willingness to maintain her own identity:

> My mother is definitely not my peer. She and I can wear the same size clothes and shoes, and her value system has made an impression upon me. But I've always been conscious of the fact that she is my mother, not my friend.

Betts gives her mother credit for helping her to form her own values: "She has shown me how to be charitable and supportive of causes." But Betts is also quick to distinguish between herself and her mother:

> I have a full-time job, and that is something she wasn't able to pull off. I have often wondered if my mother's marriage was too conventional to allow it, or if she wanted work to be second in her life to our family. Her way of doing things made me want a flexible career but a real career. I wanted something where I wouldn't have to give up time with my children, because she showed me that. But she also taught me to go beyond her, that a mother wants her daughter to do that. So I learned from my mother, especially about how to treat people with respect.

Since Betts wanted a different type of career than her mother had had, she needed another role model. She found one in the person of a former employer. This mentor was no substitute for Betts's mother, but supplemented her, providing Betts with more options in the way of both work and personality:

> When it comes to my career, I don't look to my mother but to my mentor, who was my first boss out of college. She worked full-time for years, but with hours that helped her have a balanced life. She showed me the

ropes in our industry. She is not as warm as my mother, and has another
style altogether.

Happily for Betts, neither her mother nor her mentor sees herself as
a rival for Betts's affections. Instead, the two women are each devoted
to Betts's welfare in their own way:

> I would say that these two women are the most important influences in
> my life . . . They have never even met, they just know about one another.
> Neither woman is jealous of the other but only interested in what she
> can do for me.

A fascinating portrayal of mother-daughter envy and bonding can
be seen in the film *Swimming Pool* directed by François Ozon. The
movie stars Charlotte Rampling as Sarah Morton, a middle-aged crime
writer who leads a repressed and narrow existence. Into Sarah's monas-
tic life comes Julie, the publisher's daughter, played by Ludivine Sag-
nier, all sex and sensuality. At first Sarah is threatened by the lovely
young woman who is young enough to be her daughter, envying both
Julie's self-confidence and her success with men. But Sarah's envy also
frees her desires, which gradually begin to reemerge. Instead of remaining in a self-made prison of envy and frustration, Sarah uses these emotions to reconnect with her needs. The film offers a haunting
invitation: if mothers and daughters can learn from their competition,
using their complicated feelings about each other to get in touch with
their own true selves, they can replace rivalry with an astonishing new
level of freedom and fulfillment.

Likewise, the possibility of a healthy stepmother–first wife connection
offers us hope for a female bonding that is based on cooperation rather
than rivalry. In 2003, when I wrote *Women of Divorce: Mothers, Daughters,
Stepmothers—The New Triangle*, I discovered that the first and second
wives can find ways to coparent, joining forces to care for the children of

divorce. If the stepmother and mother are both involved in the children's lives, I found, there is less competition for the children's affection. Through an effort to replace envy and competition with bonding and compromise, mothers and stepmothers were able to put the past to rest.

This was the theme of the movie *Stepmom*, in which Susan Sarandon plays Jackie, the resentful first wife, while Julia Roberts is cast as Isabel, the beautiful interloper. At first, the children remain staunchly loyal to Jackie, refusing to respond to Isabel's efforts to combine parenting and her career as a photographer. Jackie, of course, was a stay-at-home mom, giving the two women another basis for competition. But when Jackie becomes terminally ill, she realizes that she is doing them no favor in denying her children a stable home. With the children in mind, she and Isabel find ways to make concessions.

Stepmom may have obscured women's envy in a rosy glow of female bonding. But real-life women do often find ways to overcome their opposing views, particularly when children are involved. When the mother and stepmother are able to achieve this armistice, they do so for the "greater good," for the children's sake. Rosie, a forty-six-year-old consultant, told me the following story of her increasingly cordial relationship with her husband's first wife:

> I brought my stepdaughter, Doran, home to her mother's yesterday, and her mother, Patricia, asked me to stay for a cookout. I didn't stay, but it sure was enticing. Patricia and I take care of seven-year-old Doran together, and it has been a pleasure. We both love her so much, and that binds us together. I have two sons and Doran is the only girl in my life. Patricia is not like me, but we have more in common than we think. Not only do we take care of Doran, but we have similar rules about bedtime and friends on weekends. So what happens is that Doran has consistency in both houses. . . .
>
> When I met my husband, everyone warned me about the ex-wife; everyone warned me about having a stepdaughter. They said it couldn't work, that it would be a war. But they were so wrong. My experience has

been a positive one, I am happy to have someone in my life who agrees with my standards of mothering.

In Rosie's view, Patricia's willingness to share, her substitution of generosity for envy, is what makes their warm relationship possible:

I don't think that Patricia begrudges me my time with Doran. I think she is willing to share her. This gives her time with her new husband, and it keeps her life from being consumed by Doran. She has even called last-minute and asked if we will take Doran on occasion. I always say yes. If my husband makes a fuss, which he is apt to do, I'm the one defending his ex-wife. I think in another life I would have been friends with Patricia.

Mentoring is yet another form of attachment between women in which the roles of mentor/mentee provide the basis for a strong connection.

Juliet, thirty-one, a cancer researcher, describes her need for both mother and mentor:

I doubt I would have remained in this track without my mentor, Alicia, who is fifty-two. Every time I thought I should simply teach and not become a full-fledged scientist, my mentor was there, pushing me ahead and urging me to continue my work. She also showed me how to believe in myself.

The mother figures in my life—my mother, my aunts—could not have helped me here. They taught me other things, but they knew nothing of this field or how sexist it is. I am here today because I had a female mentor who was willing to extend herself to me. I feel that Alicia got something out of our relationship—a kind of payoff for her hard work, and the proof that other women would want to be in her field. . . . I plan to be a mentor for the women who start out, as soon as I am accomplished enough to do it.

As Juliet imagines, mentors do appreciate the exchange at least as much as their mentees. Natalie, for example, at age sixty-four, has had an extremely positive experience mentoring a former employee for the past ten years, not least because it seemed to be a way of paying back her own mentor:

> Janine, a talented designer, has brought me all of her sketches before she submits them to her boss. I will look them over carefully and tell her what I think. I also have helped her in her career and made suggestions over the years that have turned out well. We will meet for drinks or dinner every few weeks, and I believe that we enrich each other's lives.

Natalie views her mentoring as a specific act of female solidarity:

> I definitely consider myself a pioneer in my area and believe that very few women were around when I began. The ironic thing is that I also had someone to assist me, and this woman was so amazing, early on in the game. She really taught me everything that I know.

Another older woman with whom I spoke, sixty-three-year-old Donna, felt so strongly about mentoring that she went out of her way to make it part of the "work culture" at her current workplace. Before Donna took action, however, her story sounded very much like those we have heard in previous chapters—rivalrous women envying not only her professional success but also her marriage and her general air of contentment. To Donna, a fashion designer, other women's jealousy came as a shock:

> It took me a long time to realize that women at work resented me and my happiness on the job. I came to this place when not many women worked here, in another era. I was pleased when they invited more women, and I listened to the woes of my female coworkers. They be-

came friends, but no one liked that I loved my husband or that I was content enough with my career. No one was like that, and so the friendships
at work were built on the idea of what was missing in their lives. . . .

As Beth and Augusta reported in Chapter 7, the older women were
sometimes willing to help the youngest employees, but not the ones
who were only slightly younger:

I saw that some women who were my age would do things against the
women who were close to their ages, maybe eight or ten years younger.
Then they would help the new employees, who were just starting out.

Donna refused to accept the situation, however, and in a gesture of
generosity managed to create a new model among her female coworkers:

I felt I had to put a stop to this. . . . I gave a speech and said that we
owed it to one another to do the right thing, that as senior employees
we must include everyone in our efforts. To me, this is not just about the
workplace but about a distrust that women have of one another. I explained to all the women in my department that everyone had to do the
best job possible and teach one another. I have insisted that the senior
employees mentor the younger staff, mostly female. I think I am succeeding, the environment feels better since I laid down the law.

Donna is a vivid expression of the conclusion reached by Judith
G. Touchton in her essay, "Women's Ways of Mentoring": Women
are responsible for "the expansion and consequent redefinition of
mentoring," and for how "we think and go about mentoring." Certainly my own experience with mentoring and being mentored bears
out these positive accounts. I know that without the help of my
mentor, I would not be where I am today. I know, too, that the young

women I have mentored at the Kennedy School of Government and my students at Marymount Manhattan have enriched my life immeasurably.

Mentoring, of course, is only one of many ways that women's bonds can bring us solace, encouragement, and joy. Close relationships with coworkers, relatives, and friends can also be extremely rewarding, once we come to terms with the rivalry about which we have been silent for too long. A May 30, 2003, *New York Times* article about the Broadway production of *Nine* entitled "A Sisterhood of Self-Effacing Stars" reports on the warmth and companionship to be found among the nine female stars of the play. As described by journalist Robin Pogrebin, none of the nine women—each of whom has achieved her own measure of success on stage or screen—gets to be a star, but all enjoy being part of the ensemble. The younger women all look up to Chita Rivera, notes Pogrebin, "the den mother of the group . . . the beloved Broadway veteran to whom her younger colleagues are eager apprentices." Instead of the brutal competition depicted in *All About Eve* and countless Broadway legends, the women of *Nine* have found a means to come together, appreciating their assorted talents, ages, looks, and temperaments, as well as their common goals.

The popular film *Legally Blonde* offers a similar version of diverse women coming together. Young law student Elle Woods, a ditsy blond "California girl" dressed entirely in pink, at first faces rivalry from her serious, brunette Harvard classmate who wears the standard preppy uniform of plaid skirts and dark sweaters and has ensnared Elle's boyfriend as well as undermining her work. Elle, despite her upper-class privilege, befriends a hairdresser (played by Jennifer Coolidge, whom we met in Chapter 8), making common cause with her fellow victim of Harvard snobbery. In the end, Elle wins over her classmate as well, even as she refuses to divulge the secrets of one of her California sorority sisters. Thus, the three very different women create a new type of female solidarity. The theme is repeated in *Legally Blonde 2: Red, White, and Blonde* (2003), in which free-spirited Elle goes to Washington, D.C., overcoming the resistance of her more somber fellow interns. Elle is beautiful, chic, and an irresistible magnet for men, but instead of competing with other women, she insists on befriending them, turning rivalry into fellowship by sheer force of will.

Although the *Legally Blonde* movies offer only fantasy solutions to a very real problem, they do suggest a model for female friendship in which rivalry is first acknowledged, then overcome. In my research, I found a significant number of women who had likewise come to terms with competition and envy. When Cassandra found that her best friend was "hooking up" with her ninth-grade boyfriend, she thought their friendship was over for good. But the two women found their way back to each other seven years later, when both had started college:

> I vowed I'd wouldn't speak to Hyacinth ever again. She had basically stolen not only my boyfriend but my place in our hometown. I was known as part of a couple, and she made it into gossip that ruined me. How could I forgive her? . . .
>
> Then we ended up transferring to the same small college. When I first heard about it, I thought there'd be a war. Then I thought, this is crazy. The guy . . . was not worth it. He was a lowlife, and if both of us had to learn it by being with him, that's how it was. But I had missed Hyacinth as a friend, so I decided to give her one more chance. I made it clear that we couldn't set our eyes on the same guy, ever again. I told her that the friendship mattered and I know she felt the same. I had other girlfriends who said, "But she took from you, she stooped low." And she did, but I wanted to see if we could be friends, not enemies. . . . I had to think about it—did I really want to go on hating other girls, doing bad things to each other for the rest of our lives?

No, Cassandra decided, she didn't. She and Hyacinth agreed to end their competition and began to work together to create a new friendship. Their story shows us how female bonding triumphs over rivalry and suggests that with some soul-searching and clarity about what's really important, women can find another way.

In a similar spirit of hope, Betina, a forty-two-year-old dental assistant, feels that for the first time in her life, she has friends she can trust:

> My whole life I had to push to get somewhere. I was the cheerleader in high school, and the one everyone had to have as a friend. Already, in high school, I was worried about what would happen next and would I be able to hang on. Would someone else be prettier, more popular? Where I grew up, no one went to college, everyone got married and pregnant. I didn't do it that way so everyone talked about me. Friends dropped me because I didn't act like they did. I wanted to make something of myself and I worked hard, with my eyes in the back of my head. I had girlfriends who said one thing and did another, guy friends too.
>
> Finally I moved into the city and got a job. I've been at it for fifteen years and I'm living with a nice man. I think I can finally breathe easier. I think I know who my real women friends are, but it took a long time to figure it out. . . . My friends today are my equals. We all work hard and feel we are independent and content with our lives. This is what I wanted. It makes me feel more sure of myself.

Likewise, Samantha, forty-nine, who works as a motivational speaker in Iowa, found a similar sense of peace with four women who have been her friends since college:

> This group of friends has been there for me since we were eighteen years old. We only get together once a year or so, but it's incredible how it plays out just like it did when we were young women. . . . We're still all so close!

Initially, says Samantha, the women were close because their situations were similar:

We've been friends for years and we were never competitive. I guess it's because we all married, had careers and had kids, and no one had a rich husband or a brain child.

Now, however, the women have built a closeness that incorporates their diverse situations:

Today, two of the women are divorced, and three of us are still married. No one is setting the world afire, but no one is suffering, either, even though there were a few hard times for each of us. We . . . get closer as the years go on. . . . Maybe living in different parts of the country keeps us from being rivals. How can you compete with someone you hardly ever see?

When we were in New York last month, the five of us went to see *Menopause, the Musical.* First we had lunch and we discussed our perimenopausal or menopausal states, and found that we run the spectrum. One friend is still ovulating but not regularly, and one hasn't even begun the process. We laughed and told them they have a lot to look forward to. I'm on the quarterly system, with hot flashes thrown in. Another friend in the group is semiannual. One checked out a couple of years ago. . . .

When I think of all the competition I've encountered in my life, these friends are really an oasis. At the ripe old age of forty-nine, we all admitted that aging will be something we share, too, that we're all in it together.

Denise is a thirty-nine-year-old administrative assistant in a midwestern city. Like Samantha, she values her female friendships, in some ways even more than her relationship with a man:

There are women who are nasty, I admit, but the few select relationships I've had with female friends have worked for me. I suppose I've been fussy and careful, and it's paid off. I have friends who are there for me

24/7. I've never had that with a man—not with my ex-husband, and not with any man since. It's what I had hoped for and what I have looked for, [but] . . . I can't seem to get it right. So these friendships have been really important to me and these women are like family.

Although Denise is currently living with a man, she finds that he often doesn't meet her emotional needs. So, she explains, she turns to her girlfriends:

Now that I am not so young and easygoing, I can't be without this support system. I'd say that my girlfriends are more important to me than my male partner at this point. . . . There was a time when I would have bent over backwards to please a man. No more. Now I just choose the people who make me comfortable, and it happens to be this group of women. I feel truly blessed to have the friends I do.

When I asked Denise how she thought these friendships would hold up over time, she stressed that they did not depend on the women having identical lives:

If one of us gets engaged or goes to live with a man, we'll understand. What I wouldn't like is to see someone give up on us for that man. That's what I used to do, and where did it get me? So I've changed my ways, and it's all about trust and women I can count on. I have no doubts about my women friends like I've had about male lovers.

Utopian Visions, Real-Life Hope

Maybe it was just a coincidence, but as I was writing the final pages of this book, I felt I was suddenly seeing a wave of positive portrayals of female rivalry and solidarity, images in popular culture that suggested new possibilities for female viewers.

The movie *Miss Congeniality 2: Armed and Fabulous*, starring Sandra Bullock, was one striking example. The first movie in the series, *Miss*

Congeniality, had the FBI agent played by Bullock literally enter a beauty pageant. The brainy, tough woman, who has avoided the feminine world of looks, as well as the sphere of romance, must take a lesson from her "sisters" in the pageant, who have spent their lives mastering these traditional female arts. Although most contestants are portrayed as cutthroat competitors, and although the older beauty queen (played by Candice Bergen) is willing to kill in order to stay on top, the movie offered some hope for female bonding in the friendship Bullock's character develops with one of the contestants. Bullock's main relationship, however, was with a fellow FBI agent with whom she begins a romance as the movie ends.

In the sequel, however, Bullock is thrown in with a woman who, at least visually, seems quite unlike her, an African-American agent who is asked to serve as her bodyguard while she once again takes on a glamorous disguise. Despite the historical baggage of master and servant/slave, and despite the traditional female rivalry of two women competing for a man, Bullock and her partner manage to overcome their differences to create a true bond. Indeed, they actually throw out the man over whom they are competing, placing a higher value on their friendship.

Another utopian vision of female rivalry and friendship was the Disney movie *Ice Princess*, where the young heroine has both a mother (the scruffy feminist professor played by Joan Cusack) and a mentor (the glamorous ice-skating instructor played by *Sex in the City* alumna Kim Cattrall). Torn between these two competing models of female achievement, the heroine also has two sets of friends: a fellow science nerd, and, eventually, a group of "ice princesses," the pretty and popular girls who engage in figure-skating competitions. The high school heroine is a brilliant physics student who dreams of becoming a figure skater. Somehow she must negotiate between all the different possibilities for female accomplishment; she must also learn the difference between good competition (defined as becoming all you can be through hard work and commitment) and bad competition (sabotaging a rival's chances to improve your own). As the movie ends, the science nerd is agreeing to tutor a former ice princess, who in exchange will introduce the nerd to some cute boys, while the heroine's mother and mentor broker a deal: she'll enter a tough college but will continue to engage in ice-skating competitions so she can find out how good she really is. Although it was hard for me to imagine this set of happy endings, it's tantalizing to think that teenage girls could have such a positive perception of their future. In this perfect world, competition and friendship, ambition and compassion, mothers and mentors, all coexist harmoniously.

In real life, too, as I was finishing this book, I heard a hopeful piece of news. I was heartened to learn that even my friends Cynthia and Elinor, whose relationship I thought was irreparably damaged, had found a way back to each other. Elinor, prompted by her therapeutic journey, came to realize her role in the breakup. Although she still thought Cynthia should have let her bring a date to the wedding, she also began to realize that perhaps her own tendency to become the center of attention at every party might have been frustrating for Cynthia, who as the bride wanted to be the star of her own wedding. Moreover, as the years went by, she missed Cynthia, and the loss of their friendship came to seem more important than whatever injury the missed wedding invitation had caused.

So she called Cynthia up and apologized, fully and freely, saying that she regretted her focus on herself during what should have been Cynthia's time. Cynthia was moved to tears by Elinor's declaration, and joyfully welcomed the return of her friend. Their friendship resumed on a new level, but the surprises weren't over yet. Several months later, Cynthia finally confessed that her husband-to-be, worried about the mounting costs of their wedding, had balked at paying for Elinor's date. When Cynthia had offered to cover that expense herself, her husband refused, insisting that as a couple, they simply couldn't afford the extra guest.

Was Cynthia also motivated to please her fiancé and to keep the peace? I personally think she was. Did Elinor sometimes ignore her friends' needs in her preoccupation with her own wishes? I think that's true as well. What was moving to me about their reconciliation was not that either woman had dropped her rivalry or overcome her envy of the other. Instead, they had found a method to work through these feelings, acknowledging their own shortcomings as they became more tolerant of each other's limitations. Their reward was a profoundly satisfying resumption of a cherished friendship, and the promise of more ease and acceptance in all their future relationships. Their hard-won happy ending stands as a beacon of hope for all of us who struggle with female rivalry.

Acknowledgments

I thank many people for their support and respect for this project:

Meredith Bernstein, my visionary agent, Jennifer Enderlin, my remarkable editor, and the impressive staff at St. Martin's Press (in alphabetical order): Kim Cardascia, John Murphy, Sally Richardson, Frances Sayers, Colleen Schwartz, Matthew Shear, Dori Weintraub. For her brilliant editorial skills: Rachel Kranz. For guidance: Lori Ames, Susie Finesman, Brit Geiger, Stacey Landowe, Meryl Moss, Janis Vallely, Cynthia Vartan. For her keen insights: Jennie Ripps. For research assistance: Emilie Domer, Casey Lynch, and Ben Peryer. For legal advice: Robert Marcus, my loyal attorney. In academia: Elizabeth Irmiter, Suzanne Murphy, and Micheal Rengers at Sarah Lawrence College, Lewis Burke Frumkes at Marymount Manhattan College. In Hollywood: Jon Avnet, Michael Glassman, Deb Newmyer, Luke Sandler, Bruce Vinokour, Meredith Wagner, Allison Wallach, Ellyn Williams. The professionals who have contributed their thoughts to this book: Dr. Michele Anzilotti, Dr. Ronnie Burak, Dr. Donald Cohen, Jo League, Antoinette Michaels, Claire Owen, Amy

Reisen, Seth Shulman, Dr. Nechama Tec. To the women who have shared their deepest, darkest feelings about envy, jealousy, and competition, I am forever indebted. To preserve their anonymity and privacy, I cannot acknowledge these women by name. Their personal victories are the lifeblood of this book and evidence of the challenges women face in our culture. My parents, Selma and Herbert L. Shapiro, my in-laws, Helene and Ted Barash, and true-blue friends—each and every one of you for your constancy.

My three children, Jennie, Michael, and Elizabeth Ripps, who make it all worthwhile.

Finally I thank my husband, Gary A. Barash, infinitely wise, my safe haven in the storm.

References

Abraham, Laurie. "The Perfect Little Bump." *New York* magazine, 27 September 2004.

Adam's Rib. Directed by George Cukor. Metro-Goldwyn-Mayer, 1949.

Alice. Created by Robert Getchell. CBS and Warner Brothers, 1976.

Alice Doesn't Live Here Anymore. Directed by Martin Scorsese. Warner Brothers, 1974.

American Pie. Directed by Paul Weitz. Universal Pictures, 1999.

Anders, George. "How Traits That Helped Fiorina Climb Ladder Came to Be Fatal Flaws." *The Wall Street Journal*, 10 February 2005.

Antilla, Susan. "Money Talks, Women Don't." *The New York Times*, 21 July 2004.

Apprentice, The. Created by Mark Burnett. NBC, 2003–.

Associated Press. "Opera Soprano Booted Over Weight," 7 March 2004.

Bachelor, The. Created by Mark Fleiss. ABC, 2002–.

Bakos, Susan Crain. "The New Other Woman." *More* magazine, November 2002.

Barash, Susan Shapiro. *Mothers-in-Law, Daughters-in-Law: Love, Hate, Rivalry, and Reconciliation*. Far Hills, N.J.: New Horizons Press, 2001.

———. *A Passion for More: Wives Reveal the Affairs That Make or Break Their Marriages*. Berkeley, Calif.: Berkeley Hills Books, 2001.

————. *Women of Divorce: Mothers, Daughters, Stepmothers—The New Triangle*. Far Hills, N.J.: New Horizons Press, 2003.

Baum, L. Frank. *The Wizard of Oz*. 1900. Reprint, New York: Tor Classics, 1993.

Being Julia. Directed by István Szabó. Sony Pictures Classics, 2004.

Bend It Like Beckham. Directed by Gurinder Chadha. Fox Searchlight Pictures, 2002.

Buffy, the Vampire Slayer. Created by Joss Whedon. UPN, 1997–2003.

Buffy, the Vampire Slayer. Directed by Fran Rubel Kuzui. Twentieth Century Fox, 1992.

Business of Strangers, The. Directed by Patrick Stettner. IFC Films, 2001.

Carroll, Lewis. *Alice's Adventures in Wonderland and Through the Looking Glass*. New York: Signet Classic, 2000.

Charlie's Angels. Directed by McG. Columbia Pictures, 2000.

Collins, Nancy. "The Real Cherie Blair." *More* magazine, November 2004.

Cosby Show, The. Created by Mark Leeson, Ed Weinberger, and Bill Cosby. NBC, 1984–92.

Cox, Ana Marie. "Beauty Politic." *Elle* magazine, March 2003.

De Beauvoir, Simone. *The Second Sex*. New York: Vintage Books, 1989.

Desperate Housewives. "Ah, but Underneath." Directed by Larry Shaw. ABC. First aired 10 October 2004.

Duenwald, Mary. "Some Friends, Indeed, Do More Harm Than Good." *The New York Times*, 10 September 2002.

"The Elle 25: #9, The Women of Court TV." *Elle* magazine, September 2004.

E.R. "The Providers." Directed by David Zabel. NBC. First aired 27 January 2005.

Family Matters. Created by William Bickley and Michael Warren. ABC and CBS, 1989–98.

Family Ties. Created by Gary David Goldberg. NBC, 1982–89.

Fels, Anna. *Necessary Dreams: Ambition in Women's Changing Lives*. New York: Pantheon, 2004.

Fitch, Janet. *White Oleander*. New York: Back Bay Books, an imprint of Little, Brown, 1999.

Friedan, Betty. *The Feminine Mystique*. 1963. Reprint, New York: W. W. Norton, 1997.

Friends. Created by David Crane and Marta Kauffman. NBC, 1994–2004.

Gill, John Freeman. "Neptune's Daughters and the Ultimate Job Tryout." *The New York Times*, 12 December 2004.

Gilligan, Carol, and Lyn Mikel Brown. *Meeting at the Crossroads: Women's Psychology and Girls' Development*. New York: Random House, 1992.

Gilmore Girls. "The Lorelais' First Day at Yale." Directed by Chris Long. Warner Brothers. First aired 30 September 2003.

Golden Girls, The. Created by Susan Harris. NBC, 1985–92.

Griffin, Nancy. "Cybill Liberties." *AARP Magazine*, July–August 2004.

Grimm, Jacob, and Wilhelm. Translated by Margaret Hunt. "The Goose Girl," "Sleeping Beauty," "Snow White," "Cinderella," and "Rapunzel." In *Household Tales*. London: George Bell, 1884.

Gypsy. Directed by Mervyn LeRoy. Warner Brothers, 1962.

Hamermesh, Daniel S., and Jeff E. Biddle. "Beauty and the Labor Market." *NBER Working Papers*, no. 4518. National Bureau of Economic Research, Inc. Cambridge, Mass, 1993.

Harrington, Ann, and Petra Bartosiewicz. "Most Powerful Women in Business: Who's Up? Who's Down?" *Fortune* magazine, 4 October 2004.

Haste, Cate, and Cherie Booth. *The Goldfish Bowl: Married to the Prime Minister*. London: Chatto and Windus, 2004.

Heathers. Directed by Michael Lehmann. New World Entertainment, 1989.

His Girl Friday. Directed by Howard Hawks. Columbia Pictures, 1940.

"How Do You Like Them Apples?" *Us Weekly*, 18 October 2004.

Ice Princess. Directed by Tim Fywell. Buena Vista Pictures, 2005.

Jacobs, Alexandra. "Jennifer Coolidge, Queen of the Ugly Stepsisters." *The New York Times*, 3 October 2004.

Jerry Maguire. Directed by Cameron Crowe. TriStar Pictures, 1996.

Joan of Arcadia. Created by Barbara Hall. CBS, 2003–.

Julia. Created by Hal Kanter. NBC, 1968–71.

Just Shoot Me! Created by Steven Levitan. NBC, 1997–2003.

Kang, Stephanie. "Waist Management," *The Wall Street Journal*, 6 August 2004.

Klein, Melanie. *Envy and Gratitude and Other Works, 1946–1963*. New York: Simon and Schuster, 1975.

Kreahlin, Lorraine. "In the Relentless Pursuit of Fashion, Feet Pay the Price." *The New York Times*, 31 August 2004.

La Ferla, Ruth. "Attack of the Summer Interns." *The New York Times*, 4 August 2002.

Legally Blonde. Directed by Robert Luketic. Metro-Goldwyn-Mayer, 2001.

Legally Blonde 2: Red, White, and Blonde. Directed by Charles Herman-Wurmfeld. Metro-Goldwyn-Mayer, 2003.

Lennon, Christine. "Free for All." *Elle* magazine, October 2004.

Lerner, Gerda. *The Creation of a Feminist Consciousness*. New York: Oxford University Press, 1993.

Living Single. Created by Yvette Lee Bowser. Fox, 1993–98.

Luce, Clare Boothe. *The Women*. New York: Dramatists Play Service, 1937.

"Make Yourself Look Younger in Ten Days." *Marie Claire* magazine, March 2004.

Mary Tyler Moore Show, The. Created by James L. Brooks and Allan Burns. CBS, 1970–77.

Mean Girls. Directed by Mark S. Waters. Paramount Pictures, 2004.

Merkin, Daphne. "Keeping the Forces of Decrepitude at Bay." *The New York Times*, 2 May 2004.

Midgette, Anne. "The Curse of Beauty for Serious Musicians: Young Women Find the Playing Field Is Far from Level." *The New York Times*, 27 May 2004.

Miss Congeniality. Directed by Donald Petrie. Warner Brothers, 2000.

Miss Congeniality 2: Armed and Fabulous. Directed by John Pasquin. Warner Brothers, 2005.

Morem, Sue. "About Professionalism, Etiquette and Problems in the Workplace: Ask Sue: Jealous Coworkers." http://www.careerknowhow.com/ask_sue/jealous.htm.

Mr. and Mrs. Smith. Directed by Doug Liman. Twentieth Century Fox, 2005.

My Best Friend's Wedding. Directed by P. J. Hogan. TriStar Pictures, 1997.

Nicholson, Diane M. "Aggressive Girls: Overview Paper on Family Violence." Ottawa, Ontario: National Clearinghouse on Family Violence, 2002.

O'Donnell, Michelle. "Quarrel Over a Boy Ends in Death When Girl, 16, Stabs Another, 15." *The New York Times*, 12 October 2004.

O'Grady, Jim. "Neighborhood Report, Riverdale: Maid in Manhattan Sponsors Girls' Soccer Team in the Bronx." *The New York Times*, 22 June 2003.

O'Neil, Tom. "Oscar Watch, the Babe Factor." *The New York Times*, 14 November 2004.

Pat and Mike. Directed by George Cukor. Metro-Goldwyn-Mayer, 1952.

Pipher, Mary. *Reviving Ophelia*. New York: Ballantine Books, 1995.

Pogrobin, Robin. "Big Hair and Personality to Match." *The New York Times*, 21 August 2002.

———. "A Sisterhood of Self-Effacing Stars." *The New York Times*, 30 May 2003.

Reginato, James. "Bushwhacker." *W* magazine, September 2004.

Roseanne. Created by Matt Williams. ABC, 1988–97.

Sands, Sarah. "Do You Dress for Men or Women?" *Harper's Bazaar*, August 2004.

Saranow, Jennifer. "The New Face of Plastic Surgery." *The Wall Street Journal*, 15 April 2003.

Schnurnberger, Lynn. "Suburban Supermoms." *More* magazine, June 2002.

Schuker, Eleanor, M.D. "The Blinded Eye." *The Bulletin*, a publication of the Association for Psychoanalytic Medicine, vol. 36, fall/winter 1999.

Scrubs. Created by Bill Lawrence. NBC, 2001–.

Sex and the City. "Coulda, Woulda, Shoulda." Directed by David Frankel. HBO, 2003.

Shakespeare, William. *King Lear*. New York: Penguin Books, 1999.

Simmons, Rachel. *Odd Girl Out*. New York: Harcourt, 2002.

Simpson, Mona. *Anywhere but Here*. New York: Knopf, 1986.

Simpsons, The. Created by Matt Groening. Fox, 1989–.

Single White Female. Directed by Barbet Schroeder. Columbia Pictures Corporation, 1992.

Slagle, Matt. "Women Make Inroads in Video Game Industry." Associated Press, 9 September 2004.

Stepmom. Directed by Chris Columbus. TriStar Pictures, 1998.

Stroller, Debbie. *Stitch 'n Bitch: The Knitter's Handbook*. New York: Workman, 2004.

"Survey on Looks." *More* magazine, October 2004.

Swimming Pool. Directed by François Ozon. Focus Features, 2003.

Tannen, Mary. "Women on the Verge." *The New York Times*, 22 February 2004.

Terauds, John. "St. John Plays Beautifully As Ever." *The Toronto Star*, 13 February 2004.

That '70s Show. Created by Bonnie Turner and Terry Turner. Fox, 1998–.

13 Going on 30. Directed by Gary Winick. Sony Pictures Entertainment, 2004.

thirtysomething. Created by Marshall Herskovitz and Edward Swick. ABC, 1987–91.

Touchton, Julia G. "Women's Ways of Mentoring." AOL, p. 1. 25 February 2003.

United States Bureau of the Census. United States Census. Washington, D.C., 2000.

United States Department of Labor. "Women in the Labor Force, 2004," June 29, 2005. www.dol.gov.

Vecsey, George. "Williams Sisters in Their Own World, Don't Need an Opening Act." *The New York Times*, 8 September 2002.

Wennerstrand, Anne. "Advice for Grown-up Dancers: Toxic Envy: Two-Stepping with the Green Monster." *The Dance Insider*, 19 December 2000.

Wiseman, Rosalind. *Queen Bees and Wannabes: Helping Your Daughter Survive Cliques, Gossip, Boyfriends and Other Realities of Adolescence.* New York: Three Rivers Press, 2003.

Women, The. Directed by George Cukor. Metro-Goldwyn-Mayer, 1939.

Working Girl. Directed by Mike Nichols. Twentieth Century Fox, 1988.

Index

CPSIA information can be obtained at www.ICGtesting.com
Printed in the USA
LVOW112341170412

278072LV00001B/80/P